NEW TESTAMENT GREEK GRAMMAR

An Introduction

D1616990

NEW TESTAMENT GREEK GRAMMAR

An Introduction

REVISED EDITION

MOLLY WHITTAKER

SCM PRESS LTD

Collegis et discipulis qui, fortasse inscii,
me per multos annos in Universitate Nottinghamensi
versatam tantopere adiuverunt,
hoc opusculum dedico.

334 01134 5
First published 1969
by SCM Press Ltd
58 Bloomsbury Street London
Second edition 1980
Printed in Great Britain by
Richard Clay Ltd (The Chaucer Press)
Bungay, Suffolk

CONTENTS

5

PREFACE

This book is designed for beginners in Greek as a small, inexpensive manual which a student who has no turn for languages may discard, well thumbed with use, while the scholar will later equip himself with something more detailed and durable. I have tried to include all the basic essentials and to anticipate and explain the problems likely to confront anybody studying without the help of a teacher. There is no index of subject matter, but a detailed introductory table of contents, chiefly for the teacher's use. Vocabulary has been deliberately restricted to the words most commonly used in the New Testament, in the hope that by repetition these at least may become familiar. Elegance has been unavoidably sacrificed to terseness.

I have taken the risk of making up most of the exercises myself. Weaker students hail a familiar New Testament text with delight and rattle off a translation without thinking of the Greek, while better students complain that such texts, however much they may build up morale, are little help in practising the language. However, from Chapter 8 onwards I have added to each exercise references to New Testament texts to illustrate the new work just introduced.

Exercises are included for translation into Greek, because these are a help in memorizing new words and constructions. My main emphasis has been on translation into English, the variety and flexibility of the Koine, the subtle nuances which sometimes defy translation and prove the necessity of learning Greek in order to have a proper understanding of the New Testament. In my Key I have included a number of variants both of constructions and vocabulary, so that the student may not feel himself rigidly fettered, yet may begin to appreciate the difficulty of steering between the Scylla of literalism and the Charybdis of paraphrase.

Among the many standard works available I have made most use of J. H. Moulton, *Grammar of New Testament Greek* (Vols. 1-3);

R. Funk, *A Greek Grammar of the New Testament*; Arndt-Gingrich, *New Testament Lexicon*; Moulton and Geden, *Concordance to the New Testament*; and B. M. Metzger, *Lexical Aids for Students of New Testament Greek*. I must gratefully acknowledge a particular debt to the Rev. J. R. Bartlett of Trinity College, Dublin, who checked both my typescript and proofs and provided much helpful and constructive criticism. Finally I am deeply grateful to the editorial and production staff of the SCM Press for their patience and expertise in devising and producing such a complicated format.

University of Nottingham   MOLLY WHITTAKER

ALPHABET, DIPHTHONGS, BREATHINGS, IOTA SUBSCRIPT, ACCENTS

Alphabet

Alpha[1]	A	α	a	long as in father, short as in bat
Beta	B	β	b	
Gamma[2]	Γ	γ	g	hard as in get
Delta	Δ	δ	d	
Epsilon	E	ε	ĕ	short as in let
Zeta	Z	ζ	z	as *ds* in lords
Eta	H	η	ē	long as *a* in late
Theta	Θ	θ	th	as in thick
Iota	I	ι	i	long as *ee* in see, short as in bit
Kappa	K	κ	k	as *k* or hard *c* in cook
Lambda	Λ	λ	l	
Mu	M	μ	m	
Nu	N	ν	n	
Xi	Ξ	ξ	x	
Omicron	O	o	ŏ	short as in pot
Pi	Π	π	p	
Rho	P	ρ	r	
Sigma[3]	Σ	σ, ς	s	as in sea
Tau	T	τ	t	
Upsilon[4]	Y	υ	u	as in hub
Phi	Φ	φ	ph	as in physics
Chi	X	χ	ch	hard as in chaos, loch
Psi	Ψ	ψ	ps	as in Cyclops
Omega	Ω	ω	ō	long as in bone

[1] Capitals are normally used only for proper names, the start of a paragraph or to mark a new section, but editors vary in usage.

[2] Before a guttural (γ, κ, χ) γ is always pronounced as ν and written in English as *n* — ἄγγελος angel.

[3] σ within a word, ς at the end — relic of an old distinction in printing. Some editors use only the form c as found in early papyri and MSS.

[4] Transliterated into Latin as *y* and so passed into English usage — Κύπρος *Cyprus*.

Diphthongs
(two vowels pronounced together as one long)

$\alpha\iota$	as *ai* in aisle
$\epsilon\iota^1$	as *ei* in neigh
$o\iota$	as *oi* in oil
$\alpha\upsilon$	as *ow* in prow
$o\upsilon$	as *oo* in moose
$\epsilon\upsilon, \eta\upsilon$	as *eu* in euthanasia
$\upsilon\iota$	as *ui* in quit

Breathings
(compensation for lack of letter *h*)

A breathing, rough ' for an aspirate, smooth ' for unaspirated, is always found in front of a capital vowel (῾Ηρώδης), over a small initial vowel (ἄγγελος, ὥρα) and the second vowel of an initial diphthong (Αἰνείας, εὑρίσκω). An initial ρ is usually aspirated (ῥητορική). The breathing, whether rough or smooth, is an essential part of the word and must be written.

Iota subscript

When a small ι is written under α, η, ω it is no longer pronounced, but is an integral element, part of an ancient diphthong, and must be inserted.

Accents

Accents denoting pitch, not stress, were systematized by Aristophanes of Byzantium c. 200 BC for the use of foreigners learning Greek. They are still used in modern Greek, but the student of Greek as a dead language can disregard them as a guide to pronunciation and omit in writing. However some words can only be distinguished from one another by their accents and any scholar must be conversant with the principles of accentuation and insert them in writing, so rules for their use will be given as and when necessary.

---

[1] Pronunciation as *ei* in height is philologically unjustifiable, but used to be the conventional English pronunciation and is still sometimes found.

I Present indicative active of λύω

The great majority of verbs all have the same endings and there is no division into conjugations as in Latin. The endings show the persons and no personal pronouns are needed except for extra emphasis.

λύω	I loose, am loosing, do loose
λύεις	Thou loosest, etc. (must be used for English *you* sing.)
λύει	He, she, it looses, etc.
λύομεν	We loose, etc.
λύετε	You (pl.) loose, etc.
λύουσι(ν)[1]	They loose, etc.

Rules of Accentuation

NB In verbs the accent is regularly placed as far back from the end of the word as possible.

Rule 1. An accent can stand only on the ultimate (final syllable), penultimate (next to final) or propenultimate (next before that).

Rule 2. An acute accent can stand on any of these three syllables, whether they are long or short, but if the ultimate is long, the accent can go no further back than the penultimate.

ἀκούω	I hear	κηρύσσω	I proclaim, preach
βλέπω	I see	λαμβάνω	I take, receive
γράφω	I write	λέγω	I say
ἐσθίω	I eat	πέμπω	I send
εὑρίσκω	I find	πιστεύω	I believe, trust
θεραπεύω	I heal	σώζω	I save

[1] In CG (Classical Greek) ν was added before a following vowel to avoid hiatus or at the end of a sentence. In K (Κοινή, the 'common' tongue in which the NT was written) less sensitive writers add it before a consonant or omit before a vowel as the fancy takes them.

Translate into English: βλέπουσι, πέμπετε, ἐσθίομεν, σώζει, ἀκούεις, εὑρίσκω, θεραπεύετε, γράφεις, λέγουσι, λαμβάνομεν, πιστεύει, κηρύσσετε, λύουσιν.

Translate into Greek: We say. He hears. They believe. You (sing.) heal. I take. They write. Ye send. She is finding. We save. Thou dost preach. I am eating. Ye see. We do loose.

2   Second declension nouns and article

The Second declension is so like the Latin that it gives an easier introduction than the First declension. Greek has a definite article which precedes the noun as in English.

Singular	Masculine	Neuter
Nominative	ὁ λόγος	τὸ ἔργον
Vocative	λόγε	ἔργον
Accusative	τὸν λόγον	τὸ ἔργον
Genitive	τοῦ λόγου	τοῦ ἔργου
Dative	τῷ λόγῳ	τῷ ἔργῳ
Plural		
N.V.	οἱ λόγοι	τὰ ἔργα
A.	τοὺς λόγους	τὰ ἔργα
G.	τῶν λόγων	τῶν ἔργων
D.	τοῖς λόγοις	τοῖς ἔργοις

NB In all declensions the nominative is the same as the vocative in the plural.

In both singular (in 2nd declension always ending in -ον) and plural the nominative of a neuter noun is unchanged in vocative and accusative; the plural, whatever the form of the singular, ends in α. In CG a neuter plural subject takes a singular verb, but in K both singular and plural verbs are found.

Case Usages

Nominative for subject: σώζει ὁ λόγος.
　　　　　　　　The word saves.
Vocative for address: ὦ ἄγγελε.
　　　　　　　　O angel.
Accusative for direct object: βλέπουσι τὸ ἔργον.
　　　　　　　　They see the work.
Genitive for ownership: ὁ δοῦλος τοῦ ἀδελφοῦ.
　　　　　　　　The brother's slave.
Dative for indirect object (*to* or *for*):
　　　γράφει νόμους τοῖς ἀδελφοῖς.
　　　He writes laws for the brothers.

Rules of Accentuation

NB A noun keeps the accent of the nom. sing. unless the rules of accentuation cause a change. It is impossible to generalize about nouns as about verbs. The student who intends to practise accentuation should memorize each new word with its accent, either visually or orally.

Rule 3. A *grave* accent replaces an acute on the ultimate if this is followed by another word in the same clause — τοὺς ἀδελφοὺς βλέπω.

Rule 4. A circumflex can stand only on a long syllable, only on the ultimate or penultimate. If the accent is on a long penultimate followed by a short ultimate it must be circumflex (δοῦλος), but if the accent is on the penultimate, whether long or short, with a long ultimate, the accent must be acute (δούλου), cf. also Rule 2, ἄγγελος but ἀγγέλου.

NB Diphthongs are naturally long, but final οι and αι rank as short for purposes of accentuation, ἄγγελος, ἄγγελοι but ἀγγέλοις. In 1st and 2nd declension in gen. and dat. sing. and pl., if the accent falls on the ultimate it becomes circumflex—τοῖς ἀδελφοῖς.

13

Masculine		Neuter	
ἄγγελος -ου ὁ	messenger, angel	ἀργύριον -ου τό	silver, money
ἄρτος -ου ὁ	bread (pl. loaves)	δαιμόνιον -ου τό	demon (pl. demons, devils)
ἀδελφός -οῦ ὁ	brother	ἔργον -ου τό	work, deed
δοῦλος -ου ὁ	slave	εὐαγγέλιον -ου τό	gospel, good news
		ἱμάτιον -ου τό	cloak (pl. clothes)
θεός -οῦ ὁ[1]	god		
λόγος -ου ὁ	word	πλοῖον -ου τό	boat
νόμος -ου ὁ	law	τέκνον -ου τό	child

Nom., gen. and gender (shown in lexicons by the addition of the article) should always be learnt together, as these show the declension.

Translate: 1. ἐσθίει[2] ὁ δοῦλος τὸν ἄρτον τοῦ Θεοῦ. 2. σώζουσιν οἱ ἄγγελοι τοὺς ἀδελφούς. 3. γράφετε τοῖς δούλοις τοὺς λόγους τῶν ἀδελφῶν. 4. ὦ ἀδελφέ, πιστεύεις[3] τοῖς λόγοις τῶν ἀγγέλων. 5. πέμπει ὁ ἀδελφὸς τὸ πλοῖον. 6. λαμβάνει τὰ τέκνα τὸ ἀργύριον τῶν δούλων. 7. γράφει ὁ ἀδελφὸς τὸ εὐαγγέλιον τοῖς δούλοις. 8. λαμβάνουσι τὰ δαιμόνια τὸ ἱμάτιον τοῦ τέκνου. 9. κηρύσσομεν τὸ εὐαγγέλιον.

NB Full stop and comma are the same as in English.

Translate: 1. We see the works of God. 2. The brothers find the gospels. 3. O angel, you write the words of the gospel for the children. 4. The children of God receive the gospel. 5. She is saving the clothes for the brothers. 6. The slaves send the boats. 7. The demons are eating the children's bread. 8. I hear the words of the law.

[1] To denote God, as distinct from gods, generally used with the article and often written with a capital.
[2] Greek word order is extremely flexible, but the verb tends to precede the subject.
[3] Used with the dative or preposition, εἰς with acc., ἐν with dat.

3   Present indicative active of contracted verbs with stem in ε. εἰς, ἐκ, ἐν

NB In a lexicon the uncontracted form is given to show the stem-vowel and this should be learnt, but in writing there is always contraction. The fact that a circumflex accent replaces acute if before contraction the accent falls on a contracting vowel is a useful indication of a contracted verb.

It will be worthwhile to memorize the following rules:

ε drops out before ει, η, ου and ω; ε+ε=ει; ε+ο=ου.

Present indicative active

φιλέ-ω	φιλῶ	I love, am loving, do love
φιλέ-εις	φιλεῖς	
φιλέ-ει	φιλεῖ	
φιλέ-ομεν	φιλοῦμεν	
φιλέ-ετε	φιλεῖτε	
φιλέ-ουσι(ν)	φιλοῦσι(ν)	

ἄγω	lead, drive	φιλέω	love
αἰτέω	ask (request)	ἀπόστολος -ου ὁ	apostle
ζητέω	(w. acc.) seek (for)	θάνατος -ου ὁ	death
		κόσμος -ου ὁ	world
καλέω	call	κύριος -ου ὁ	master, sir (w. capital, Lord)
κρύπτω	hide		
λαλέω	speak, talk		
μαρτυρέω	(w. dat.) bear witness	οἶκος -ου ὁ	house
		καί	and, even, also
ποιέω	make, do		
τελέω	end, finish	καί — καί	both — and
τηρέω	keep, observe (i.e. keep)	οὐ	not (οὐκ before ', οὐχ before ')

15

εἰς	(w. acc.) in, into		vowel becomes ἐξ)
ἐκ	(w. gen.) from, out of (before	ἐν	(w. dat.) in, inside, on

---

Translate: 1. ἄγουσιν οἱ δοῦλοι τοὺς ἀποστόλους εἰς τὸν οἶκον.
2. τηρεῖ καὶ σώζει ὁ Κύριος τὸν κόσμον. 3. οὐ μαρτυρεῖτε τῷ
εὐαγγελίῳ, ὦ ἀδελφέ. 4. καλεῖ ὁ ἀπόστολος τὰ δαιμόνια ἐκ τῶν
τέκνων. 5. ζητοῦμεν τὸ ἀργύριον ἐν τῷ οἴκῳ. 6. ποιεῖτε ἄρτους
τῷ κυρίῳ, δοῦλοι. 7. λαλοῦσιν οἱ ἄγγελοι τοὺς λόγους τοῦ
Θεοῦ. 8. αἰτεῖ τὰ τέκνα ἄρτον. 9. σώζεις, Κύριε, τοὺς ἀδελφοὺς ἐκ τοῦ θανάτου. 10. οὐχ εὑρίσκομεν τὰ ἱμάτια ἐν τῷ οἴκῳ
τοῦ δούλου.

Translate: 1. The law bears witness to the words of God. 2.
We hide the bread in the house. 3. The apostles are writing
gospels for the world. 4. You (sing.) take the child's clothes out
of the house. 5. You (pl.) call the slave's child. 6. The demons
do not find the children's money. 7. She is finishing the apostle's
work. 8. The messengers are asking for loaves. 9. The brothers
believe in the law of the Lord. 10. The master hears and observes
God's word.

---

4 First declension feminine nouns. Conspectus of definite article. Punctuation. Simple particles

All First declension nouns ending in α or η are feminine and
decline alike in the pl. In the sing. nouns whose final α follows a
vowel (ἀλήθεια) or ρ (ἡμέρα) retain α in gen. and dat., but nouns
whose final α follows a consonant other than ρ (θάλασσα) change
to η.

Sing. N.V.	ἡ ἡμέρα	ἐντολή	θάλασσα
A.	τὴν ἡμέραν	ἐντολήν	θάλασσαν
G.	τῆς ἡμέρας	ἐντολῆς	θαλάσσης
D.	τῇ ἡμέρᾳ	ἐντολῇ	θαλάσσῃ
Pl. N.V.	αἱ ἡμέραι	ἐντολαί	θάλασσαι
A.	τὰς ἡμέρας	ἐντολάς	θαλάσσας
G.	τῶν ἡμερῶν	ἐντολῶν	θαλασσῶν
D.	ταῖς ἡμέραις	ἐντολαῖς	θαλάσσαις

Complete conspectus of the definite article

Sing. N.	ὁ	ἡ	τό	Pl.	οἱ	αἱ	τά
A.	τόν	τήν	τό		τούς	τάς	τά
G.	τοῦ	τῆς	τοῦ		τῶν	τῶν	τῶν
D.	τῷ	τῇ	τῷ		τοῖς	ταῖς	τοῖς

ἀγάπη -ης ἡ — love
ἀλήθεια -ας ἡ — truth
ἁμαρτία -ας ἡ — sin
βασιλεία -ας ἡ — kingdom
δικαιοσύνη -ης ἡ — righteousness
δόξα -ης ἡ — glory
εἰρήνη -ης ἡ — peace
ἐκκλησία -ας ἡ — church
ἐντολή -ῆς ἡ — commandment
ἐξουσία -ας ἡ — authority
ἡμέρα -ας ἡ — day
θάλασσα -ης ἡ — sea, lake
ἄνθρωπος -ου ὁ — man, human being
ἔχω — have
ἱερόν -οῦ τό — temple
πῶς — how?

σάββατον -ου τό — sabbath, week
σημεῖον -ου τό — sign, miracle
ἀλλά — but (strong) (may be ἀλλ' before a vowel)
δέ — and, but (weak)
γάρ — for (not to be confused w. dat.)
οὖν — therefore

These last three never begin a sentence, but generally stand as second word.

NB All 1st declension nouns accent -ῶν in gen. pl. In gen. and dat. sing. and acc. pl. the α is long.

17

Punctuation

The Greek semi-colon is · and is used much more often than in English. The Greek question mark is ;

Translate: 1. ζητοῦσιν οὖν οἱ ἀδελφοὶ τὴν βασιλείαν τοῦ Θεοῦ· φιλοῦσι γὰρ τὴν ἀλήθειαν.[1] 2. πῶς ἐν τῷ σαββάτῳ λαλεῖς τοὺς λόγους τοῦ εὐαγγελίου ἐν τῇ ἐκκλησίᾳ, ἀλλ᾽ οὐ τηρεῖς τὰς ἐντολάς; 3. ποιοῦμεν τὰ ἔργα τοῦ νόμου, πιστεύομεν δὲ ἐν τῷ εὐαγγελίῳ· ἐν γὰρ τοῖς λόγοις τῶν ἀποστόλων εὑρίσκομεν τὴν ἀλήθειαν. 4. σώζει ὁ ἄγγελος τοὺς ἀνθρώπους ἐκ τῆς ἁμαρτίας, τὰ δὲ δαιμόνια ἄγουσιν εἰς θάνατον· ἐν γὰρ τῷ κόσμῳ ἔχουσιν ἐξουσίαν. 5. ποιοῦσι τὰ ἔργα οἱ δοῦλοι ἐν τῇ θαλάσσῃ, τὸ δὲ ἀργύριον λαμβάνει ὁ κύριος καὶ τηρεῖ τοῖς τέκνοις.

Translate: 1. You (pl.) find love and peace in the church, for the brethren trust in the words of the Lord. 2. Therefore we seek righteousness in the commandments of the law, but the law does not save from sin. 3. God does miracles for the world, but men believe the demons, for sin leads even (καί) the brethren to death. 4. The children therefore are talking to the apostle in the temple, for he loves children, but in men he sees the sins of the world. 5. O brother, you ask for loaves, but we eat the bread of angels, not of men. 6. How do you (sing.) do the works of God on the sabbath?

[1] Except in simple prepositional phrases the article is generally used with abstract nouns, when it will not be translated in English, also to mark a collective group — οἱ ἄνθρωποι men or *mankind*.

All nouns ending in -ης or -ας are masculine, differing from feminine only in having a separate voc. sing. and a gen. sing. in -ου.

		disciple	young man
Sing.	N.	ὁ μαθητής	νεανίας
	V.	μαθητά	νεανία
	A.	τὸν μαθητήν	νεανίαν
	G.	τοῦ μαθητοῦ	νεανίου
	D.	τῷ μαθητῇ	νεανίᾳ
Pl.	N.V.	οἱ μαθηταί	νεανίαι
	A.	τοὺς μαθητάς	νεανίας
	G.	τῶν μαθητῶν	νεανιῶν
	D.	τοῖς μαθηταῖς	νεανίαις

ἀπό (w. gen.)	from	οἰκοδομέω	build
βαπτιστής -οῦ ὁ	baptist	παρθένος -ου ἡ	girl
γλῶσσα -ης ἡ	tongue		
δεσπότης -ου ὁ	master	πρό	(w. gen.)
ἔρημος -ου ἡ[1]	desert		before, of
κώμη -ης ἡ	village		place or
μαθητής -οῦ ὁ	disciple		time
νεανίας -ου ὁ	young man	προφήτης -ου ὁ	prophet
νόσος -ου ἡ	disease	σύν	(w. dat.) with
ὁδός -οῦ ἡ	way, road	υἱός -οῦ ὁ	son
οἰκοδεσπότης -ου ὁ	householder		

[1] There are a few feminine 2nd declension nouns in -ος. Note that the feminine article must be used with these, just as the masculine must be used with 1st declension masculine nouns, in spite of the discrepancy in endings.

Translate: 1. οἱ νεανίαι σὺν τοῖς δούλοις τοῦ προφήτου οἰκοδο-
μοῦσιν τὸ ἱερόν, ὁ δὲ Κύριος οὐκ αἰτεῖ οἶκον. 2. ἡ παρθένος ἔχει
νόσον· ὁ δὲ υἱὸς τοῦ ἀνθρώπου θεραπεύει τὰς νόσους. 3. ὦ
δέσποτα, οὐκ ἀκούεις τοὺς λόγους τῆς γλώσσης, ἀλλὰ βλέπεις
τὰ ἔργα τῶν ἀνθρώπων. 4. φιλεῖ ὁ βαπτιστὴς τὴν δικαιοσύνην
καὶ κηρύσσει ἐν τῇ ἐρήμῳ τὴν βασιλείαν τοῦ Θεοῦ· τηροῦμεν
οὖν τὰς ἐντολὰς τοῦ προφήτου. 5. ὦ μαθηταί, λαμβάνετε
ἐξουσίαν ἐν τῇ κώμῃ, οἱ δὲ ἀπόστολοι μαρτυροῦσι τῷ κόσμῳ.
6. ὦ νεανία, λαλῶ ταῖς παρθένοις πρὸ τοῦ ἱεροῦ· ζητοῦσι γὰρ
τὴν εἰρήνην καὶ τὴν ἀλήθειαν ἀπὸ τοῦ εὐαγγελίου.

Translate: 1. The slaves are leading the girls out of the house
into the village, but the householder is keeping the children with
the young men before the temple. 2. In the church we see the
glory of God, for the brothers bear witness to righteousness and
truth. 3. You (pl.) call the young men out of the boats before the
sabbath; therefore they are asking bread for the children. 4. O
Lord, you save the world and mankind from the authority of
demons; therefore we believe in the truth of the gospel. 5. The
girl does not heal diseases, O prophet, but she loves children and
observes God's commandments. 6. The son of man is preaching
from the boat to the disciples and they listen and write the words
for the householder's children.

6   Second declension adjectives. πρός

These fall into two groups, masculine and neuter always like
λόγος and ἔργον, feminine like *either* ἡμέρα if the stem ends in a
vowel or ρ, *or* ἐντολή if it ends in any other consonant.

	holy			first		
Sing. N.	ἅγιος	ἁγία	ἅγιον	πρῶτος	πρώτη	πρῶτον
V.	ἅγιε	ἁγία	ἅγιον	πρῶτε	πρώτη	πρῶτον
A.	ἅγιον	ἁγίαν	ἅγιον	πρῶτον	πρώτην	πρῶτον
G.	ἁγίου	ἁγίας	ἁγίου	πρώτου	πρώτης	πρώτου
D.	ἁγίῳ	ἁγίᾳ	ἁγίῳ	πρώτῳ	πρώτῃ	πρώτῳ
Pl. N.V.	ἅγιοι	ἅγιαι	ἅγια	πρῶτοι	πρῶται	πρῶτα

ἀγαθός -ή -όν	good	παιδίον -ου τό	little child
ἅγιος -α -ον	holy, saintly	πείθω	persuade
ἄδικος -ον[1]	unjust, un-righteous	περιπατέω	walk
		πιστός -ή -όν	faithful
δίκαιος -α -ον	just, righteous	πονηρός -ά -όν	evil, wicked
ἐμός -ή -όν[2]	my	πρός	(w. acc.) to,
ἔσχατος -η -ον	last		towards
ἡμέτερος -α -ον	our	πρῶτος -η -ον	first
καρδία -ας ἡ	heart	σός σή σόν	thy
οὐρανός -οῦ ὁ	sky, heaven	ὑμέτερος -α -ον	your

Translate: 1. περιπατεῖ οὖν τὰ ἐμὰ παιδία σὺν τοῖς ἁγίοις νεανίαις ἀπὸ τῆς θαλάσσης πρὸς τὴν πρώτην κώμην· καλεῖ γὰρ ὁ ἄδικος οἰκοδεσπότης. 2. οὐ βλέπουσιν οἱ ἄνθρωποι τὴν βασιλείαν τοῦ οὐρανοῦ ἐν τῷ κόσμῳ, ἐν δὲ ταῖς ἡμετέραις καρδίαις πιστεύομεν εἰς τὸν υἱόν. 3. ἐν δὲ ταῖς ἐσχάταις ἡμέραις κηρύσσουσι οἱ ἅγιοι ἀπόστολοι τὸ ἐμὸν εὐαγγέλιον τοῖς πιστοῖς μαθηταῖς. 4. οἱ δίκαιοι λόγοι τοῦ σοῦ ἀγαθοῦ υἱοῦ, ἀδελφέ, σώζουσι τὰ ἡμέτερα πονηρὰ τέκνα ἐκ τοῦ θανάτου· μαρτυροῦσι γὰρ τῇ ἀληθείᾳ τῶν πρώτων προφητῶν. 5. οὐκ ἔχετε ἀργύριον ἐν τοῖς ὑμετέροις οἴκοις, τοῖς δὲ πιστοῖς δούλοις σώζετε τοὺς ἐσχάτους ἄρτους. 6. ἐν ἀγάπῃ λέγεις λόγους ἀγαθούς.

Translate: 1. Peace and love bear witness to the truth of the gospel. 2. In our village the righteous brethren keep God's holy

---

[1] There is no separate feminine form in compound adjectives and a few others, e.g. ἔρημος, which is used as a feminine noun because γῆ, land, is understood.

[2] Possessive adjectives are used with the article..

commandments; but in your church the disciples do not find truth. 3. The first young man loves little children and is talking to the faithful girls in the last house of my village. 4. You (sing.) hide your righteousness, but your works speak before the Lord. 5. How does the evil tongue of demons persuade even our good and holy slaves?

---

7 Imperfect indicative active. μέγας, πολύς, διά

The imperfect active is used for habitual or continuous action.

Distinguishing Marks:

(1) tense endings[1]

(2) prefix of temporal augment to show past time, *either* ε before initial consonant *or* lengthening of initial vowel as follows:

α	becomes	η	ἀκούω	ἤκουον
αι		η	αἰτέω	ἤτουν
ε		η	ἐσθίω	ἤσθιον
ο		ω	ὀνομάζω	ὠνόμαζον
οι		ῳ	οἰκοδομέω	ᾠκοδόμουν

ἔλυον I was loosing *or* I used to loose	ἐφίλε-ον -ουν
ἔλυες	ἐφίλε-ες -εις
ἔλυε(ν)[2]	ἐφίλε-ε -ει
ἐλύομεν	ἐφιλέ-ομεν -οῦμεν
ἐλύετε	ἐφιλέ-ετε -εῖτε
ἔλυον	ἐφίλε-ον -ουν

[1] When the ending of a new verb is imperfect, remember to look for the unaugmented form in a lexicon.

[2] ν occurs after a final ε of the 3rd sing. in this and other tenses to avoid hiatus before a following vowel or to mark a pause.

When verbs were compounded with a preposition, as often happened (cf. p. 128), in the present the preposition was written in full before a consonant, ἀπο-θνήσκω, but if it ended in a vowel this elided before a following vowel, ἀπ-άγω. Before the augment such elision always happened except with περί: ἀπ-έθνησκον, ἀν-εγίνωσκον, παρ-εκάλουν but περι-επάτουν.[1]

μέγας, πολύς

Two very common 2nd declension adjectives which are irregular only in masculine and neuter nom. and acc. sing.

Sing.	great			much		
N.V.	μέγας	μεγάλη	μέγα	πολύς	πολλή	πολύ
A.	μέγαν	μεγάλην	μέγα	πολύν	πολλήν	πολύ
G.	μεγάλου	μεγάλης	μεγάλου	πολλοῦ	πολλῆς	πολλοῦ
D.	μεγάλῳ	μεγάλῃ	μεγάλῳ	πολλῷ	πολλῇ	πολλῷ
Pl.	μεγάλοι	μεγάλαι	μεγάλα	πολλοί	πολλαί	πολλά

Until prepositions become familiar, division between preposition and stem will be shown in the vocabularies.

αἰώνιος -ον	eternal (separate fem. rare)	δίκτυον -ου τό	net
ἀκολουθέω	(w. dat.) follow	ἐκ-βάλλω	cast out
ἀνα-γινώσκω	read	ζωή -ῆς ἡ	life
ἀπ-άγω	lead away	Ἰησοῦς[2] -οῦ	Jesus
ἀπο-θνήσκω	die	μέγας -άλη -α	big, great
ἀπο-κτείνω	kill	ὀνομάζω	name
βάλλω	throw	παρα-καλέω	exhort, comfort
βιβλίον -ου τό	book	πολύς πολλή	much (plural
γινώσκω	know	πολύ	many)

[1] This sensitivity to hiatus also led sometimes before a word beginning with a vowel to elision of the final vowel of a preposition or common particle, e.g. ἀλλ', δ'. When the consonant before the elided vowel was π or τ it changed to the aspirated form φ or θ before a rough breathing, ἀπ' οἴκου but ἀφ' ἁμαρτίας Such elision is marked by an apostrophe replacing the elided vowel, which makes it easily recognizable.

[2] Transliterated from Aramaic into quasi 2nd declension:

N. Ἰησοῦς   V. Ἰησοῦ   A. Ἰησοῦν   G. Ἰησοῦ   D. Ἰησοῦ

The article tends to be used with the names of well-known people.

διά   (w. acc.) because of, on account of, (w. gen.) through

Translate: 1. περιεπάτει οὖν ὁ Ἰησοῦς σὺν τοῖς μαθηταῖς πρὸς τὴν θάλασσαν· ἠκολούθουν δὲ πολλοί. 2. ἐν δὲ τῇ μεγάλῃ κώμῃ εὕρισκον[1] πολλὰ παιδία καὶ ἀπῆγον[2] διὰ τῶν ὁδῶν εἰς τὸν ἡμέτε- ρον οἶκον· φιλῶ γὰρ τὰ ἀγαθὰ τέκνα. 3. πῶς ἔβαλλον οἱ πιστοὶ δοῦλοι τὰ δίκτυα ἐκ τοῦ πλοίου εἰς τὴν μεγάλην θάλασσαν; 4. ᾐτεῖτε τὸν ἅγιον ἄρτον ἐκ τοῦ ἱεροῦ, οὐκ ἐκ τοῦ οὐρανοῦ. 5. ἀπὸ τῆς γλώσσης τοῦ Ἰησοῦ ἤκουον οἱ ἀδελφοὶ τοὺς λόγους τῆς αἰωνίου ζωῆς. 6. διὰ τὴν σὴν δικαιοσύνην ἀνεγίνωσκες τὸ πρῶτον βιβλίον τοῦ νόμου, ἀλλ᾽ οὐκ ἐγίνωσκες τὸ εὐαγγέλιον. 7. ἠκολουθοῦμεν οὖν τῷ Ἰησοῦ καὶ εἰς τὴν ἔρημον. 8. ἐξέβαλλεν ὁ Ἰησοῦς τὰ δαιμόνια, παρεκάλει δέ τὰ παιδία.

Translate: 1. Because of disease many disciples used to die in the desert, but the righteous apostle heals faithful men. 2. We used to name Jesus the son of man and write the commandments of the holy gospel in our books. 3. The evil householder sends many children into the desert; therefore they die. 4. Your (pl.) unjust master used to kill many of my faithful slaves, for he did not know the words of the law. 5. You, young man, were seeking the kingdom of heaven; therefore because of your good works you see God's signs and they persuade your heart.

[1] As ευ and ηυ were pronounced alike, initial ευ often takes no augment.
[2] In any tense the accent cannot go further back than the augment.

8 The verb *to be*. οὗτος, ἐκεῖνος

The irregular verb *to be* has three tenses, present, imperfect and future (cf. p. 35). In the present, except for the 2nd person sing., εἰμί is enclitic, i.e. so weak that it cannot stand at the beginning of a sentence and throws back its accent onto the preceding word whenever possible.[1]

Present Indicative		Imperfect Indicative	
εἰμί	I am	ἤμην	I was
εἶ	thou art	ἦσθα, ἦς[2]	thou wast
ἐστί(ν)	he, she, it is	ἦν	he, she, it was
ἐσμέν	we are	ἦμεν, ἤμεθα	we were
ἐστέ	you are	ἦτε	you were
εἰσί(ν)	they are	ἦσαν	they were

This verb is followed by a predicate telling something about the subject, not by a direct object, so it takes the same case after it as before it:

ἡ παρθένος ἐστὶν ἀγαθή. ὁ Ἰησοῦς ἦν ὁ υἱὸς τοῦ Θεοῦ.
The girl is good. Jesus was the son of God.

When there is a predicate the verb *to be* is often omitted, but must be supplied in English:

μακάριοι οἱ πτωχοί. Blessed are the poor.

NB The article is used to form a noun of the corresponding gender:
  (*a*) with adjectives, e.g. οἱ ἅγιοι, the holy men, i.e. the saints, τὸ πονηρόν, the evil thing, i.e. evil in the abstract.
  (*b*) with adverbs, e.g. the common Lucan ἀπὸ τοῦ νῦν, from the present time, i.e. henceforth.
  (*c*) with prepositional phrases used adjectivally, e.g. οἱ ἐν Ἰουδαίᾳ, those in Judaea.

---

[1] See p. 154 for a list of enclitics and rules for their accentuation.
[2] When two forms are given this means that CG and K forms were used indifferently.

οὗτος, ἐκεῖνος

Two common 2nd declension demonstratives which must be carefully learnt:

οὗτος	αὕτη	τοῦτο	οὗτοι	αὗται	ταῦτα
τοῦτον	ταύτην	τοῦτο	τούτους	ταύτας	ταῦτα
τούτου	ταύτης	τούτου	τούτων	τούτων	τούτων
τούτῳ	ταύτῃ	τούτῳ	τούτοις	ταύταις	τούτοις

The diphthong before an ending in o or ω is ου, before an ending
in η or α is αυ. Hence τούτων gen. pl. for all genders.

ἐκεῖνος has no peculiarities except for the neuter sing. in -o, which
is common to all 2nd declension demonstratives.

NB Both οὗτος (this) and ἐκεῖνος (that) stand either before or after
the combination of article and noun, never between:

οὗτος ὁ μαθητής   ἐκείνη ἡ κώμη
this disciple   that village

Both may stand alone without any article and noun, when a noun
must be supplied in English from the gender of the demonstrative:[1]

οὗτοι   ἐκεῖναι   ταῦτα
these men   those women   these things

διδάσκω	teach	ὄχλος -ου ὁ	crowd, multi-
ἐκεῖνος -η -o	that		tude
Ἰουδαῖος -ου ὁ	Jew	πλούσιος -α -ον	rich
καλός -ή -όν	beautiful,	πτωχός -ή -όν	poor
	good	Ῥωμαῖος -ου ὁ	Roman
μακάριος -α -ον	blessed,	σταυρός -οῦ ὁ	cross
	happy	τότε	then
νῦν	now	τυφλός -ή -όν	blind
οὗτος αὕτη τοῦτο	this	Φαρισαῖος -ου ὁ	Pharisee

---

[1] Sometimes when they stand alone as the subject of a verb they are no more
than an emphatic *he*, cf. Luke 1.32.

Translate: 1. οἱ Φαρισαῖοι οὐ φιλοῦσι τούτους τοὺς πλουσίους
Ῥωμαίους· διὰ γὰρ τὰς ἁμαρτίας οὐχ ἅγιοί εἰσιν. 2. τότε ἐν
ταῖς ἡμέραις ἐκείναις ἐδίδασκες τὸν ὄχλον· νῦν δὲ τυφλὸς εἶ· ὁ
γὰρ ἀπόστολος οὐ θεραπεύει ταύτην τὴν νόσον. 3. ἔβαλλε ταῦτα
τὰ ὑμέτερα τέκνα τὰ ἐμὰ ἱμάτια ἐξ ἐκείνου τοῦ πρώτου πλοίου
εἰς τὴν θάλασσαν· πολλοὶ¹ γάρ εἰσι καὶ πονηροί. 4. καλά ἐστι
τὰ ἔργα ταύτης τῆς παρθένου, ἀλλ' οὐ πιστὴ ἡ καρδία. 5. ὦ
μακάριοι προφῆται, ἐμαρτυρεῖτε τῇ ἀληθείᾳ· κηρύσσει δὲ ὁ
βαπτιστὴς τοῖς πτωχοῖς ἐν τῇ ἐρήμῳ· δίκαιος γάρ ἐστι καὶ ἅγιος
ὁ ἔσχατος τῶν προφητῶν.

Matt. 22.14; 25.2; 25.36 (ἐν — ἤμην); John 1.19a; 5.9b; 17.17b

[From now on references to NT texts will be given, illustrating
forms and constructions already met. Inevitably there will be new
vocabulary; this should be looked up in a lexicon and the student
should make his own word-book, learning new words as they occur.
It is assumed that the Bible Society's Greek Testament, 2nd edition, will be used. Translation may be checked by reference to the
Revised Version (RV), Revised Standard Version (RSV) or the Bible
Society's Greek-English N.T. (Diglot). The New English Bible
(NEB) will best be used in conjunction with one of the preceding
more literal translations.]

In continuous narrative the historic present, used vividly for past
time, will often be met.

Translate: 1. In the days of the prophets rich men used to build
many houses in this village. 2. We were teaching the sons of
these beautiful girls with those children. 3. You (pl.) used to eat
this good bread and send loaves for the faithful slaves. 4. You
(sing.) were in this boat and you were reading to these little children
the last commandments of that good law. 5. On account of these
evil deeds the Roman used to kill slaves on the cross. 6. This rich
man was seeking a big house for the happy son of the householder.

¹ Such constructions according to sense are common. τέκνον is neuter, but
a child is a person, so the subject contained in the verb εἰσι is thought of as
masculine.

Future active—formed by adding σ to present stem and then present endings: λύω λύ-σ-ω

Aorist[1] **active**—formed by prefixing augment, adding σ to stem as in future, then aorist endings in which α is the distinctive vowel.

This is the historic tense most often used in narrative for a single completed action.

λύσω	I shall loose	ἔλυσα	I loosed or I did loose
λύσεις		ἔλυσας	
λύσει		ἔλυσε(ν)	
λύσομεν		ἐλύσαμεν	
λύσετε		ἐλύσατε	
λύσουσι(ν)		ἔλυσαν	

Contracted verbs lengthen the stem vowel before adding σ:

φιλέω φιλήσω ἐφίλησα but καλέσω, ἐκάλεσα; τελέσω, ἐτέλεσα

When the stem ends in a consonant, combination with σ follows certain rules:[2]

Gutturals

(1) κ, χ, γ + σ = ξ: διώκω διώξω ἐδίωξα
(2) a longer present stem in σσ conceals a guttural:[3]

κηρύσσω κηρύξω ἐκήρυξα

Labials

(1) π, φ, β + σ = ψ: πέμπω πέμψω ἔπεμψα
(2) a longer present stem in ππ conceals a labial:

ἀποκαλύπτω ἀποκαλύψω ἀπεκάλυψα

[1] See p. 49 for explanation of name.
[2] Rules for forming the future and aorist of liquid and nasal stems ending in λ, μ, ν, ρ are not given until p. 71.
[3] Verbs with a longer present stem use this for present and imperfect, but the stem proper is used for forming all other tenses.

Dentals

(1) τ, θ, δ drop out before σ: πείθω πείσω ἔπεισα

(2) a present stem in ζ usually conceals a dental, but occasionally a guttural:

σώζω   σώσω   ἔσωσα   κράζω[1] κράξω   ἔκραξα

ἀγοράζω	buy	ἐκ-κόπτω	cut down
ἀπο-καλύπτω	reveal, un-cover	ἑτοιμάζω	prepare
		κράζω	cry out
βαστάζω	carry	λῃστής -οῦ ὁ	robber, bandit
γῆ -ῆς ἡ	earth, land	ὅτι	(conjunction)
δέκα	(indecl.) ten		because
δένδρον -ου τό	tree	πράσσω	do
διώκω	pursue, perse-cute	φυλάσσω	guard

Give 1st person sing. of fut. indic. active of ἄγω, γράφω, βλέπω; 3rd sing. of aorist indic. active of verbs in vocabulary above; 3rd pl. of aorist indic. active of ἀκούω, αἰτέω, παρακαλέω, θεραπεύω.

Translate: 1. ἔπεμψαν οὖν οἱ Ἰουδαῖοι τοὺς πονηροὺς λῃστὰς τούτους πρὸς τοὺς Ῥωμαίους· ἐξουσίαν γὰρ οὐκ εἶχον.[2] 2. γράψομεν τούτους τοὺς ἁγίους λόγους ἐν τῷ βιβλίῳ καὶ οὐκ ἀποκαλύψομεν τῷ ὄχλῳ τῷ ἀδίκῳ.[3] 3. τότε ἐβάστασεν ὁ Ἰησοῦς τὸν σταυρόν, οἱ δέ μαθηταὶ οὐκ ἠκολούθησαν. 4. ὦ πλούσιε νεανία, ἠγόρασας ἱμάτια τοῖς πτωχοῖς, πολὺ δὲ ἀργύριον φυλάσσεις ἐν τῷ ἱερῷ. 5. διώξουσιν ἐκεῖνοι οἱ δοῦλοι τὸν πονηρὸν ἄγγελον εἰς ταύτην τὴν γῆν· καλοὶ γάρ εἰσι καὶ πιστοί. 6. ὅτι ἔκραξεν ἐν τῇ ἐρήμῳ ἤκουσαν οἱ ὄχλοι τὸν βαπτιστὴν καὶ ἔπραξαν τὰς ἐντολὰς τοῦ νόμου. 7. πῶς ἐξέκοψας ἐκεῖνα τὰ μεγάλα δένδρα;

Matt. 5.12b; 13.3 (καὶ — παρ.); 26.19b; I Cor. 15.11b

---

[1] All other verbs in -ζω given in this book conceal a dental.

[2] ἔχω has an irregular augment in the imperfect. Notice too the future ἕξω, where the smooth breathing changes to rough.

[3] Instead of standing between article and noun an adjective may less commonly follow a repetition of the article.

Translate: 1. The Jews bought a cross for the son of man and you finished your work, O Jesus. 2. Because of this sin of the world God sent Jesus to the earth and saved mankind. 3. You (pl.) will prepare a way for the Lord in the desert; for he guards and will save the faithful and holy. 4. On this day ten apostles preached the gospel to many in that great crowd. 5. I asked for a book (acc.) and wrote these things for my children, because they believe in God and will bear witness to the signs of Jesus. 6. We hid the blind man in this house, for the robbers used to kill rich men and take the money of the poor. 7. How did the first apostle reveal the gospel?

IO Personal and reflexive pronouns. αὐτός. Article with μέν and δέ. κατά, μετά

Personal Pronouns

Sing.	ἐγώ		I	σύ	thou (you sing.)
	ἐμέ	με		σέ	
	ἐμοῦ	μου		σοῦ	
	ἐμοί	μοι		σοί	

The nominative is used only to emphasize the subject of the verb; the longer forms of ἐγώ, always accented, and the acc., gen. and dative of σύ, if accented, are used only to give emphasis or with a preposition. The shorter forms of ἐγώ and these cases of σύ are used as enclitics (cf. p. 154) when they are not emphatic, and cannot stand at the beginning of a sentence.

πιστεύουσι δι' ἐμέ.
They trust because of me.

τὸ παιδίον μου
my little child

σὺ λέγεις.　　　　　　διώκουσί σε.
You say (it).　　　　　They are pursuing you.

Pl.　ἡμεῖς[1]　we　　　ὑμεῖς　ye (you pl.)
　　ἡμᾶς　　　　　　　ὑμᾶς
　　ἡμῶν　　　　　　　ὑμῶν
　　ἡμῖν　　　　　　　ὑμῖν

These personal pronouns used possessively in the genitive with a combination of article and noun were in common use, with the same meaning as the possessive adjective:

　οἱ δοῦλοι ἡμῶν　　　τὸ ἀργύριόν σου　　　οἱ οἶκοι ὑμῶν

αὐτός -ή -ό

αὐτός has three uses:

1. 3rd person pronoun in oblique cases meaning *him, her, it, them* (Latin *is, ea, id*):

　τὸ βιβλίον αὐτοῦ　　　φιλοῦμεν αὐτήν.
　his book　　　　　　　We love her.

　τὰ ἱμάτια αὐτῶν　　　πέμπει ἄρτον αὐτοῖς.
　their clothes　　　　　He sends bread for them.

There is no 3rd person possessive adjective, so the genitive of the pronoun must be used (cf. Latin *eius, eorum*).

2. in apposition to subject contained in verb or to combination of article and noun means *self* (Latin *ipse*):

　αὐτὸς λέγει.　　　　　ἐβλέψαμεν τὸν προφήτην αὐτόν.
　He himself says.　　　We saw the prophet himself.

3. standing between article and noun means *same* (Latin *idem*):[2]

　ὁ αὐτὸς νόμος　the same law

---

[1] The circumflex accent marking an original contraction of two vowels.

[2] The neuter sing. and pl. are sometimes fused with the article, ταὐτό=τὸ αὐτό *the same thing*; ταὐτά=τὰ αὐτά *the same things*, to be distinguished from ταῦτα *these things* by retention of breathing and difference in accentuation.

Reflexive Pronouns

1st and 2nd person sing. αὐτός is fused with the pronoun:

ἐμαυτόν -ήν   σεαυτόν -ήν
ἐμαυτοῦ -ῆς   σεαυτοῦ -ῆς
ἐμαυτῷ -ῇ   σεαυτῷ -ῇ
λύω ἐμαυτόν.   οὐ θεραπεύεις σεαυτόν.
I am releasing myself.   You do not heal yourself.

3rd person sing.

ἑαυτόν -ήν -ό   ἑαυτοῦ -ῆς -οῦ   ἑαυτῷ -ῇ -ῷ

1st, 2nd and 3rd person pl.

ἑαυτούς -άς -ά   ἑαυτῶν[1]   ἑαυτοῖς -αῖς -οῖς
μαρτυροῦμεν ἑαυτοῖς.   φιλοῦσιν ἑαυτούς.
We bear witness to ourselves.   They love themselves.

Article with μέν and δέ

The article retains a trace of an ancient pronominal use, found with δέ to mark a change of subject, ὁ δέ *but he*, οἱ δέ *but they*, often used in the NT with verbs of saying:

ἐκάλεσα τὸν ἀδελφόν μου, ὁ δέ οὐκ ἤκουσεν.

I called my brother, but he did not hear.

Akin to this is the use with μέν . . . δέ (μέν is an emphasizing particle, often untranslated, anticipating a following δέ and marking a balanced antithesis, a stylistic nicety common in CG):

ἐγὼ μέν εἰμι Ῥωμαῖος, σὺ δὲ δοῦλος.

I on the one hand am a Roman, you on the other hand are a slave.

or (more commonly) I am a Roman, but you are a slave.

With the article used as a pronoun:

ὁ μέν (οἱ μέν) . . . ὁ δέ (οἱ δέ)

He (they) on the one hand . . . he (they) on the other hand

i.e. one . . . another (sing.), some . . . others (pl.)

οἱ μὲν γράφουσιν, οἱ δὲ ἀναγινώσκουσι.

Some are writing, others are reading.

---

[1] At times some MSS may read the CG variant αὐτῶν, but modern editors prefer ἑαυτῶν or αὐτῶν, which in K were often used indiscriminately.

ἁμαρτωλός -όν	sinful	μετά	(w. acc.) after
δεσμός -οῦ ὁ	chain		(w. gen.)
ἐχθρός -ά -όν	hostile		with
ἰατρός -οῦ ὁ	doctor	οἶνος -ου ὁ	wine
ἴδιος -α -ον[1]	one's own	πίνω	drink
κατά	(w. acc.) according to	πότε	when?
		πρόβατον -ου τό	sheep
	(w. gen.) down from, against	συν-άγω	gather, drive together
		τελώνης -ου ὁ	tax-collector

Translate: 1. ἔλυσα τοὺς δεσμοὺς αὐτῶν καὶ ἔπεμψα τοὺς μὲν πρὸς τὴν θάλασσαν, τοὺς δὲ εἰς ταύτην τὴν κώμην. 2. ἀνεγίνωσκον οἱ δοῦλοί σου καὶ τὰ παιδία ἡμῶν ταῦτα (τὰ αὐτὰ) βιβλία· φιλοῦσι γὰρ τοὺς λόγους τοῦ ἁγίου ἀποστόλου. 3. ὁ πλούσιος καὶ ἄδικος τελώνης αὐτὸς ἐλάμβανεν ἀπὸ τοῦ πτωχοῦ τὰ ἱμάτια αὐτοῦ· οὗτος γὰρ οὐκ εἶχεν ἀργύριον. 4. μετὰ δὲ τὰς ἡμέρας ταύτας βλέψουσι καὶ οἱ ἁμαρτωλοὶ τὴν βασιλείαν τῶν οὐρανῶν·[2] ὁ γὰρ Ἰησοῦς πείσει αὐτούς. 5. σύ, ὦ δέσποτα, ἐλάλησας ταῦτα κατὰ τοῦ προφήτου τούτου ὅτι ἐχθρὸς εἶ καὶ διώκεις ἡμᾶς. 6. κατὰ τὸν νόμον ὑμῶν ἐπέμψαμεν τὸν ἁμαρτωλὸν ἐκεῖνον μετὰ τῶν αὐτῶν δούλων πρὸς αὐτὸν τὸν Ῥωμαῖον· ὁ δὲ οὐκ ἐτήρησεν αὐτοὺς ἐν τῷ ἰδίῳ οἴκῳ αὐτοῦ. 7. πότε ἔβλεψας σὺ τὸν Κύριον;

Matt. 1.21b; 3.17 (οὗτ. — ἀγαπ.); 9.37; 22.16 (καὶ — Ἡρ.); Mark 14.7a; 14.56; John 1.41a; 17.14b

Translate: 1. Some were drinking wine with the tax-collectors, others were eating bread with you (pl.) in the same village. 2. My enemies[3] are seeking our land and will gather together our sheep and will pursue us into the desert. 3. You (pl.) yourselves

---

[1] In CG the article was sufficient to describe something as belonging to the subject of the verb, φιλεῖ τὸν υἱόν *He loves his son*, but in κ this was reinforced by a possessive pronoun, φιλεῖ τὸν υἱὸν αὐτοῦ (ἑαυτοῦ), or by ἴδιος, φιλεῖ τὸν ἴδιον υἱόν, with or without the genitive pronoun.

[2] Some NT writers prefer the pl. because the Semitic word for sky only existed as a plural.

[3] ἐχθροί used as a noun. The Greek plural must be used for the English collective *enemy*.

guarded the good doctor, because he healed your blind sons; but they bore witness against him. 4. The righteous householder did not trust in himself, but in the commandments of God, for the gospel of Jesus revealed them to him. 5. Because of this, O young man, you wrote the same things in the tax-collector's book against our brother, but he will not believe you and will tell me the truth. 6. This poor girl was beautiful; therefore many used to seek her, but she herself loved the rich man's blind son, because he had a big house and much money.

II   Middle voice: present, imperfect, future, aorist

The Middle voice was used, as distinct from the Active, to show that the subject was doing something or getting something done in his own interest. In κ it was falling out of use and often the distinction hardly permits translation. $\kappa\epsilon\acute{\iota}\rho\omega$, Active, is used of a man shearing a sheep in Acts 8.32 (Isa. 53.7), the Middle used properly in Acts 18.18 when Paul 'had his hair cut off' (NEB), but 'having shorn his head' (RV). $\nu\acute{\iota}\pi\tau\omega$, Active, is used of Jesus' washing the disciples' feet, John 13.14, the Middle invariably of personal washing, but the translation is still *wash*. In Matt. 27.5 $\dot{\alpha}\pi\acute{\eta}\gamma\xi\alpha\tau o$ (from $\dot{\alpha}\pi\acute{\alpha}\gamma\chi\omega$) is used when Judas *hanged himself*, but an Active with a reflexive pronoun is more common. Active and Middle of $\alpha\grave{\iota}\tau\acute{\epsilon}\omega$ seem to be used interchangeably, although the Middle might be expected to imply asking or claiming for oneself.

There are also some common verbs which are deponent, i.e. have laid aside their active forms, but are active in meaning. These may be either Middle or Passive in form or may have a Middle future and Passive aorist. To differentiate, (M) or (P) will be added to deponent verbs in the vocabularies and irregularities noted.

34

Present Indicative Middle

λύομαι[1]	αἰτέομαι -οῦμαι
λύει or λύῃ	αἰτέει -εῖ or -έῃ -ῇ
λύεται	αἰτέεται -εῖται
λυόμεθα	αἰτεόμεθα -ούμεθα
λύεσθε	αἰτέεσθε -εῖσθε
λύονται	αἰτέονται -οῦνται

Imperfect Indicative Middle — formed as in the Active by prefixing the augment and adding the proper endings.

ἐλυόμην	ᾐτεόμην -ούμην
ἐλύου	ᾐτέου -οῦ
ἐλύετο	ᾐτέετο -εῖτο
ἐλυόμεθα	ᾐτεόμεθα -ούμεθα
ἐλύεσθε	ᾐτέεσθε -εῖσθε
ἐλύοντο	ᾐτέοντο -οῦντο

Future and Aorist Middle are formed like the Active, future by adding σ to the stem proper (lengthened in contracted verbs, αἰτήσομαι) and then the present endings, aorist by prefixing the augment, adding σ and then aorist endings in which the distinctive vowel is α (ᾐτησάμην).

Future Indicative Middle	Aorist Indicative Middle
λύσομαι	ἐλυσάμην
λύσει or λύσῃ	ἐλύσω
λύσεται	ἐλύσατο
λυσόμεθα	ἐλυσάμεθα
λύσεσθε	ἐλύσασθε
λύσονται	ἐλύσαντο

NB The verb *to be* has a regular middle future, ἔσομαι, except for 3rd sing. ἔσται.

[1] In CG the Middle was used meaning *loose for one's own purpose*, i.e. *ransom*, but is not found in the NT.

δέχομαι (M)	receive	νεκρός -ά -όν	dead (as
διάβολος -ου ὁ[1]	devil		noun,
ἐκ-λέγομαι (M)	choose		corpse)
ἔρχομαι (M)[2]	come or go	νίπτω	wash
Ἰωάννης -ου ὁ	John	προσ-εύχομαι (M)	pray
κεφαλή -ῆς ἡ	head	προσ-καλέομαι (M)	summon
λαός -οῦ ὁ	people	χωλός -ή -όν	lame

Translate: 1. κατ' ἐμοῦ. πέμπει σοι τὰ τέκνα ἑαυτοῦ. φιλεῖτε ἑαυτούς. ἐζήτουν ἡμᾶς. ἐκηρύξαμεν ὑμῖν. 2. ὁ μὲν προσηύξατο τῷ Θεῷ, ὁ δὲ ἔκραξεν ἐν τῇ ἐρήμῳ. 3. πῶς ἔρχονται οἱ τελῶναι καὶ οἱ ἁμαρτωλοὶ εἰς τὴν βασιλείαν τῶν οὐρανῶν πρὸ ἡμῶν τῶν Φαρισαίων; 4. ἐξελέξατο ὁ Ἰησοῦς τοὺς ἀποστόλους αὐτοῦ ἐκ τοῦ λαοῦ· οἱ δὲ ἠκολούθησαν αὐτῷ. 5. δεχόμεθα οὖν εἰς τὴν ἁγίαν ἐκκλησίαν καὶ τοὺς χωλοὺς καὶ τοὺς πτωχοὺς κατὰ τὴν ἐντολὴν αὐτοῦ τοῦ Κυρίου ἡμῶν. 6. ἐν δὲ ταῖς ἐσχάταις ἡμέραις ἐλεύσεται ὁ Ἰησοῦς αὐτὸς καὶ προσκαλέσεται τοὺς νεκροὺς καὶ σώσει αὐτοὺς ἐκ τῆς ἐξουσίας τοῦ διαβόλου. 7. ἐδέχου τοὺς ἀδίκους εἰς τὸν οἶκόν σου καὶ ἡτοίμαζες αὐτοῖς ἄρτον καὶ οἶνον· διὰ τοῦτ' οὖν πολλοὶ ἤρχοντο πρός σε καὶ ἐφίλουν. 8. ἔνιπτεν ἡ δούλη τὸ τέκνον, ἀλλ' αὐτὸς ἐνίπτετο τὴν κεφαλὴν ἑαυτοῦ. 9. μέγας οὖν ἔσται καὶ σώσει τὸν λαόν.

Mark 6.7 (καὶ — δω.); Luke 8.27 (οὐκ — ἔμεν.); John 1.20a; 15.16a; Gal. 4.14b-15a

Translate: 1. Some heal, others preach. His son. Our little children. We shall follow you (sing.). I do not bear witness to myself. 2. You, O Lord, chose this man; and he will lead many and reveal to them your gospel in his books. 3. Wicked men pray to the devil himself, but Jesus casts out demons because of his authority. 4. You (pl.) used to teach many blind men with these ten girls; and they (fem.) used to read to them the words of eternal life. 5. I composed (made for myself) the first book, O

---

[1] Properly *slanderer* and as such represents ᴏᴛ Satan.
[2] Very common verb with irregular future middle ἐλεύσομαι and aorist and perfect active (cf. pp. 42, 98).

Theophilus, because my brothers were not praying in their hearts, but were saying evil things[1] against the church. 6. That lame man will receive the bread because he is asking according to the law.

---

12 Passive voice: present, imperfect. Temporal clauses. ὑπό

Passive is used when the inactive subject suffers treatment, as opposed to the Active when the subject takes action or the Middle when the subject takes action in his own interest or accepts treatment. Passive and Middle are the same in form in present and imperfect, but differ in formation of future and aorist (cf. p. 45). Sometimes there is little distinction in meaning. Compare I Cor. 10.2, *received baptism* (NEB), *were baptized* (RV) with Gal. 3.27 where the passive is used in a similar phrase.

A personal agent is expressed by ὑπό with the genitive, instrument by the dative (cf. Latin ablative) or in κ often by ἐν with the dative.

συνάγεται τὰ πρόβατά μου ὑπὸ τῶν λῃστῶν (ἐν) λίθοις.
My sheep are being gathered together by the robbers with stones.

Temporal clauses

Temporal conjunctions:

when	ὅτε, ὡς
while	ὡς, ἐν ᾧ, ἕως
until	ἕως, μέχρι(ς), ἄχρι(ς)

---

[1] Neuter pl. of the adjective, which implies *things*.

(These three are used alone or with the gen. sing. neuter of the relative, οὗ or ὅτου (cf. p. 91), as conjunctions meaning *until*, prepositionally with the genitive, meaning *as far as* (cf. p. 131).)

All these conjunctions are found with the appropriate tense of the indicative expressing definite action.

βαπτίζω	baptize, wash	μισθός -οῦ ὁ	pay, reward
γραφή -ῆς ἡ	writing (pl. scriptures)	ὀφθαλμός -οῦ ὁ	eye
		περιβλέπομαι (M)	look round
ἐλεέω[1]	pity	πορεύομαι (P)[3]	journey, (walk, figura- tively)
ἐργάτης -ου ὁ	workman		
Ἰορδάνης -ου ὁ	Jordan		
λίθος -ου ὁ	stone	ποταμός -οῦ ὁ	river
μάχαιρα -ης ἡ[2]	sword	ὑπό	(w. acc.) under, (w. gen.) by, (of agent)
μετάνοια -ας ἡ	change of mind, re- pentance		

Give the 3rd sing. aorist indic. active of ἐλεέω, ἀποκαλύπτω; 2nd sing. imperfect indic. active and passive of ἔχω; 1st pl. present indic. passive of ζητέω, σώζω; 3rd pl. fut. indic. of δέχομαι, πορεύομαι; 3rd sing. present and fut. indic. of ἔρχομαι; 2nd pl. aorist indic. middle of αἰτέω, περιβλέπομαι.

[From now on words used in the translation from Greek which are easily identifiable from their English derivatives or because they are cognate with words already learnt will not be included in the vocabularies prefixed to exercises.]

Translate: 1. ἀπεκτείνοντο οἱ πτωχοὶ μαχαίρῃ ὑπὸ τῶν πονηρῶν τελωνῶν, ὡς ἐπορεύοντο διὰ τῆς ἐρήμου εἰς ταύτην τὴν γῆν. 2. οἰκοδομεῖται ἡ συναγωγὴ μεγάλοις λίθοις ὑπὸ τῶν αὐτῶν ἐργα- τῶν· μετὰ δὲ πολλὰς ἡμέρας τελέσουσι τὸ ἔργον, ἀλλ' οὐκ ἐν τῷ

---

[1] Note that it is only the final ε which contracts — ἐλεῶ.
[2] Irregular gen. and dat. sing. in -ης, -ῃ.
[3] This has a middle future πορεύσομαι.

σαββάτῳ. 3. ὅτι ἠλέησε τὸν ὄχλον προσεκαλέσατο αὐτοὺς ὁ
'Ιησοῦς· οἱ δὲ οὐκ ἐπείθοντο τοῖς λόγοις αὐτοῦ. 4. μέχρι
ἐβαπτισάμην ἐν τῷ 'Ιορδάνῃ ποταμῷ οὐ προσηυχόμην ἐν μετα-
νοίᾳ τῷ Θεῷ· ἠγόμην γὰρ εἰς ἁμαρτίαν ὑπὸ τοῦ διαβόλου καὶ
τῶν δαιμονίων αὐτοῦ. 5. βάλλεται τὰ δίκτυα ἐκ τοῦ πλοίου εἰς
τὴν θάλασσαν ὑπὸ τοῦ Πέτρου. 6. πολλοὶ ἐβαπτίζοντο καὶ
πορεύονται ἐν τῇ ὁδῷ τῆς δικαιοσύνης.

Mark 6.20a; Luke 24.32 (ὡς — γρ.); John 4.50b; 5.7b (ἐν
ᾧ — κατ.); 17.12 (ὅτε — αὐτ.); 19.8 (ὅτε — λόγ.)

Translate: 1. The big cross is carried by Jesus, but he is not
pitied by the crowd. 2. We looked round the temple and talked
to the little children, for we pitied them. 3. While the last gospel
was being written the scriptures used to be hidden by this faithful
apostle under the stones. 4. You (sing.) received the reward of
your righteousness when you saw Jesus with your own eyes; but
in the last days he will come in his glory with the holy angels. 5.
You (pl.) were being pursued into the desert by many robbers
until our master sent his slaves. 6. These scriptures were not
being read by the youths, for they were being guarded by the
unrighteous tax-collector in his own house.

13   Second aorist active and middle. Relative pronoun

The rules already given were for the 1st or weak aorist and apply
to the great majority of verbs. Some verbs, however, instead of
adding σ to the stem and then aorist endings, after prefixing the
augment add the *imperfect* endings to a strong stem. There is no
way of predicting that a verb will have a strong aorist. Such verbs

are few, but in common use and must be accepted as irregular and learnt carefully.

Aorist indic. active		Aorist indic. middle	
λαμβάνω		γίνομαι	
ἔλαβον	I took *or* received	ἐγενόμην	I became
ἔλαβες		ἐγένου	
ἔλαβε(ν)		ἐγένετο	
ἐλάβομεν		ἐγενόμεθα	
ἐλάβετε		ἐγένεσθε	
ἔλαβον		ἐγένοντο	

As there is often irregularity also in forming the future this is given below as well as the strong aorist:

ἄγω	ἄξω	ἤγαγον	lead *or* drive
ἁμαρτάνω	ἁμαρτήσω	ἡμάρτησα ἥμαρτον	sin
ἀπο-θνήσκω	ἀποθανοῦμαι	ἀπέθανον	die
γίνομαι[1]	γενήσομαι	ἐγενόμην	become, happen
εὑρίσκω	εὑρήσω	εὗρον	find
λαμβάνω	λήμψομαι[1]	ἔλαβον	take *or* receive
λείπω	λείψω	ἔλιπον	leave
μανθάνω		ἔμαθον	learn
πάσχω		ἔπαθον	suffer
πίνω	πίομαι	ἔπιον	drink
πίπτω	πεσοῦμαι	ἔπεσον	fall
τίκτω	τέξομαι	ἔτεκον	bring forth, bear a child
φεύγω	φεύξομαι	ἔφυγον	flee

In the κ there is a strong tendency to assimilate to better known forms; hence ἡμάρτησα along with ἥμαρτον, κατέλειψα (stronger form of λείπω *abandon*) along with κατέλιπον, without any difference of meaning.

The future middle forms ἀποθανοῦμαι and πεσοῦμαι are simply contracted forms with -ε (cf. p. 71).

[1] Spelling of κ instead of CG γίγνομαι, λήψομαι.

40

Relative Pronoun

Except in the nom. sing. masc. ὅς and the accented ἥ, οἵ, αἵ this can be memorized as the definite article without initial τ.

ὅς	ἥ	ὅ	οἵ	αἵ	ἅ
ὅν	ἥν	ὅ	οὕς	ἅς	ἅ
οὗ	ἧς	οὗ	ὧν	ὧν	ὧν
ᾧ	ᾗ	ᾧ	οἷς	αἷς	οἷς

The relative must agree with its antecedent in number and gender, but not necessarily in case, as this is dictated by the pronoun's function in its own clause:

ἄγεται πρὸς τὸν σταυρὸν ὁ διδάσκαλος ὃν φιλοῦμεν.
The teacher whom we love is being led to the cross.

ἔρχεται τὸ τέκνον οὗ τὸ ἱμάτιον ἔλαβον.
The child whose cloak I took is coming.

ἀποθανοῦνται οἱ νεανίαι οἳ ἐποίησαν τοῦτο.
The young men who did this will die.

ἐκεῖ	there	σωτηρία -ας ἡ	salvation
κακός -ή -όν	bad	χρόνος -ου ὁ	time
πέντε	five	ὧδε	here

Translate: 1. οὐχ ἥμαρτεν ὁ τυφλὸς οὗτος οὗ ἐθεράπευσε τοὺς ὀφθαλμοὺς ὁ Ἰησοῦς. 2. οἱ μὲν Γαλιλαῖοι φεύξονται εἰς τὴν Σαμάρειαν, οἱ δὲ ἐχθροὶ εὑρήσουσιν αὐτοὺς ἐκεῖ. 3. ἔμαθον οἱ μαθηταὶ ταῦτα ἐν τῇ Ῥώμῃ, ἐν ᾗ ἔλιπεν αὐτοὺς ὁ Παῦλος. 4. καὶ[1] ἐγένετο μετὰ πολὺν χρόνον ἔτεκεν ἡ παρθένος υἱόν, ὃς πολλοὺς ἤγαγεν εἰς σωτηρίαν. 5. οὐκ ἐπίομεν οἶνον ἕως οὗ περιεβλεψάμεθα τὸ ἱερόν. 6. ἔπεσε τὰ παιδία μου ἐκ τοῦ πλοίου καὶ ἀπέθανον πέντε ἐν τῇ θαλάσσῃ· διὰ τοῦτο πολλὰ ἔπαθεν ὁ κακὸς διδάσκαλος αὐτῶν. 7. ὡς ἔλεγε τοῦτο ἐγένετο μέγα σημεῖον ἐκ τοῦ οὐρανοῦ.

Matt. 10.38; Mark 1.36-37a; 2.27a; Luke 10.30 (Ἄνθ. — περι.); 20.31-2; John 1.42a; 14.24; (καὶ — ἐμός); Rev. 17.11

[1] A Semitism frequent in the NT to represent 'it came to pass' of the OT. The simplest construction is used here when the main verb is not linked to ἐγένετο by any conjunction, known technically as parataxis (cf. p. 151).

Translate: 1. Five took their pay and will depart (ἀπέρχομαι) in peace, but this workman has a disease which the doctor will heal here. 2. We drove our sheep to the great river into which they fell; there we left them. 3. You (pl.) will receive salvation from your enemies, who sinned when they talked against God. 4. He will become great and the people of the Jews will call him John the baptist, because he will baptize many in the river Jordan. 5. You (sing.) found here the money which my brother left under that big stone, which is guarded by the swords of the slaves.

---

14   Second aorist (continued). Indirect statement introduced by ὅτι

Some verbs very commonly used in the strong aorist have no cognate present form, but are attached to a present of the same meaning under which they are found in lexicons and in lists of principal parts (cf. pp. 155-61). Because of frequent use these were often assimilated to the weak aorist and NT writers attach weak aorist endings at will (e.g. ἦλθαν for ἦλθον).

ἔρχομαι	ἐλεύσομαι (M)	ἦλθον	come *or* go
ἐσθίω	φάγομαι (M)	ἔφαγον	eat
ἔχω	ἕξω	ἔσχον	have
			(ε augment, not stem)
λέγω	ἐρῶ (-έω)	εἶπον[1]	say
	(cf. p. 71)		
ὁράω	ὄψομαι (M)	εἶδον	see
φέρω	οἴσω	ἤνεγκον	bear, bring

[1] εἶπε is the commonest verb for *he said* in the NT; ἔφη is also found (cf. p. 118) and the imperfect ἔλεγε may occur to link on further sayings, translated as an aorist. Cf. Mark 4.21, 26, 30.

Indirect Statement

In κ the usual construction is a clause introduced by ὅτι meaning *that*: [1]

λέγει ὅτι ὁ Ἰησοῦς ἐστιν ἐν τῇ κώμῃ.
He says that Jesus is in the village.

Greek, however, uses a *vivid* or *graphic* construction, keeping in the clause after a historic main verb of saying or thinking what was actually said or thought:

εἶπεν ὅτι ὁ Ἰησοῦς ἐστιν ἐν τῇ κώμῃ.
He said that Jesus was in the village.

This contrasts with the English Sequence of Tenses when the verb of the reported statement is put a stage back into the past in chronological relation to the main verb:

ἄγει ὁ δοῦλος τὰ πρόβατα.
The slave drives the sheep.

εἶπεν ὅτι ἄγει ὁ δοῦλος τὰ πρόβατα.
He said that the slave was driving the sheep (ἄγει unchanged).

ἄξει ὁ δοῦλος τὰ πρόβατα.
The slave will drive the sheep.

εἶπεν ὅτι ἄξει ὁ δοῦλος τὰ πρόβατα.
He said that the slave would drive the sheep (ἄξει unchanged).

ἤγαγεν ὁ δοῦλος τὰ πρόβατα.
The slave drove the sheep.

εἶπεν ὅτι ἤγαγεν ὁ δοῦλος τὰ πρόβατα.
He said that the slave had driven the sheep (ἤγαγεν unchanged).

It follows that in translation after a historic main verb the Greek present will be translated as imperfect, the aorist strictly speaking as pluperfect, but here English usage is permissive and often the aorist will be retained:

ἔμαθε τὸ τέκνον ταῦτα.
The child learnt these things.

[1] Not to be confused with ὅτι meaning *because*. Context generally prevents ambiguity. There is also a redundant and untranslatable ὅτι equivalent to inverted commas, introducing direct quotation (cf. p. 101).

εἶπεν ὅτι ἔμαθε τὸ τέκνον ταῦτα.

He said that the child learnt (*or* had learnt) these things.

ἀγρός -οῦ ὁ	field	φυλακή -ῆς ἡ	prison,
βασανίζω	torment		watch
διάκονος -ου ὁ	servant,		(time of
	minister		night)
ἕτερος -α -ον	other,	φωνή -ῆς ἡ	voice
	different	χήρα -ας ἡ	widow
εὐθύς	immediately	Χριστός -οῦ	Christ
στρατιώτης -ου ὁ	soldier		(literally
τόπος -ου ὁ	place		anointed,
ὑπηρέτης -ου ὁ	attendant		i.e. Mes-
φοβέομαι (P)	fear		siah)

Notice the following compounds of ἔρχομαι. Generally a preposition is needed too, but not necessarily the preposition of the compound.

ἀπέρχομαι	(w. preposition)	go away, depart
διέρχομαι	(w. acc. or διά w. gen.)	go through
εἰσέρχομαι	(w. preposition)	enter
ἐξέρχομαι	(w. preposition)	go out from
προσέρχομαι	(w. dat. or preposition)	approach
συνέρχομαι	(w. dat. or preposition)	go with

Give the 2nd sing. aorist indic. active of μανθάνω, τίκτω; 1st pl. aorist indic. active of φεύγω, ἀποθνήσκω; 3rd sing. aorist indic. middle of λαμβάνω, γίνομαι; 3rd pl. fut. indic. middle of εὑρίσκω, πίνω; 2nd sing. aorist indic. active and middle of γράφω, αἰτέω, ἀγοράζω.

Translate: 1. ἤνεγκεν οὖν ὁ Σίμων τὸν σταυρὸν τοῦ Χριστοῦ ἕως ἦλθον πρὸς τὸν τόπον ἐν ᾧ ἀπέθανεν. 2. εἶπον δὲ οἱ ὑπηρέται ὅτι οὐχ εὗρον τοὺς ἀποστόλους ἐν τῇ φυλακῇ ἐν ᾗ ἔλιπον αὐτούς. 3. καὶ ἐγένετο ὡς ἐξήλθομεν ἐκ Ναζαρετ εἶδε χήραν καὶ εἶπεν ὅτι ἐλεεῖ αὐτήν. 4. καὶ ὅτε ἔφαγον τοὺς πέντε ἄρτους ἀπῆλθον εἰς τὰς ἰδίας οἰκίας αὐτῶν. 5. καὶ εὐθὺς ἦλθον εἰς τὴν χώραν τῶν Γερασηνῶν· ἐκεῖ δὲ εἶδον ὅτε ἐξῆλθον ἐκ τοῦ πλοίου ἄνθρωπον ὃς ἐβασανίζετο ὑπὸ πολλῶν δαιμονίων ἃ ἐκαλεῖτο Λεγιών. 6. ὑμεῖς μὲν οἱ Φαρισαῖοι εἴπετε ἡμῖν ὅτι γινώσκετε τὰς ἐντολὰς τοῦ νόμου· οὗτος δὲ ὁ Στέφανος ἐμαρτύρησε τῇ ἀληθείᾳ καὶ περιπατεῖ ἐν τῇ ὁδῷ τῆς αἰωνίου ζωῆς· πιστὸς γάρ ἐστι καὶ ἀγαθὸς διάκονος τῆς ἐκκλησίας.

Mark 2.13a; 3.13 (καὶ [third] — αὐτ.); Luke 5.33 (οἱ — νηστ.); John 4.50; 6.24a; Acts 9.9b; 16.6a

Translate: 1. When we heard our master's voice we immediately said that he was praying. 2. Another soldier said that Jesus had cried out with a loud (μέγας) voice. 3. You (pl.) went through our land and learnt that many children were dying in the fields. 4. Many used to fear the devil, until they saw Jesus and he saved them. 5. Because I pitied this lame man I said that I would go with him and lead him to the doctor. 6. The faithful slave said that his master had gone through the desert and had left his sheep there.

---

15   Future and aorist passive

The aorist passive is formed by prefixing the augment, adding θ to the stem and then the aorist endings. **The future passive** is formed from the aorist passive (so that any irregularity will be found in both), i.e. normally stem + θ + ησ + present endings.

ἐλύθην	I was loosed	λυθήσομαι	I shall be loosed
ἐλύθης		λυθήσει or -η	
ἐλύθη		λυθήσεται	
ἐλύθημεν		λυθησόμεθα	
ἐλύθητε		λυθήσεσθε	
ἐλύθησαν		λυθήσονται	

Consonantal stems before θ are aspirated if possible.

Gutturals κ, χ, γ before θ become χ $\delta\iota\omega\kappa\omega$ $\dot{\epsilon}\delta\iota\omega\chi\theta\eta\nu$
Labials π, ϕ, β before θ become ϕ $\pi\dot{\epsilon}\mu\pi\omega$ $\dot{\epsilon}\pi\dot{\epsilon}\mu\phi\theta\eta\nu$
Dentals τ, θ, δ before θ become σ $\pi\epsilon\dot{\iota}\theta\omega$ $\dot{\epsilon}\pi\epsilon\dot{\iota}\sigma\theta\eta\nu$

Strong aorists are also found, but the endings are the same for both weak and strong. The strong aorist is distinguished by the absence of θ.

$\gamma\rho\dot{\alpha}\phi\omega$ $\dot{\epsilon}\gamma\rho\dot{\alpha}\phi\eta\nu$ $\gamma\rho\alpha\phi\dot{\eta}\sigma\omega\mu\alpha\iota$
$\sigma\pi\epsilon\dot{\iota}\rho\omega$ $\dot{\epsilon}\sigma\pi\dot{\alpha}\rho\eta\nu$ $\sigma\pi\alpha\rho\dot{\eta}\sigma\omega\mu\alpha\iota$

The strong aorist passive is like an old intransitive aorist active form, still found in κ in $\beta\alpha\dot{\iota}\nu\omega$[1] $\dot{\epsilon}\beta\eta\nu$, $\chi\alpha\dot{\iota}\rho\omega$ $\dot{\epsilon}\chi\dot{\alpha}\rho\eta\nu$. Like these is $\gamma\iota\nu\dot{\omega}\sigma\kappa\omega$, except that the vowel of the endings is ω.

$-\ddot{\epsilon}\beta\eta\nu$	$\dot{\epsilon}\chi\dot{\alpha}\rho\eta\nu$	$\dot{\epsilon}\gamma\rho\dot{\alpha}\phi\eta\nu$	$\ddot{\epsilon}\gamma\nu\omega\nu$
$-\ddot{\epsilon}\beta\eta\varsigma$	$\dot{\epsilon}\chi\dot{\alpha}\rho\eta\varsigma$	$\dot{\epsilon}\gamma\rho\dot{\alpha}\phi\eta\varsigma$	$\ddot{\epsilon}\gamma\nu\omega\varsigma$
$-\ddot{\epsilon}\beta\eta$	$\dot{\epsilon}\chi\dot{\alpha}\rho\eta$	$\dot{\epsilon}\gamma\rho\dot{\alpha}\phi\eta$	$\ddot{\epsilon}\gamma\nu\omega$
$-\ddot{\epsilon}\beta\eta\mu\epsilon\nu$	$\dot{\epsilon}\chi\dot{\alpha}\rho\eta\mu\epsilon\nu$	$\dot{\epsilon}\gamma\rho\dot{\alpha}\phi\eta\mu\epsilon\nu$	$\ddot{\epsilon}\gamma\nu\omega\mu\epsilon\nu$
$-\ddot{\epsilon}\beta\eta\tau\epsilon$	$\dot{\epsilon}\chi\dot{\alpha}\rho\eta\tau\epsilon$	$\dot{\epsilon}\gamma\rho\dot{\alpha}\phi\eta\tau\epsilon$	$\ddot{\epsilon}\gamma\nu\omega\tau\epsilon$
$-\ddot{\epsilon}\beta\eta\sigma\alpha\nu$	$\dot{\epsilon}\chi\dot{\alpha}\rho\eta\sigma\alpha\nu$	$\dot{\epsilon}\gamma\rho\dot{\alpha}\phi\eta\sigma\alpha\nu$	$\ddot{\epsilon}\gamma\nu\omega\sigma\alpha\nu$

The futures conform to the strong stems:

$-\beta\dot{\eta}\sigma\omega\mu\alpha\iota$ $\chi\alpha\rho\dot{\eta}\sigma\omega\mu\alpha\iota$ $\gamma\rho\alpha\phi\dot{\eta}\sigma\omega\mu\alpha\iota$ $\gamma\nu\dot{\omega}\sigma\omega\mu\alpha\iota$

Some common irregular aorist passives:

$\dot{\alpha}\kappa\omega\dot{\nu}\omega$	$\dot{\eta}\kappa\omega\dot{\nu}\sigma\theta\eta\nu$	$\dot{\alpha}\kappa\omega\nu\sigma\theta\dot{\eta}\sigma\omega\mu\alpha\iota$	hear
$\kappa\alpha\lambda\dot{\epsilon}\omega$	$\dot{\epsilon}\kappa\lambda\dot{\eta}\theta\eta\nu$	$\kappa\lambda\eta\theta\dot{\eta}\sigma\omega\mu\alpha\iota$	call
$\kappa\rho\dot{\nu}\pi\tau\omega$	$\dot{\epsilon}\kappa\rho\dot{\nu}\beta\eta\nu$	$\kappa\rho\nu\beta\dot{\eta}\sigma\omega\mu\alpha\iota$	hide
$\lambda\alpha\mu\beta\dot{\alpha}\nu\omega$	$\dot{\epsilon}\lambda\dot{\eta}\mu\phi\theta\eta\nu$	$\lambda\eta\mu\phi\theta\dot{\eta}\sigma\omega\mu\alpha\iota$	take or receive
$\lambda\dot{\epsilon}\gamma\omega$	$\dot{\epsilon}\rho\rho\dot{\epsilon}\theta\eta\nu,$		say
	$\dot{\epsilon}\rho\rho\dot{\eta}\theta\eta\nu$[2]		
$\mu\iota\mu\nu\dot{\eta}\sigma\kappa\omega\mu\alpha\iota$ (P)	$\dot{\epsilon}\mu\nu\dot{\eta}\sigma\theta\eta\nu$	$\mu\nu\eta\sigma\theta\dot{\eta}\sigma\omega\mu\alpha\iota$	(w. gen.) remember
$\sigma\dot{\omega}\zeta\omega$	$\dot{\epsilon}\sigma\dot{\omega}\theta\eta\nu$	$\sigma\omega\theta\dot{\eta}\sigma\omega\mu\alpha\iota$	save
$\tau\epsilon\lambda\dot{\epsilon}\omega$	$\dot{\epsilon}\tau\epsilon\lambda\dot{\epsilon}\sigma\theta\eta\nu$	$\tau\epsilon\lambda\epsilon\sigma\theta\dot{\eta}\sigma\omega\mu\alpha\iota$	end

[1] The simple verb $\beta\alpha\dot{\iota}\nu\omega$ had become obsolete in κ, but various compounds are frequently used in the NT.

[2] $\lambda\dot{\epsilon}\gamma\omega$ was only used in present and imperfect, so these forms along with the strong aorist active $\epsilon\dot{\hat{\iota}}\pi\omega\nu$ were used to supply the other tenses.

Contracted verbs lengthen ε to η as in active and middle:
ἐφιλήθην.

ἀναβαίνω	come *or* go up	σοφός -ή -όν	wise
ἀναλαμβάνω	take up	σπείρω	sow
ἀσπάζομαι (Μ)	greet	τεσσεράκοντα	forty
καθαρίζω	cleanse	ὕστερον	(adverb) later
καρπός -οῦ ὁ	fruit		(neuter sing.
καταβαίνω	come *or* go down		of adjective)
		χαίρω	rejoice
νηστεύω	fast	ὡς	as (of manner)
πειράζω	try, tempt		

Translate: 1. ἐχάρη δὲ ἡ Μαρία ὅτε ἠσπάσατο αὐτὴν ὁ ἄγγελος· οὗτος γὰρ εἶπεν αὐτῇ ὅτι τέξεται υἱὸν ὃς κληθήσεται Ἰησοῦς ὅτι σώσει τὸν λαὸν αὐτοῦ. εἶπεν οὖν αὐτῷ ἡ παρθένος ὅτι δούλη ἐστὶ τοῦ Κυρίου. 2. κατέβη οὖν ὁ Ἰησοῦς εἰς τὴν ἔρημον καὶ ἐκεῖ ἡμέρας[1] τεσσεράκοντα ἐνήστευσεν· ὕστερον δὲ ὅτε ἐπειράσθη ὑπὸ τοῦ διαβόλου εἶπεν αὐτῷ ὅτι ἐγράφη, Οὐκ ἐκπειράσεις Κύριον τὸν Θεόν σου. 3. ὡς ἐρρήθη ἐν τῇ παραβολῇ, οὗτοι ἐσπάρησαν εἰς τὴν γῆν τὴν καλὴν καὶ φέρουσι πολὺν καρπόν. 4. μετὰ τὸν θάνατον τοῦ Ἰησοῦ ἦμεν μετ' αὐτοῦ ἕως οὗ ἀνελήμφθη ἀφ' ἡμῶν εἰς τὸν οὐρανόν. 5. ἐχάρησαν οἱ δέκα λεπροὶ ὅτε ἐκαθαρίσθησαν ὑπὸ τοῦ Ἰησοῦ. 6. ἔγνωτε ἐν ταῖς ἰδίαις καρδίαις ἑαυτῶν ὅτι οὐκ ἀκουσθήσονται οἱ λόγοι ὑμῶν, ἀλλὰ προσηύξασθε τῷ Θεῷ· ὁ δὲ ἔσωσεν ὑμᾶς. 7. πότε ἐμνήσθης τοῦ λόγου ὃς ἐρρέθη ὑπὸ τοῦ σοφοῦ νεανίου;

Matt. 28.16a; Mark 1.9; 12.12 (ἔγν. — εἶπ.); Luke 1.60 (Οὐχί — Ἰω.); John 2.2b; Heb. 11.37 (ἐλιθ. — μηλ.)

Translate: 1. Blessed are the poor, for later they shall be rich. 2. You (pl.) will be persecuted by the Jews because you knew me and my works. 3. This writing will be hidden from the wise, but will be revealed to little children. 4. Five loaves were bought but they were not saved from the enemy, who ate them immediately.

[1] The accusative is used as in Latin for duration of time.

5. Jesus journeyed with his disciples towards the lake; there they found a great crowd of Jews, some of whom were persuaded by him, but others were not led to repentance. 6. It was said by the prophet that sinners would see God's salvation and would rejoice.

16   Infinitive: formation, prolate, purpose, indirect command

Infinitives are formed as follows:

ACTIVE

Present — stem + ειν:

     λύ-ω   λύειν   φιλέ-ω   φιλέειν   φιλεῖν

Future — future stem + present ending ειν:

     λύσ-ω   λύσειν

1st Aorist — remove augment, then aorist stem + αι:

     ἔ-λυσ-α   λῦσαι

2nd Aorist—remove augment,[1] then aorist stem + present ending ειν:

     ἔ-λαβ-ον   λαβεῖν

MIDDLE

Present — stem + εσθαι:

     λύ-ομαι   λύεσθαι   φιλέ-ομαι   φιλέεσθαι   φιλεῖσθαι

Future — future stem + present ending εσθαι:

     λύσ-ομαι   λύσεσθαι

1st Aorist — remove augment, then aorist stem + ασθαι:

     ἐ-λυσ-άμην   λύσασθαι

---

[1] NB εἶπον εἰπεῖν, εἶδον ἰδεῖν.

2nd Aorist — remove augment, then aorist stem + present ending
ἐσθαι:

ἐ-γεν-όμην   γενέσθαι

Present — identical with middle:

λύ-ομαι   λύεσθαι

Future — future stem + present ending ἐσθαι:

λυθήσομαι   λυθήσεσθαι

1st and 2nd Aorist — remove augment, then aorist stem + ῆναι:

ἐ-λύθ-ην   λυθῆναι   ἐ-γράφ-ην   γραφῆναι

NB -ἔβην, -βῆναι   ἔγνων, γνῶναι.

	Active	Middle	Passive
Present	λύειν	λύεσθαι	λύεσθαι
Future	λύσειν	λύσεσθαι	λυθήσεσθαι
1st Aorist[1]	λῦσαι	λύσασθαι	λυθῆναι
2nd Aorist	λαβεῖν	γενέσθαι	γραφῆναι

The verb *to be* has only present infinitive εἶναι and regularly
formed future, ἔσεσθαι from ἔσομαι.

Meanings of the tenses

In shedding the augment the aorist infinitive loses the sense of
past time[2] and refers simply to single as opposed to continuous
actions; it may be compared with a point · in some undefined
(ἀόριστος) period of time as opposed to an unbroken line ——.
Present and aorist infinitives are generally translated alike in
English, both λύειν and λῦσαι *to loose*, but there is a subtle differentiation in Greek and in translating into Greek the student must

---

[1] Note the following irregularities in the accentuation of the infinitive, when
the accent does not retract as far back as possible:
   (1) 1st aorist active — accent does not retract beyond penultimate: διῶξαι
      καλέσαι
   (2) 2nd aorist active takes a circumflex on ultimate: λαβεῖν
   (3) 2nd aorist middle accents on penultimate: γενέσθαι
   (4) aorist passive — all infinitives ending in ναι (there are others) accent on
      penultimate: λυθῆναι γραφῆναι

[2] It does retain a past sense when it replaces an aorist indicative in accusative
and infinitive construction for reported statement (cf. p.101).

be careful to preserve the distinction. When either tense seems possible the aorist is the more common:

> ἐκέλευσεν ἡμᾶς ἀναγινώσκειν τὰς γραφάς.
> He ordered us to read (keep on reading) the scriptures.

> ἐκέλευσεν ἡμᾶς ἀναγνῶναι τοῦτο τὸ βιβλίον.
> He ordered us to read this book (one single act).

The future infinitive will be found replacing the future indicative in the accusative and infinitive construction for reported statement (cf. p. 101).

The following three constructions have English parallels and should present no difficulty:

1. **Prolate infinitive** extending meaning of certain verbs:

ἄρχομαι (M)	ἄρξομαι	ἠρξάμην	begin
βούλομαι		ἐβουλήθην	wish, be willing
θέλω	θελήσω	ἠθέλησα	wish
μέλλω	μελλήσω	ἤμελλον (imperf.)	be about to, delay

> ἤρξατο διδάσκειν αὐτούς.
> He began to teach them.

> μέλλει γὰρ ὁ υἱὸς τοῦ ἀνθρώπου ἔρχεσθαι.
> For the Son of Man is about to go.

2. **Infinitive expressing purpose** after verbs of *motion* or *sending* :

> ἀπῆλθεν ὁ Ἰησοῦς προσεύχεσθαι.
> Jesus went away to pray.

3. **Indirect Command**—each new verb of commanding or requesting must be learnt with the case that it governs:

κελεύω	w. acc.	command
δέομαι (P)	w. gen.	beg[1]
διατάσσω	w. dat.	order, command[2]
ἐπιτάσσω	w. dat.	,,
προστάσσω	w. dat.	,,

[1] Like other monosyllabic stems in ε the vowel ε only contracts before a following ε; the aorist is ἐδεήθην.

[2] With this compound, though not with the other two, active and middle are used indifferently.

δέομαί σου θεραπεῦσαι τὸν υἱόν μου.

I beg you to heal my son.

ἐκέλευσε τὸν δοῦλον ἀπελθεῖν.

He ordered the slave to depart.

διέταξέ (διετάξατό) μοι φαγεῖν τοῦτον τὸν ἄρτον.

She commanded me to eat this bread.

NB The negative with the infinitive is always μή.

Translate: 1. ἀνέβη ὁ Ἰησοῦς εἰς Ἱερουσαλημ·[1] ἔγνω γὰρ ὅτι ἐκεῖ μέλλει πολλὰ πάσχειν· παρεκάλεσεν οὖν καὶ τοὺς μαθητὰς αὐτοῦ φέρειν τοὺς ἰδίους σταυροὺς αὐτῶν καὶ ἀκολουθεῖν αὐτῷ. 2. καὶ ἐγένετο ὅτε ἐτέλεσεν τοὺς λόγους τούτους ἀπῆλθεν ὁ Ἰησοῦς εἰς τοὺς ἀγροὺς διδάσκειν ἑτέρους. 3. ἤρξαντο οὖν οἱ ἀπόστολοι ἐξελθεῖν εἰς τὰ ἔσχατα τῆς γῆς· διετάξατο γὰρ αὐτοῖς ὁ Ἰησοῦς κηρύσσειν τοῖς ἀνθρώποις ὅτι προσέρχεται ἡ βασιλεία τῶν οὐρανῶν. 4. ὅτε ἤμελλεν[2] ἀποθνήσκειν ὁ Ἰησοῦς ἔκραξε φωνῇ μεγάλῃ. 5. ἐδεήθημεν τοῦ ὑπηρέτου μὴ δέξασθαι τὸ ἀργύριον· ὁ δὲ οὐκ ἠθέλησεν ἀκοῦσαι, ἀλλ' ἐχάρη ὅτε ἔλαβε τὸν μισθὸν τῆς ἀδικίας αὐτοῦ. 6. οὐκ ἐβούλου πορευθῆναι μεθ' ἡμῶν διὰ τῶν ἀγρῶν· διὰ τοῦτ' οὖν νῦν ἐπιτάσσομέν σοι μὴ συνελθεῖν ἡμῖν ἰδεῖν τὰ σημεῖα ταῦτα.

Matt. 20.22 (τὸ — πιν.); Mark 2.17b; 5.17; Luke 12.1 (ἤρξ. — πρῶτ.); 15.15 (καὶ [second] — χοίρ.); John 12.21 (Κύρ. — ἰδ.); Acts 21.34 (ἐκέλ. — παρ.)

Translate: 1. The prophet ordered the people to prepare a way for the Lord. 2. We did not wish to keep on writing the same things to you. 3. You (sing.) asked me to pity this poor man and send him to my house. 4. Jesus began to teach the people many things. 5. I beg you to keep this wine, because my master ordered the girls not to drink. 6. You (pl.) went with your brother to be taught in this place. 7. These sinners were persuaded by his wise words to fear the Lord in their hearts and to do righteous works.

[1] In modern texts Semitic words which did not fit into a Greek declinable pattern are transliterated without accent or breathing. There is also Ἱεροσόλυμα 2nd declension, neuter pl. (fem. Matt. 2.3).

[2] μέλλω generally takes a present infinitive even when the action is not continuous.

17   Articular infinitive.   Adverbs formed from second declension adjectives

The infinitive is used as a neuter verbal noun, itself indeclinable, qualified by an adverb instead of an adjective, given cases by prefixing the article:

> ἀγαθὸν τὸ εὖ γράφειν.
> It is a good thing to write well.

> τῷ μανθάνειν γινόμεθα σοφοί.
> By learning we become wise.

This verbal noun may have a subject which is expressed by the accusative and, like the indicative verb, a direct or indirect object:

> μετὰ τὸ γράψαι ἡμᾶς ταύτην τὴν ἐπιστολήν
> After our writing this letter

> i.e. After we wrote this letter

In κ this use of prepositions with articular infinitive forming a noun clause is more common than in cg and is used for the following constructions:

1. Temporal clauses

> μετά (w. acc.) — after the subject's action or treatment

> μετὰ τὸ ἀπαχθῆναι τοὺς ἀποστόλους
> After the apostles had been led away

> ἐν (w. dat.) — in the process of the subject's action or treatment

> ἐν τῷ πορεύεσθαι τὸν Ἰησοῦν διὰ τῆς Γαλιλαίας
> While Jesus was going through Galilee

> πρό (w. gen.) — before the subject's action or treatment

> πρὸ τοῦ πειρασθῆναι τὸν Ἰησοῦν ὑπὸ τοῦ διαβόλου
> Before Jesus was tempted by the devil

2. Causal clauses

διά (w. acc.) — on account of the subject's action or treatment

διὰ τὸ φοβεῖσθαι τὸν Πειλᾶτον τοὺς Ἰουδαίους
Because Pilate feared the Jews

3. Purpose clauses

εἰς ⎫ (w. acc.) — towards, with a view to the subject's action or
πρός ⎭ treatment

εἰς (πρὸς) τὸ ἰδεῖν τὰ παιδία τὸν Ἰησοῦν
In order that the little children might see Jesus

The infinitive is also used as a noun clause when it occurs as the subject of the verb *to be* or of an impersonal verb.

καλόν ἐστιν ἡμᾶς ὧδε εἶναι.   Mark 9.5
It is a good thing that we are here.
or It is good for us to be here.

δεῖ takes this acc. and infin. construction (like Latin *oportet*):

δεῖ τοὺς ἀνθρώπους ἀποθανεῖν.
It is necessary for men to die.

Often the verb is translated personally: Men must die.

ἔξεστι(ν) takes a dative of the person to whom licence is allowed (like Latin *licet*):

οὐκ ἔξεστιν ὑμῖν κηρύσσειν.
It is not lawful for you to preach (*or* to continue preaching).

Adverbs from 2nd declension adjectives

These may be formed by changing the final -ων of the gen. pl. into -ως.

ἄδικος, ἀδίκων, ἀδίκως — δίκαιος, δικαίως — κακός, κακῶς
— καλός, καλῶς

δεῖ[1]   (w. acc. and infin.) it is necessary, right
ἔξεστι   (w. dat. and infin.) it is lawful, possible

[1] δεῖ is contracted, as shown by the accent, so the imperfect is ἔδει.

εὖ[1]	well	κριτής -οῦ ὁ	judge
εὐαγγελίζομαι (M)	preach the gospel, evangelize	παλαιός -ά -όν	old
		πάλιν	again, back
		χαρά -ᾶς ἡ	joy
		χρεία -ας ἡ	need
ἥλιος -ου ὁ	sun	ὠφελέω	help
κράββατος -ου ὁ	mattress		

Give the fut. infin. active, middle and passive of ἄγω, σώζω, πέμπω; present infin. active and passive of ζητέω, πειράζω; aorist infin. active of μανθάνω, κρύπτω; aorist infin. middle of αἰτέω, προσεύχομαι; aorist infin. passive of κηρύσσω, καλέω.

Translate: 1. ἐν δὲ τῷ πορεύεσθαι τὸν Ἰησοῦν καὶ τοὺς μαθητὰς αὐτοῦ πρὸς Ιερουσαλημ εἶπεν ὅτι δεῖ τὸν υἱὸν τοῦ ἀνθρώπου πολλὰ παθεῖν. 2. οὐκ ἔξεστιν ἡμῖν εὖ γνῶναι τὸν χρόνον ἐν ᾧ ἐλεύσεται ὁ Χριστός· διὰ δὲ τὸ εἰπεῖν αὐτὸν ταῦτα ἐμάθομεν ὅτι ἐν ἐκείνῃ τῇ ἡμέρᾳ ὄψονται αὐτὸν οἱ ἅγιοι. 3. μετὰ δὲ τὸ τὸν Ἰωάννην ἀκοῦσαι ἐν τῷ δεσμωτηρίῳ τὰ ἔργα τοῦ Χριστοῦ ἔπεμψε μαθητὰς λαλεῖν αὐτῷ· ὁ δὲ ἐκέλευσεν αὐτοὺς εἰπεῖν τῷ διδασκάλῳ ἑαυτῶν ἃ ἤκουσαν καὶ ἔβλεψαν. 4. καλῶς οὖν εἶπεν ὅτι οὐ χρείαν ἔχουσιν οἱ δίκαιοι μετανοίας διὰ τὸ μὴ ἁμαρτωλοὺς εἶναι αὐτούς. 5. ἀδίκως προσηύχοντο οἱ Φαρισαῖοι ἐν ταῖς ὁδοῖς πρὸς τὸ ἀκουσθῆναι ὑπὸ τῶν ἀνθρώπων καὶ δόξαν λαβεῖν. 6. ἐν δὲ ταῖς ἐσχάταις ἡμέραις κρυβήσεται μὲν ὁ ἥλιος, χαρήσονται δὲ οἱ ἅγιοι διὰ τὸ πάλιν ἐλθεῖν τὸν Χριστὸν εἰς τὴν γῆν. 7. εἶπεν οὖν ὅτι πρὸ τοῦ ἀναγνῶναι αὐτὸν τὰς παλαιὰς γραφὰς οὐκ ἐπίστευσε τοῖς λόγοις τοῦ διδασκάλου ὃς ἐκέλευσε τοὺς πλουσίους δικαίως ὠφελεῖν τοὺς πτωχούς. 8. κακῶς μὲν ἔχει[2] αὕτη ἡ παρθένος, θεραπεύσει δὲ τὴν νόσον ὁ σοφὸς ἰατρός. 9. πῶς σώσει ὁ Κύριος τὸν κόσμον;

Luke 2.4 (διὰ — Δ.); 8.42b; Acts 12.20 (ἤτ. — βασ.); 19.21 (Μετὰ — ἰδ.); Rom. 8.29 (εἰς — ἀδ.)

---

[1] εὖ is used as an adverb of ἀγαθός, which has no formation of its own. It is common as a prefix, e.g. εὐαγγελίζομαι, which augments εὐη- as if compounded with a preposition.

[2] ἔχω is used colloquially with adverbs to express a state or condition, like the verb εἰμί with an adjective. κακῶς ἔχω means I am ill, like our colloquial I am in a bad way.

[Use the articular infinitive in this exercise wherever possible.]
Translate: Because the apostles evangelized in this place, my brothers, great will be your joy. 2. These young men brought a mattress in order that Jesus might see the lame man and heal him. 3. Justly did the judges bear witness to the old law while they were guarding the people. 4. After Jesus came again to the lake he ordered the disciple to cast his net from the boat. 5. It is necessary for a good judge to keep the commandments well because they were written by God through the great prophet. 6. We were not willing to journey through this land in order to learn from the wise soldier.

18 Third declension nouns with consonantal stems

NB It is more than ever essential to learn the gen. sing. and gender of each noun, because the nom. alone is not necessarily a guide to either.

Consonantal stems

These all have the same case endings, but in the dative pl. the stem combines with the ending -σι(ν), giving rise to the variations already met in forming fut. and aorist active and middle.

Sing.	guard	hope	body	saviour
N.	φύλαξ ὁ	ἐλπίς ἡ	σῶμα[1] τό	σωτήρ[2] ὁ
V.	φύλαξ	ἐλπίς	σῶμα	σῶτερ
A.	φύλακα	ἐλπίδα	σῶμα	σωτῆρα
G.	φύλακος	ἐλπίδος	σώματος	σωτῆρος
D.	φύλακι	ἐλπίδι	σώματι	σωτῆρι

[1] All 3rd declension nouns ending in α are neuter and generally have a stem in -ατ.

[2] Normally the accent stays in the same relation to the stem as in the nom. sing., but note the irregularity in this vocative.

Pl.

N.V.	φύλακες	ἐλπίδες	σώματα	σωτῆρες
A.	φύλακας	ἐλπίδας	σώματα	σωτῆρας
G.	φυλάκων	ἐλπίδων	σωμάτων	σωτήρων
D.	φύλαξι(ν)	ἐλπίσι(ν)	σώμασι(ν)	σωτῆρσι(ν)

Gutturals   κ, χ, γ + σ = ξ
Labials   π, φ, β + σ = ψ[1]
Dentals   τ, θ, δ before σ drop out.
Liquid   ρ remains unchanged before σ.

Sing.	shepherd	age	ruler	governor
N.	ποιμήν ὁ	αἰών ὁ	ἄρχων ὁ[2]	ἡγεμών ὁ
G.	ποιμένος	αἰῶνος	ἄρχοντος	ἡγεμόνος

Pl.

D.	ποιμέσι(ν)	αἰῶσι(ν)	ἄρχουσι(ν)	ἡγεμόσι(ν)

Liquid ν before σ drops out.
-οντ before σ — the ντ drops out and ο lengthens to ου.

αἷμα -ατος τό	blood	πνεῦμα -ατος τό	spirit
ἀλέκτωρ -ορος ὁ	cock	ποῦ	where?
ἀμπελών -ῶνος ὁ	vineyard	ῥῆμα -ατος τό	saying
ἄρχω	(w. gen.)	σάρξ σαρκός[3] ἡ	flesh
	rule	στόμα -ατος τό	mouth
ὄνομα -ατος τό	name	τέσσαρες -α	four
πατρίς -ίδος ἡ	native place		

Translate: 1. εὐθὺς οὖν ἐπορεύθησαν τέσσαρες φύλακες εἰς τὴν πατρίδα ἑαυτῶν πρὸς τὸ ἰδεῖν τὸ σημεῖον τοῦτο τὸ μέγα. 2. μετὰ τὸ φωνῆσαι τὸν ἀλέκτορα πάλιν ἐλευσόμεθα πρὸς τὸν ἀμπελῶνα τοῦ ἄρχοντος ὅτι θέλομεν πιεῖν τὸν καλὸν οἶνον μετὰ τῶν ποιμένων. 3. ἐν ἐλπίδι ἀποθνήσκετε διὰ τὸ πιστεύειν ὅτι

---

[1] Given for completeness, but few such words exist.
[2] Noun formed from present participle of ἄρχω. The active is rare in NT, but middle deponent ἄρχομαι begin is often found.
[3] Most 3rd declension monosyllables accent on the ultimate in the gen. and dative sing. and pl.

ἕξει ἡ ψυχὴ ζωὴν εἰς τὸν αἰῶνα.[1] 4. πῶς ὄψονται σὰρξ καὶ αἷμα τὴν βασιλείαν τοῦ οὐρανοῦ, ἢ μέλλει ἔρχεσθαι ἐν ἐκείναις ταῖς ἡμέραις; 5. ἐπέμφθη ὁ σωτὴρ εἰς τὸν κόσμον κηρῦξαι τὸν λόγον τοῖς ἡγεμόσι καὶ τοῖς ἄρχουσι καὶ τοῖς πτωχοῖς. 6. ἐν δὲ τῷ ὀνόματι τοῦ Χριστοῦ ποιήσουσι μεγάλα ἔργα εἰς τὸ πείθειν τοὺς ἀνθρώπους ὅτι ἔλεγε τὸ στόμα αὐτοῦ ῥήματα πιστὰ καὶ δίκαια. 7. πάλιν ἔκραξεν ὅτι διὰ τοῦ σώματος εὑρίσκομεν τὸν μισθὸν τοῦ θανάτου, διὰ δὲ τοῦ ἁγίου πνεύματος σωζόμεθα ἐκ τῆς ἐξουσίας τοῦ διαβόλου. 8. ποῦ εὗρες τὸν καλὸν ἀλέκτορα τοῦτον;

John 5.47; 10.14; Acts 13.23; Rom. 8.10; 8.24a; I Cor. 2.6 (Σοφ. — τούτου [second])

Translate: 1. He knew that the rich ruler ought to help the poor judges. 2. The wicked guards brought much fruit for the unjust governor from the ruler's vineyard. 3. The ten good shepherds wisely led their sheep from the desert to their own native land. 4. Through the holy spirit good sayings came out from the saviour's mouth. 5. In this age you (pl.) will be persecuted by wicked men, but later you will receive your reward and will become great in heaven. 6. Then Jesus said that we must eat his flesh and drink his blood.

---

19   Third declension irregular nouns. ἐπί

Some common **Third declension irregular or misleading nouns:**

γόνυ τό   γόνατος   γόνασι(ν)   knee

[1] αἰών means *age* in the sense of the world-age in which we live, coeval with the world, so εἰς τὸν αἰῶνα implies *to the end of the age, for ever* (cf. Latin *in saeculum*).

θρίξ ἡ[1]	τριχός	θριξί(ν)	hair
κύων ὁ, ἡ	κυνός	κυσί(ν)	dog
νύξ ἡ	νυκτός	νυξί(ν)	night
ὀδούς ὁ	ὀδόντος	ὀδοῦσι(ν)	tooth
οὖς τό	ὠτός	ὠσί(ν)	ear
πούς ὁ	ποδός	ποσί(ν)	foot
ὕδωρ τό	ὕδατος	ὕδασι(ν)	water
χάρις ἡ	χάριτος	χάρισι(ν) (acc. sing. χάριν)	grace, favour
χείρ ἡ	χειρός	χερσί(ν)	hand

Sing.	man, husband	woman, wife	father
N.	ἀνήρ ὁ	γυνή ἡ	πατήρ ὁ
V.	ἄνερ	γύναι	πάτερ
A.	ἄνδρα	γυναῖκα	πατέρα
G.	ἀνδρός	γυναικός	πατρός
D.	ἀνδρί	γυναικί	πατρί
Pl.			
N.V.	ἄνδρες	γυναῖκες	πατέρες
A.	ἄνδρας	γυναῖκας	πατέρας
G.	ἀνδρῶν	γυναικῶν	πατέρων
D.	ἀνδράσι(ν)	γυναιξί(ν)	πατράσι(ν)

μήτηρ (mother), θυγάτηρ (daughter) are declined like πατήρ.

ἐπί

ἐπί is found with three cases and in κ the basic meaning of *on* occurs almost indiscriminately with all three.

w. acc.

> *on*, properly with some idea of motion
>
> > ἔπεσεν ἐπὶ τὴν γῆν.
> > It fell upon the ground.

w. gen.

(1) *on*

> > ἐπὶ τῶν νεφελῶν
> > On the clouds

---

[1] One single hair; the plural must be used if collective.

(2) *in the time of*

ἐπὶ τῶν προφητῶν

In the time of the prophets

(3) *in the presence of, before*

ἐπὶ τοῦ Καίσαρος

In the presence of Caesar

w. dat.

(1) *on* or *at* in local sense

ἐπὶ τῇ θύρᾳ

At the door

(2) *at* giving reason, especially with verbs of emotion

ἐθαύμασεν ἐπὶ τῇ ἀπιστίᾳ αὐτῶν.

He marvelled at their disbelief.

ἁγιάζω	sanctify	θαυμάζω	marvel
ἔλαιον -ου τό	oil	θύρα -ας ἡ	door
ἐπεί	when, since	λαμπάς -άδος ἡ	lamp
	(causal or	νεφέλη -ης ἡ	cloud
	temporal)	φρόνιμος -ον	wise

Translate: 1. ἀριθμεῖ ὁ πατὴρ ὑμῶν ὁ ἐν οὐρανοῖς καὶ τὰς τρίχας τῶν κεφαλῶν ὑμῶν. 2. μετὰ δὲ τὸ βαπτισθῆναι τὸν Ἰησοῦν ἐν τῷ ποταμῷ ἐπεὶ ἀνέβη ἐκ τοῦ ὕδατος ἠκούσθη φωνὴ ἐκ τῶν νεφελῶν. 3. ὦτα ἔχουσιν οἱ ἄνθρωποι εἰς τὸ ἀκούειν καὶ πόδας εἰς τὸ περιπατεῖν. 4. ἔπεσεν ὁ πατὴρ πρὸς τὰ γόνατα τοῦ Ἰησοῦ καὶ ἐδεήθη αὐτοῦ ὠφελῆσαι τὸν υἱόν· ὁ δὲ εὐθὺς ἐθεράπευσεν αὐτόν. 5. ὦ γύναι, λέγω σοι ὅτι πέντε ἔσχες ἄνδρας καὶ νῦν ὃν ἔχεις οὐκ ἔστιν σου ἀνήρ. 6. αἱ μὲν ἠγόρασαν ἔλαιον ταῖς λαμπάσιν, αἱ δὲ οὐκ εἶχον καὶ ἐθαύμαζον ἐπὶ τῇ σοφίᾳ τῶν φρονίμων παρθένων. 7. ὦ πάτερ, ἐλεήσεις ἡμᾶς· οἱ γὰρ τελῶναι καὶ ἁμαρτωλοὶ ἁγιάζονται τῇ σῇ χάριτι. 8. οὐ δεῖ τὰς γυναῖκας ἀποκαλύψαι τὰς τρίχας ἐν τῇ ἐκκλησίᾳ.

Luke 1.34; 6.6b; 12.3b; 13.28a; John 1.13; Eph. 3.14-15; 5.23

59

Translate: 1. Because of God's grace he became an apostle after he had heard the Lord's voice with his own ears. 2. The good governor wished to send my mother and daughter to their own country in order that they might be saved from the enemy. 3. It was night and Jesus began to walk on the water from the land to the boat: the disciples saw him with their own eyes and were afraid. 4. You (sing.) carried the fruit from the vineyard in your hands and left it at the door of the shepherd's house. 5. The dogs ate the corpse's flesh with their teeth. 6. Husbands and wives ought to persuade their children to walk righteously in the way of the Lord.

---

20 Third declension nouns with vowel stems. περί

Third declension vowel stems fall into four main small groups:

Sing.	city	fish	king	nation (pl. Gentiles)
N.	πόλις¹ ἡ	ἰχθύς² ὁ	βασιλεύς ὁ	ἔθνος³ τό
V.	πόλι	ἰχθύ	βασιλεῦ	ἔθνος
A.	πόλιν	ἰχθύν	βασιλέα	ἔθνος
G.	πόλεως	ἰχθύος	βασιλέως	ἔθνους
D.	πόλει	ἰχθύι	βασιλεῖ	ἔθνει
Pl. N.V.	πόλεις	ἰχθύες	βασιλεῖς	ἔθνη
A.	πόλεις	ἰχθύας	βασιλεῖς -έας	ἔθνη
G.	πόλεων	ἰχθύων	βασιλέων	ἐθνέων -ῶν
D.	πόλεσι(ν)	ἰχθύσι(ν)	βασιλεῦσι(ν)	ἔθνεσι

¹ All abstract nouns like πόλις are feminine.
² Symbol of the early church because the letters are the initials of Ἰησοῦς Χριστὸς Θεοῦ Υἱὸς Σωτήρ.
³ Peculiarities from an original stem ἔθνεσ which dropped the σ, so ε contracts. This group is always neuter.

60

ἀνάστασις -εως ἡ	resurrec-	ὄρος -ους τό	mountain
	tion	ὀσφύς -ύος ἡ	loins
γραμματεύς -έως ὁ	scribe	περί	(w. acc.) about, around
δύναμις -εως ἡ	power		(w. gen.) about, con-
ἔτος -ους τό	year		cerning
θλῖψις -εως ἡ	tribula-	πίστις -εως ἡ	faith
	tion	πλῆθος -ους τό	multitude
ἱερεύς -έως ὁ	priest	τέλος -ους τό	end
κρίσις -εως ἡ	judgment		

Give the gen. sing. of γλῶσσα, μαθητής, φύλαξ; acc. sing. of πρόβατον, λαμπάς, σωτήρ; acc. pl. of χείρ, θρίξ, γόνυ; dat. pl. of πούς, κύων, αἰών, ἄρχων; 3rd sing. aorist indic. active, middle, passive of ἄρχω, πέμπω, ἀγοράζω, αἰτέω.

Translate: 1. διὰ τῶν χειρῶν τῶν ἀποστόλων ἐποίησεν ὁ Θεὸς πολλὰς δυνάμεις·[1] πολλοὺς γὰρ οἳ νόσους εἶχον ἐθεράπευσαν ἐλαίῳ καὶ ἀπέλυσαν ἀπὸ τῶν θλίψεων αὐτῶν. 2. μετὰ τὴν ἀνάστασιν τῶν νεκρῶν ἔσται κρίσις ἐπὶ τῆς γῆς καὶ ὑμεῖς οἱ δώδεκα ἀπόστολοι θρόνους ἕξετε καὶ κριταὶ ἔσεσθε τῶν ἐθνῶν. 3. πιστὴ δ' ἦν ἡ καρδία τοῦ πλήθους[2] καὶ οὐκ ἐφοβοῦντο τὸν βασιλέα καὶ τοὺς φύλακας καὶ ὑπηρέτας αὐτοῦ. 4. εἶχεν ὁ Ἰωάννης ζωνὴν περὶ τὴν ὀσφὺν αὐτοῦ καὶ ἱμάτιον ὃ ἐποιήθη ἐκ τριχῶν καμήλου. 5. ὦ βασιλεῦ, ἐλεύσεται ὁ ἀρχιερεὺς καὶ παρακαλέσει σε πάλιν πέμψαι τὸν Ἰησοῦν πρὸς τὸν ἡγεμόνα. 6. ἀπῆλθεν ὁ σωτὴρ πρὸς τὸ ὄρος καὶ ἐκεῖ ἐδίδαξε τοὺς ὄχλους ἀχρὶ οὗ νὺξ ἐγένετο. 7. ἔλαβε τοῦτο τὸ παιδίον μέγαν ἰχθὺν ἐκ τοῦ ὕδατος ὃν ἠγόρασεν ὁ κύριος τοῦ ἀμπελῶνος. 8. οὗτοι ἀπέθανον ἐν ἐλπίδι· ἔγνωσαν γὰρ ὅτι ὁ ἄρχων τοῦ κόσμου τούτου οὐ μέλλει ἔχειν δύναμιν καὶ ἐξουσίαν εἰς τὸν αἰῶνα.

Mark 2.21a; 9.2; Luke 1.5; 1.33; 8.25 (εἶπ. — ὑμ.); Philemon 10

Translate: 1. In this year because of God's grace I was released from my bonds by the soldiers who were guarding me in the

---

[1] In NT often as a *mighty work*, implying a miracle.
[2] In Acts often refers to the body of the Christians.

prison. 2. This city became great among the Gentiles; for many brought their sons to see the temple and the king's beautiful house. 3. Jesus talked to the disciples about his own end and said that there would be a resurrection. 4. By faith we know that after Jesus died the disciples saw him again in the body. 5. With their teeth the dogs saved the money from the robbers who tried to take it.

2I Participles : adjectival use

Participles, like the infinitive, are found for every voice and tense, except the imperfect and pluperfect.

ACTIVE

Active participles are all 3rd declension with a 1st declension fem.

Present — present stem +-ων -ουσα -ον, masc. and neuter (except for nom. and acc.) declined like ἄρχων, fem. like θάλασσα, as the final α of the nom. follows a consonant other than ρ.

Sing.	N.V.	λύων	λύουσα	λῦον
	A.	λύοντα	λύουσαν	λῦον
	G.	λύοντος	λυούσης	λύοντος
	D.	λύοντι	λυούσῃ	λύοντι
Pl.	N.V.	λύοντες	λύουσαι	λύοντα
	A.	λύοντας	λυούσας	λύοντα
	G.	λυόντων	λυουσῶν	λυόντων
	D.	λύουσι(ν)	λυούσαις	λύουσι(ν)

Contracted verbs with stem in ε follow the now familiar rules:

φιλῶν (-έων) φιλοῦσα (-έουσα) φιλοῦν (-έον)
φιλοῦντος (-έοντος)

Future — future stem +present endings:

N. sing.	λύσων	λύσουσα	λῦσον
G. sing.	λύσοντος	λυσούσης	λύσοντος
D. pl.	λύσουσι(ν)	λυσούσαις	λύσουσι(ν)

1st Aorist — drop augment, aorist stem +-ας -άσα -αν:

N. sing.	λύσας	λύσασα	λῦσαν
G. sing.	λύσαντος	λυσάσης	λύσαντος
D. pl.	λύσασι(ν)	λυσάσαις	λύσασι(ν)

NB In dat. pl. ντ drops out before σι(ν), α lengthened in pronunciation.

2nd Aorist — drop augment, aorist stem +present endings:

N. sing.	λαβών[1]	λαβοῦσα	λαβόν
G. sing.	λαβόντος	λαβούσης	λαβόντος
D. pl.	λαβοῦσι(ν)	λαβούσαις	λαβοῦσι(ν)

MIDDLE

Middle participles are all like 2nd declension adjectives.

Present — present stem +-όμενος -η -ον:

λυόμενος λυομένη λυόμενον
φιλούμενος φιλουμένη φιλούμενον

Future — future stem +present endings:

λυσόμενος λυσομένη λυσόμενον

1st Aorist — drop augment, aorist stem +-άμενος -η -ον:

λυσάμενος λυσαμένη λυσάμενον

2nd Aorist — drop augment, aorist stem +present endings:

γενόμενος γενομένη γενόμενον

PASSIVE

Present — identical with middle:

λυόμενος λυομένη λυόμενον

Future — future stem +present endings:

λυθησόμενος λυθησομένη λυθησόμενον

[1] Note the irregular accentuation, a means of identifying the strong aorist participle active.

1st and 2nd Aorist — drop augment, aorist stem + 3rd declension
endings -εἰς -εἶσα -έν:[1]

N. sing.	λυθείς (γραφείς)	λυθεῖσα	λυθέν
G. sing.	λυθέντος	λυθείσης	λυθέντος
D. pl.	λυθεῖσι(ν)	λυθείσαις	λυθεῖσι(ν)

	Active	*Middle*
Present	λύων -ουσα -ον	λυόμενος -η -ον
Future	λύσων -ουσα -ον	λυσόμενος -η -ον
1st Aorist	λύσας -ασα -αν	λυσάμενος -η -ον
2nd Aorist	λαβών -οῦσα -όν	γενόμενος -η -ον

	Passive
Present	λυόμενος -η -ον
Future	λυθησόμενος -η -ον
1st Aorist	λυθείς -εῖσα -έν
2nd Aorist	γραφείς -εῖσα -έν

NB -βαίνω and γινώσκω form their aorist active participles:

N. sing.	-βάς	-βᾶσα	-βάν
G. sing.	-βάντος	-βάσης	-βάντος
D. pl.	-βᾶσι(ν)	-βάσαις	-βᾶσι(ν)

N. sing.	γνούς	γνοῦσα	γνόν
G. sing.	γνόντος	γνούσης	γνόντος
D. pl.	γνοῦσι(ν)	γνούσαις	γνοῦσι(ν)

The verb *to be* forms its present participle:

ὤν οὖσα ὄν   ὄντος οὔσης ὄντος
οὖσι(ν) οὔσαις οὖσι(ν)

The future participle is ἐσόμενος, formed regularly from ἔσομαι.

Adjectival use of participle

When the participle is used adjectivally, sometimes with the
article it will be best translated by a noun: ὁ σπείρων — the sower.
Usually the idiomatic translation will be by a relative clause:

μακάριοι οἱ ζητοῦντες τὸν Θεόν.
Blessed are the (men) seeking God.
i.e. Blessed are those who seek God.

[1] NB Irregular accentuation on the ultimate.

NB The negative with the participle, as with infinitive, is always μή. The aorist participle usually denotes past action, previous to that of the main verb:

οἱ ἐλθόντες εἰς τὴν πόλιν εἶδον αὐτόν.

Those who came into the city saw him.

ἀγαπητός -ή -όν	beloved	κατοικέω	inhabit (w.
ἄφεσις -εως ἡ	forgiveness		acc.), dwell
δοξάζω	glorify		(w. ἐν + dat.)
ἐπαγγελία -ας ἡ	promise	μετανοέω	repent
εὐλογέω	bless	ποτήριον -ου τό	cup
θεωρέω	behold	πῦρ -ός τό	fire
καιρός -οῦ ὁ	season, due time	σπέρμα -ατος τό	seed

Translate: 1. οἱ εὐλογοῦντες τὸν Θεὸν δέξονται τὸν ἴδιον μισθὸν αὐτῶν. 2. οἱ Ἰουδαῖοι αὐτοὶ οἱ λαβόντες τὰς ἐπαγγελίας οὐκ ἠθέλησαν γνῶναι τὸν Χριστόν. 3. ὁ θεωρῶν τὸν υἱὸν καὶ πιστεύων εἰς αὐτὸν ἕξει ζωὴν αἰώνιον. 4. τοῦτο τὸ σπέρμα τὸ εἰς καλὴν γῆν σπαρὲν εὐλογεῖται ὑπὸ τοῦ Θεοῦ. 5. δεῖ τοὺς μετανοήσαντας δοξάζειν τὸν Θεὸν διὰ τὴν ἄφεσιν τῶν ἁμαρτιῶν. 6. οὗτος ὁ ἀδίκως γενόμενος ἀρχιερεὺς πονηρός ἐστι. 7. ὑμεῖς οἱ πιόντες τὸ ἐμὸν ποτήριον μέλλετε πάσχειν τὴν αὐτὴν θλῖψιν. 8. ἐξῆλθον οἱ κατοικοῦντες ἐν Ἰερουσαλημ πρὸς τὸν Ἰωάννην εἰς τὸ βαπτισθῆναι ὑπ' αὐτοῦ. 9. ἔπιπτεν εἰς τὸ πῦρ καὶ εἰς τὸ ὕδωρ τοῦτο τὸ ἀγαπητὸν τέκνον τὸ δαιμονιζόμενον. 10. οὗτός ἐστιν ὁ Χριστὸς ὁ σώσων τὸν κόσμον. 11. ὁ γὰρ ἄρτος τοῦ Θεοῦ ἐστιν ὁ καταβαίνων ἐκ τοῦ οὐρανοῦ. 12. δεῖ τὸν ἀκολουθοῦντά μοι βαστάζειν τὸν ἑαυτοῦ σταυρόν.

Matt. 4.21; Luke 10.38-39; John 10.1-3; I Cor. 14.2-4

[Whenever possible, use the participle]

Translate: 1. Blessed are those who prepare a way for the Lord; for they shall rejoice. 2. The lady who carries the lamp heals those who suffer. 3. My mother who bore five sons and four daughters used to say that she loved these her children. 4. The Father who sent me ordered me to proclaim forgiveness of sins to men and women. 5. Those who were led away by the guards died on the cross. 6. He who has ears to hear will receive these sayings.

---

22   Participles: adverbial use.   παρά

Adverbial use of participles. Here the participle is closely linked with the verb and is generally to be translated by one of the following constructions:

1. Temporal clause — the commonest use.

> διερχόμενος τὴν γῆν ἐδίδασκε τοὺς ὄχλους.
> Passing through the land he was teaching the crowds.

i.e. As he was passing . . .

> λαβὼν τὸ ἀργύριον οὐκ ἤθελε τηρεῖν αὐτό.
> Having taken the money he was unwilling to keep it.

i.e. When he had taken . . .

2. Causal

> φοβούμενος τοὺς Ἰουδαίους ἔφυγεν ἐκ τῆς πόλεως.
> Fearing the Jews he fled from the city.

i.e. Because he feared . . .

3. Concessive

> καίπερ ὢν υἱὸς ἔμαθεν ἀφ᾽ ὧν ἔπαθεν τὴν ὑπακοήν.
> Even (καί with emphasizing suffix περ) being a son he learnt
> obedience from what he suffered.   Heb. 5.8

i.e. Although he was a son . . .

This is the normal CG construction, but rare in NT and not necessarily introduced by καίπερ. The concessive nature will be shown by the context.

4. Conditional

πῶς ἡμεῖς ἐκφευξόμεθα τηλικαύτης ἀμελήσαντες σωτηρίας;
How shall we escape if we neglect so great salvation?

Heb. 2.3

Here the context makes it quite clear that the participle is used conditionally and to translate it by a straightforward participle would obscure the whole argument.

Sometimes English idiom will prefer two verbs linked by *and*:

κράξας εἶπε.
Having cried out he said.
i.e. He cried out and said.

Note the common NT expression, bad Greek but modelled on Semitic idiom:

ἀποκριθείς[1] εἶπε.
Having answered he said.
i.e. He answered and said.

Sometimes a participle giving attendant circumstances will be best translated by a participle:

περιῆγεν τὰς κώμας διδάσκων.
He went round the villages teaching.

Always start by translating the Greek participle literally, then think whether it would be turned into better English by using a clause, for the participle is used much more often in Greek than in English.

ἀνοίγω	open	ὁμολογέω	confess
ἀποκρίνομαι	answer	ὀνειδίζω	reproach
ἔξω	(adverb) outside, (w. gen.) outside		

[1] In CG this was a middle deponent, in K more often passive, but both forms are found in the NT.

οὕτως	so, thus		(persons),
παρά	(w. acc.) beside,		(w. dat.) near,
	to the side		beside[1]
	of (persons),	ὑπάγω	depart
	contrary to,	ὑπακούω	(w. dat.) obey
	(w. gen.) from		

Translate: 1. καὶ ἀποκριθεὶς εἶπεν ὅτι οἱ ὀνειδίζοντες τὸν Θεὸν οὐ φέρουσι τὸν καρπὸν τῆς δικαιοσύνης. 2. καταβὰς οὖν ἀπὸ τοῦ ὄρους εἰσῆλθε πάλιν εἰς τὴν πόλιν εὑρεῖν ἐκεῖ τὴν θυγατέρα αὐτοῦ τὴν δαιμόνιον ἔχουσαν. 3. λέγοντες οὖν ὅτι ἁμαρτίαν οὐκ ἔχομεν οὐ λέγομεν τὴν ἀλήθειαν περὶ ἑαυτῶν. 4. ἀνοίξας δὲ τὴν θύραν ὁ λῃστὴς ἀπήγαγε πολλὰ πρόβατα. 5. καίπερ πολλὰ παθοῦσα ἐν τῷ τεκεῖν τὸν υἱὸν τὸν ἀγαπητὸν ἐχάρη ἡ μήτηρ ἰδοῦσα τὸ πρωτότοκον παιδίον. 6. ὁμολογήσαντες τὰς ἁμαρτίας ἡμῶν λημψόμεθα ἄφεσιν παρὰ τοῦ Πατρός. 7. παρὰ τῷ τελώνῃ ἔπιες πολὺν οἶνον καὶ ὑπήκουσας αὐτῷ κελεύοντί σε ἀδίκως λαβεῖν τὸ ἀργύριον τῶν πτωχῶν χηρῶν. 8. οὕτως οὖν παρεκάλεσε τὸ πλῆθος δέχεσθαι τὸν λόγον· ἀλλ' οὐκ ἐβούλοντο ἀκούειν μὴ πιστεύοντες τῷ εὐαγγελίῳ. 9. πορευόμενοι δὲ διὰ τῶν ἀγρῶν ἐθεωρήσαμεν πολὺν καρπὸν καὶ τέσσαρας ἡμέρας νηστεύσαντες ἠθέλομεν φαγεῖν. 10. καὶ πολλὰ ποιήσαντες παρὰ τὸν νόμον ἤχθησαν εἰς τὴν πόλιν ὑπὸ τῶν φυλάκων· ἐπὶ δὲ τοῦ κριτοῦ εἶπον ὅτι κατὰ νόμον πορεύονται ἐν τῇ ὁδῷ τοῦ Κυρίου.

Matt. 2.11-12; Mark 1.9-13; Luke 5.39; Acts 13.4-7; Heb. 12.17b

[Whenever possible use a participle]

Translate: 1. While we were departing we beheld a great crowd marvelling at the blind man's faith. 2. He answered and said that the Son came forth from the Father who sent him into the world. 3. When they had confessed their sins they walked beside the river until they came to the city. 4. Although I am so poor I try to help those who do not receive pay, for I sent a fish to this

[1] With the dative of a person it often means *at the house of*, like Latin *apud* or French *chez*.

widow. 5. As Jesus was coming up out of the water he saw the Holy Spirit coming down upon him. 6. When he had prayed outside in desert places he entered the city again in order to evangelize there.

---

23   Genitive absolute.   Periphrastic tenses

Genitive absolute. When a combination of pronoun or noun with participle stands independent of the rest of the sentence this participle phrase is put in the genitive. Often editors put a comma after it to mark its self-sufficiency. Such a phrase will correspond to one of the clauses given above in Chapter 22 and should be translated accordingly rather than by the stilted English Nominative Absolute:

ἐξελθόντος τοῦ τέκνου, εἰσῆλθεν ὁ πατήρ.
The child having gone out, the father entered.
i.e. When the child had gone out, . . .

NB (1) This construction corresponds to the Latin Ablative Absolute, but is much more flexible and common because of the wider range of voices and tenses available.

(2) In κ the Genitive Absolute is used loosely, even when the noun or pronoun occurs elsewhere in the sentence, but this causes no difficulty in translation:

Καὶ ἐκπορευομένου αὐτοῦ ἐκ τοῦ ἱεροῦ λέγει αὐτῷ εἷς τῶν μαθητῶν αὐτοῦ (αὐτοῦ followed by αὐτῷ, instead of ἐκπορευομένῳ αὐτῷ)
And as he was going out of the temple one of his disciples said to him . . .   Mark 13.1

Periphrastic Tenses (i.e. formed in a round-about way)

In κ combinations of the verb *to be* with the present participle sometimes occur, chiefly in Mark and Luke and therefore probably influenced by οτ Semitic idiom.

Imperfect

καὶ ἦσαν οἱ μαθηταὶ Ἰωάννου καὶ οἱ Φαρισαῖοι νηστεύοντες.
And the disciples of John and the Pharisees were fasting.

Mark 2.18

Future (emphasizing continuity)

καὶ οἱ ἀστέρες ἔσονται ἐκ τοῦ οὐρανοῦ πίπτοντες.
And the stars will be falling from heaven.

Mark 13.25

ἀστήρ -έρος ὁ	star	ἤδη	already,
ἀτενίζω	gaze		now
ἐγγίζω	(w. dat.)	θέλημα -ατος τό	wish, will
	approach,	παράγω	pass by
	draw near	πρεσβύτερος -ου ὁ	elder
ἔτι	still	σκότος -ους τό	darkness
οὐκέτι[1]	no longer	φῶς φωτός τό	light
μηκέτι[1]	no longer		

Translate: 1. καὶ ἀναλημφθέντος τοῦ Ἰησοῦ, ὡς οἱ μαθηταὶ ἀτενίζοντες ἦσαν εἰς τὸν οὐρανόν, νεφέλη ἔλαβεν αὐτὸν ἀπὸ τῶν ὀφθαλμῶν αὐτῶν. 2. τοῦ δὲ Παύλου ἐκλεξαμένου πρεσβυτέρους τῇ ἡμετέρᾳ ἐκκλησίᾳ, οἱ κατοικοῦντες τὴν πόλιν ἤμελλον ἀποκτείνειν αὐτόν. 3. τῶν δέ ποιμένων ἰδόντων τὸν ἀστέρα, οἱ νεανίαι ἤθελον λιπεῖν τὰ πρόβατα ἐπὶ τοῦ ὄρους. 4. ὁ δὲ πατήρ μου ἔτι ὢν παιδίον εἶδε τὸν Ἰησοῦν παράγοντα παρὰ τὴν θάλασσαν, πολλῶν ἀκολουθούντων. 5. μηκέτι ἀκούοντος τοῦ ὄχλου, εὐθὺς ἐκέλευσε τοὺς μαθητὰς ἐμβῆναι εἰς τὸ πλοῖον. 6. οὐκέτι μεθ' ὑμῶν ἔσομαι πολὺν χρόνον· τοῦ γὰρ ἡγεμόνος ἐν Ῥώμῃ ὄντος, ἤδη μέλλει κρίνειν με ὁ κεντυρίων ὁ πολλοὺς ὑφ' ἑαυτὸν ἔχων στρατιώτας. 7. ἔσεσθε οὖν διωκόμενοι ὑπὸ τῶν ἐθνῶν·

[1] Compounds of οὐ and μή have no difference in meaning, but like οὐ and μή are used, the former with the indicative for statements of fact, the latter with infinitive and participle.

οὗτοι γάρ, μὴ εὐαγγελισαμένων ὧδε τῶν ἀποστόλων, πείθονται ὅτι ἀδίκως πράσσετε παρὰ τὸν νόμον. 8. ἐπὶ δὲ Ἡσαίου τοῦ προφήτου φυγόντος τοῦ ἱερέως ἐκείνου ἐκ τῆς πόλεως, οἱ μὲν ἐβουλήθησαν τηρεῖν ἐν φυλακῇ τὴν γυναῖκα αὐτοῦ, οἱ δὲ μὴ δέχεσθαι τὰ παιδία εἰς τὰς οἰκίας αὐτῶν. 9. μὴ μαρτυρούντων ὑμῶν τῇ πίστει, πολλοὶ περιπατοῦντες ἔσονται ἐν τῷ σκότει· οὐ γὰρ ἀκούσουσι περὶ Ἰησοῦ τοῦ φωτὸς τοῦ κόσμου. 10. κατὰ δὲ τὸ θέλημα τοῦ πατρὸς αὐτοῦ, μὴ θελούσης τῆς μητρός, λῃστὴς ἐγένετο ὁ σὸς ἀδελφός· δικαίως οὖν ἀπέθανεν ἐπὶ σταυρῷ.

Matt. 8.16a; 19.22; 25.10; Mark 1.22; Luke 4.20b; 15.1; 21.17a; 23.8

Translate: 1. When Jesus was already walking towards them on the water, the disciples began to cry out, because they marvelled at his power. 2. The soldiers who guarded me were persuaded by my mother to release me, although many were afraid. 3. While the women are still approaching the city, we will prepare houses for them; for they will wish to dwell here with their husbands. 4. When John had preached to the multitude, many wished to be baptized. 5. Jesus was passing by the lake and saw John and his brother casting their nets from the boat into the water in order to take fish. 6. Because they wished to see the star with their own eyes these kings left their own country; then they found the little child beside his mother with the shepherds and they marvelled.

24 Future and aorist of verbs with liquid stems. πᾶς, τις

Liquid Verbs with stem ending in λ μ ν ρ
Most of these verbs have some irregularity, but there are some general principles:

1. The future active and middle were originally formed by adding
εσ; the σ dropped out, leaving a contracted ending like present
of φιλῶ.

2. In these verbs the present stem may be longer than the stem
proper, which is found in the future:

   (a) a double λ in the present always drops one λ:

   ἀγγέλλω (ἀγγελέω) ἀγγελῶ

   (b) a diphthong in the present drops ι:

   ἐγείρω ἐγερῶ αἴρω ἀρῶ

3. The 1st aorist active and middle lengthen a short vowel of
present or future; this stem is not followed by σ but directly by
the aorist endings.

   α, ι lengthen to the ear, but no change appears in writing:

   αἴρω ἦρα[1] κρίνω ἔκρινα

   ε lengthens to a diphthong by addition of ι:

   μένω ἔμεινα
   ἐγείρω ἤγειρα

4. 1st aorist passive — if the stem ends in ρ this is followed by θ,
ἐγείρω ἠγέρθην, but ν drops out before θ in κρίνω, ἐκρίθην.

ἀγγέλλω	ἀγγελῶ	ἤγγειλα	ἠγγέλην	announce, report
αἴρω	ἀρῶ	ἦρα		take up
ἀποθνήσκω	ἀποθανοῦμαι	ἀπέθανον		die
ἀποκτείνω	ἀποκτενῶ	ἀπέκτεινα	ἀπεκτάνθην	kill
ἀπόλλυμι[2]	ἀπολῶ	ἀπώλεσα		(active) destroy, lose
	ἀπολοῦμαι	ἀπωλόμην		(middle) perish
ἀποστέλλω	ἀποστελῶ	ἀπέστειλα	ἀπεστάλην	send forth
βάλλω	βαλῶ	ἔβαλον	ἐβλήθην	throw

[1] η is due to the augment; in infinitive and participle etc. α is found—
ἆραι ἄρας.
[2] This belongs to an irregular group of verbs (cf. p. 115), but as the stem
proper is -ολ it has been given here, as it is a very common verb in the NT.

ἐγείρω	ἐγερῶ	ἤγειρα	ἠγέρθην	rouse, raise (from dead)
κρίνω	κρινῶ	ἔκρινα	ἐκρίθην	judge
μένω	μενῶ	ἔμεινα		remain
ὀφείλω		ὤφειλον	(imperfect only)	owe (w. infin., ought)
σπείρω		ἔσπειρα	ἐσπάρην	sow
φθείρω	φθερῶ	ἔφθειρα	ἐφθάρην	destroy

Formation of participles and infinitives follows normal rules:

From ἐγείρω

Future active   ἐγερ(έων)ῶν -(έουσα)οῦσα -(έον)οῦν   ἐγερεῖν
               ἐγεροῦντος ἐγερούσης ἐγεροῦντος
Aorist active   ἐγείρας -ασα -αν   ἐγεῖραι
Aorist passive   ἐγερθείς -εῖσα -έν   ἐγερθῆναι

NB In the future of such verbs ʾas μένω and κρίνω where there is no change of stem, in some persons only the circumflex marks the tense.

    μενῶ   μενεῖς   μενεῖ   μενοῦμεν   μενεῖτε   μενοῦσι(ν)

    πᾶς   πᾶσα   πᾶν
    παντός   πάσης   παντός
    πᾶσι(ν)   πάσαις   πᾶσι(ν)

This common adjective meaning *all*, declined like the 1st aorist participle active (cf. p. 63), stands outside article and noun, as also ὅλος *whole*:

πᾶσα ἡ πόλις.   ὅλη ἡ πόλις.
All the city.   The whole city.

    τίς   τί
    τίνος   τίνος
    τίσι(ν)   τίσι(ν)

Accented[1] and standing at the beginning of the sentence this is a 3rd declension interrogative pronoun or adjective, with no separate feminine:

[1] Before another word the interrogative τίς retains the acute accent and does not change to grave.

τίς τοῦτο ἐποίησεν;   τί ἀκούομεν;
Who did this?   What do we hear?

τί alone from an original διὰ τί is also common, meaning *why*:

τί τοῦτο λέγεις;   Why do you say this?

τις as an enclitic (cf. p. 154) is like an indefinite article, *a* or *a certain* (Latin *quidam*), in plural *some*:

ἄνθρωπός τις.   ἔλεγόν τινες.
A man *or* a certain man.   Some were saying.

κατακρίνω	condemn	σήμερον	(adverb) today
ὅλος -η -ον	whole	τίς τί	who?,
παῖς παιδός	(m. or f.) child		(neuter)
πᾶς πᾶσα πᾶν[1]	all		what?, why?,
πρωΐ	(adverb)		(enclitic) a
	early		

Translate: 1. τοῦ δὲ ἀλέκτορος τὸν παῖδα ἐγείραντος, ἡ μήτηρ ἐκέλευσεν αὐτὸν μένειν ἐπὶ τῷ κραββάτῳ, ὅτι πρωΐ ἔτι ἦν. 2. τίς ὧδε ὀφείλει ἀργύριον τῷ τελώνῃ; κατακρινεῖ γὰρ πάντας τοὺς μὴ κατὰ νόμον πράσσοντας. 3. πάντες οὖν οἱ ἀποσταλέντες εἰς τὰς πόλεις εὐαγγελίσασθαι πάλιν ἐπορεύθησαν εἰς Καφαρναυμ μετὰ χαρᾶς μεγάλης, πολλῶν τὸν λόγον δεξαμένων. 4. τί σήμερον ἀπωλέσατε ἐκεῖνα τὰ καλὰ πρόβατα ἐπὶ τοῦ ὄρους; ἠγόρασε γὰρ αὐτὰ ὁ βασιλεὺς αὐτὸς καὶ ἀπέστειλεν εἰς τοῦτον τὸν ἀγρὸν μετὰ τοῦ ποιμένος αὐτῶν. 5. ἄρας οὖν τὸν σταυρὸν τοῦ Ἰησοῦ Κυρηναῖός τις Σίμων ὀνόματι ἤνεγκεν αὐτὸν ἕως οὗ ἦλθον εἰς τὸν τόπον ἐν ᾧ ἔδει αὐτὸν ἀποθανεῖν. 6. ὀφείλω ἀγγεῖλαι ταῦτα τὰ πιστὰ ῥήματα καὶ εἰς Ῥώμην· ἐκεῖ γὰρ δεῖ με ἐπὶ Καίσαρος κριθῆναι. 7. ἀπέκτειναν λῃσταί τινες τὸν ἄνδρα μου μαχαίρῃ διερχόμενον τὴν Γαλιλαίαν πρὸς τὴν ἑαυτοῦ πατρίδα. 8. τί οὐκ ἔχομεν ἐξουσίαν ἐκβαλεῖν τοῦτο τὸ δαιμόνιον τὸ πειράζον ἀπολέσαι τὸν παῖδα; 9. ἐγερθεὶς δὲ ἐκ νεκρῶν μετὰ τεσσεράκοντα ἡμέρας ἤρθη ὁ Ἰησοῦς εἰς τὰς νεφέλας, ἀτενι-

---

[1] There is also a strengthened form ἅπας, ἅπασα, ἅπαν, but both are translated as *all*.

74

ζόντων τῶν μαθητῶν εἰς τὸν οὐρανόν. 10. φθαρείσης ταύτης τῆς πόλεως, ἐβουλήθησαν οἱ ἐχθροὶ ἀποκτεῖναι τοὺς πολίτας.

Matt. 4.23-25; 13.37-43b; 25.7; Mark 5.31-32; Luke 9.25; John 1.49

Translate: 1. We ought to send all the fruits from the vineyard to those who remain in the city; for some[1] are fasting and will die. 2. After killing the king the wicked soldiers begged the guards to keep them hidden in the temple. 3. We shall not condemn the widows who killed their husbands, because they were unrighteous men and did everything contrary to the law. 4. Why did some dogs flee from the house when they saw the boy approaching with four girls? 5. Who reads the whole book of the prophet and after reading it keeps in his heart all the commandments and promises? 6. When he had sown the seeds on the earth the sower went home again blessing and glorifying God.

25   Imperative. Multiplication of negatives

Imperatives are formed for both the 2nd and 3rd person present and aorist.

	Active present		Middle and Passive present	
2nd sing.	λῦε	φίλει (ε-ε)	λύου	φιλοῦ (έ-ου)
3rd sing.	λυέτω	φιλείτω (ε-έτω)	λυέσθω	φιλείσθω (ε-έσθω)
2nd pl.	λύετε	φιλεῖτε (έ-ετε)	λύεσθε	φιλεῖσθε (έ-εσθε)
3rd pl.	λυέτωσαν	φιλείτωσαν (ε-έτωσαν)	λυέσθωσαν	φιλείσθωσαν (ε-έσθωσαν)

[1] τις being enclitic will not normally stand as first word in a sentence.

75

	Active		Middle	
	1st aorist	2nd aorist	1st aorist	2nd aorist
2nd sing.	λῦσον	λάβε	λῦσαι	γενοῦ[1]
3rd sing.	λυσάτω	λαβέτω	λυσάσθω	γενέσθω
2nd pl.	λύσατε	λάβετε	λύσασθε	γένεσθε
3rd pl.	λυσάτωσαν	λαβέτωσαν	λυσάσθωσαν	γενέσθωσαν

Passive

	1st aorist	2nd aorist	Verb *to be*
2nd sing.	λύθητι	ἀποστάληθι	ἴσθι
3rd sing.	λυθήτω	ἀποσταλήτω	ἔστω, ἤτω
2nd pl.	λύθητε	ἀποστάλητε	ἔστε
3rd pl.	λυθήτωσαν	ἀποσταλήτωσαν	ἔστωσαν

To form the aorist the augment is dropped. In the 1st aorist active and middle the endings are characterized by α; in the 2nd aorist the strong stem is followed by the present endings. In the aorist passive note the difference between the endings of the 2nd sing. of the 1st and 2nd aorist.

A command necessarily refers to the future, but the difference between positive commands in present and aorist is the same as for the infinitive, i.e. present for continuous or repeated action, aorist for one single act, although in English both are usually translated alike.

> λάβετε, φάγετε· τοῦτό ἐστιν τὸ σῶμά μου.
> Take, eat; this is my body.　　　　　　　　　　　　　　Matt. 26.26
> (Aorist for the particular occasion of the Last Supper)

> τοῦτο ποιεῖτε εἰς τὴν ἐμὴν ἀνάμνησιν.
> Do this in remembrance of me.　　　　　　　　　　　　I Cor. 11.24
> (Present implying that the rite will be continually repeated)

> Ἡ φιλαδελφία μενέτω.
> Let love of the brethren continue.　　　　　　　　　　　Heb. 13.1

Numerals 1 to 4 are 3rd declension, but except for 4, τέσσαρες -α, have some peculiarities:

---

[1] The 2nd sing. 2nd aorist middle accents on the ultimate. Two common 2nd sing. 2nd aorist actives accent irregularly — ἐλθέ εἰπέ. Note the difference between εἶπε *he said* and εἰπέ *say*.

1	εἷς	μία	ἕν	2	δύο	3	τρεῖς	τρία
	ἕνα	μίαν	ἕν		δύο		τρεῖς	τρία
	ἑνός	μιᾶς	ἑνός		δύο		τριῶν	τριῶν
	ἑνί	μιᾷ	ἑνί		δυσί(ν)		τρισί(ν)	τρισί(ν)

Multiplication of negatives

When a compound negative precedes the simple negative the two cancel each other out, as in English. When, however, the simple negative is followed by one or more compound negatives or compound negatives are piled up, then the negative emphasis is increased, though only one negative will be translated.

Compound negatives:

οὐδείς	οὐδεμία	οὐδέν	no one,
μηδείς	μηδεμία	μηδέν	nothing
οὐδέποτε	μηδέποτε		never
οὐκέτι	μηκέτι		no longer
οὔπω	μήπω		
οὐδέπω	μηδέπω		not yet

οὐδεὶς οὐ λέγει τοῦτο.
Nobody does not say this.   i.e. Everybody says this.

οὐ λέγει τοῦτο οὐδείς.   οὐ λέγει τοῦτο οὐδεὶς οὐδέποτε.
Nobody says this.   Nobody ever says this.

ἐκέλευσε μὴ αἰτεῖν μηδένα μηδέν.
He ordered that nobody should ask for anything.

δεξιός -ά -όν	right	πάντοτε	always
εἰ	if	παραγγέλλω	(w. dat.) command
ἰδού[1]	lo !		
ἰσχυρός -ά -όν	strong	τρίτος -η -ον	third
κλαίω	weep	σκανδαλίζω	cause to fall away, offend
κλέπτης -ου ὁ	thief		
κωφός -ή -όν	dumb, deaf		
μνημεῖον -ου τό	tomb		

---

[1] This is the 2nd sing. middle imperative of εἶδον, which supplies the aorist forms for ὁράω, but is frequently used as an interjection, as is also, though less often, the imperative active ἴδε.

Translate: 1. καὶ εἰ ἡ δεξιά σου χεὶρ σκανδαλίζει σε, ἔκκοψον αὐτὴν καὶ βάλε ἀπὸ σοῦ. 2. ἔγειρε[1] καὶ περιπάτει· παραγγέλλω δέ σοι μὴ ἁμαρτάνειν μηκέτι. 3. ὁ ἄνθρωπος ὁ ἔχων τὰ δαιμόνια ἀποκριθεὶς εἶπε· πέμψον ἡμᾶς εἰς τοὺς χοίρους. 4. τῇ δὲ τρίτῃ ἡμέρᾳ ἐγερθεὶς ἐξῆλθεν ἐκ τοῦ μνημείου καὶ εἶπε τῇ Μαριαμ· γύναι, τί κλαίεις; 5. εἰ ἰσχυρός τις ἔχει πολὺ ἀργύριον φυλασσέτω αὐτὸ ἐν τῇ ἰδίᾳ οἰκίᾳ αὐτοῦ. 6. ἀκουέτωσαν πάντες οἱ κωφοὶ καὶ δεχέσθωσαν εἰς τὰ ὦτα τοὺς ἐμοὺς λόγους. 7. ἀρθήτω τὸ σῶμα ἐπὶ τὸν σταυρὸν καὶ ἐκεῖ μενέτω πρὸς τὸ πάντας θεωρεῖν τοῦτον τὸν ἄδικον καὶ πονηρὸν λῃστὴν οὕτως ἀποθνήσκοντα. 8. διὰ τί ἔκραξας; οὐ γινώσκει γὰρ οὐδεὶς τὴν ὥραν ἐν ᾗ μέλλει ἔρχεσθαι ὁ οἰκοδεσπότης· λέγω οὖν ὑμῖν πᾶσι· προσεύχεσθε. 9. ἰδοῦσα δὲ τὸν ἄγγελον καὶ ἀκούσασα ἃ εἶπεν αὐτῇ ἡ παρθένος ἀπεκρίθη λέγουσα· γενέσθω μοι κατὰ τὸ ῥῆμά σου. 10. ἰδού, λέγω σοι, αἰτοῦ πάντοτε παρὰ τοῦ Θεοῦ ἃ θέλεις λαβεῖν· οὗτος γὰρ ἐλεήσει σε πιστεύοντα ὅτι ἀγαθός ἐστιν.

Matt. 6.9-10; 6.19-21; 10.8a; 14.25-30; Luke 4.23 ('Ιατ. — σε.); 16.29; John 1.43-44; Eph. 6.5-7; 6.11a

Translate: 1. Open your mouth and announce now to all these Gentiles the Lord's miracles and mighty works. 2. Let all the earth and those who dwell in it bless the Lord. 3. Remain by the tomb all night (cf. p. 47) and guard it; for the dogs must not approach. 4. Always carry oil in your lamps. 5. Send one of these two fish to the king; for he wishes to eat a fish taken in this lake. 6. Who will condemn the sons of God? Let them be blessed and glorified even by the angels.

[1] In the imperative commonly used intransitively (*rise*) and in the present, where an aorist might be expected. The same holds for ἄγω, used intransitively to mean *come* or *go*.

26 Subjunctive: hortatory, prohibitions, with ἵνα or ὅπως in indirect command and purpose clauses

In the **subjunctive** all present endings resemble the indicative, but are distinguished by long vowels—NB η for ει.

	Active	Middle and Passive		Verb *to be*
λύω	φιλῶ	λύωμαι	φιλῶμαι	ὦ
λύῃς	φιλῇς	λύῃ	φιλῇ	ᾖς
λύῃ	φιλῇ	λύηται	φιλῆται	ᾖ
λύωμεν	φιλῶμεν	λυώμεθα	φιλώμεθα	ὦμεν
λύητε	φιλῆτε	λύησθε	φιλῆσθε	ἦτε
λύωσι(ν)	φιλῶσι(ν)	λύωνται	φιλῶνται	ὦσι(ν)

1st and 2nd Aorist Active and Middle drop augment, then aorist stem is followed by present endings:

ἔλυσα	λύσω	ἔλαβον	λάβω
ἐλυσάμην	λύσωμαι	ἐγενόμην	γένωμαι

1st and 2nd Aorist Passive drop augment, but aorist stem is then followed by present endings of the subjunctive of the verb *to be*:

ἐλύθην	λυθῶ	ἀπεστάλην	ἀποσταλῶ

The distinction between present and aorist subjunctive is the same as for the infinitive and imperative, i.e. between continuous and momentary action (cf. p. 49).

Four constructions in which the subjunctive is used:

1. **Hortatory** to express a 1st person command, as in Latin:

    πάντοτε εὐλογῶμεν τὸν Θεόν.
    Let us always praise God (i.e. keep on praising him).

    σήμερον φάγωμεν καὶ πίωμεν.
    Let us eat and drink today (i.e. on this particular occasion).

The negative is μή.

2. **Prohibitions** in the 2nd person:[1]

    (a) μή is used with the present imperative for prohibition of an action already begun:

        μὴ φοβεῖσθε. Do not fear (i.e. Stop being afraid).

    (b) μή is used with the aorist subjunctive to prohibit embarking on a course of action:

        μὴ ψευδομαρτυρήσῃς. Do not bear false witness.

3. **Indirect command** or request may be expressed by a subjunctive clause introduced by ἵνα or less often ὅπως, negative μή:

    ἐδεήθην αὐτοῦ ἵνα θεραπεύσῃ τὸν παῖδά μου.
    I begged him to heal my boy.

4. **Purpose** may also be expressed by a subjunctive clause with ἵνα or ὅπως ; negative μή, often μή alone without a conjunction:

    ἦλθον πρὸς τῆς πόλιν ἵνα μένω παρὰ τῷ πατρί.
    I came to the city in order to stay at my father's.

    μενοῦμεν ὧδε μὴ (ἵνα μὴ) εὕρωσιν ἡμᾶς οἱ ἐχθροί.
    We shall stay here lest the enemy find us (that the enemy may not find us).

ἅπτομαι (M)	(w. gen.) touch	θηρίον -ου τό	wild beast
ἀρχή -ῆς ἡ	beginning, rule	καθίζω	sit
ἀρχιερεύς -έως ὁ	high priest	μέσος -η -ον	middle
δοκέω	seem, think	οὔτε — οὔτε	neither — nor
ἕκαστος -η -ον	each	μήτε — μήτε	
ἐλπίζω	hope	προσκυνέω	(usually w. dat.)
ἐντέλλομαι (M)	(w. dat.) command		worship, prostrate oneself
ἑπτά	(indecl.) seven		

Give the 1st pl. future indic. active of ἀπόλλυμι, ἀποκτείνω, αἴρω; aorist infin. middle and passive of ἀποκρίνομαι; 3rd sing. aorist imperative active, middle and passive of αἰτέω; 3rd pl. present imperative active and middle of τηρέω; gen. sing. and dat. pl. of αἰών, γένος, δύναμις, δόξα; acc. sing. of ἰχθύς, χάρις.

[1] Distinction between the two types (a) and (b) is not always clear cut.

Translate: 1. ἀσπάσασθε πάντας τοὺς ἀδελφούς· οὗτοι γὰρ ἐν ἀρχῇ¹ ὠφέλησάν με χρείαν ἔχοντα ἄρτου, ὅτε κατῴκουν ἐν τῇ πόλει αὐτῶν. 2. εἶπεν οὖν τοῖς μαθηταῖς ἵνα ἐμβάντες εἰς τὸ πλοῖον ἀπέλθωσιν. 3. μηκέτι μηδὲν αἰτώμεθα, μὴ λέγῃ τὰ ἔθνη ὅτι πάντοτε δεόμεθα. 4. λεπρὸς δέ τις προσελθὼν προσεκύνησεν αὐτῷ καὶ ἐδεήθη ἵνα καθαρίσῃ αὐτόν. 5. καὶ ἥψατο τῆς γλώσσης τοῦ κωφοῦ λέγων αὐτῷ· Ἰδού, ἔσῃ λαλῶν. 6. ὦ γύναι, οὐδέποτε βλέψω οὐδεμίαν οὕτω καλήν· μακάριος ὁ ἀνήρ σου καὶ προστάξω αὐτῷ ἵνα εὖ σε ποιῇ. 7. μὴ κατακρίνῃς μηδένα πρὸ τοῦ ἀκοῦσαι ὅλον τὸν λόγον αὐτοῦ. 8. ἥμαρτεν οὔτε ὁ πατὴρ οὔτε ἡ μήτηρ μου· μὴ οὖν ἐντείλῃ ἵνα φθαρῶσιν ὑπὸ τῶν θηρίων. 9. μηκέτι κάθιζε ἐπὶ τῆς γῆς, ἀλλ᾽ ἔγειρε εἰς τὸ μέσον· θέλω γὰρ ἅψασθαί σου ἵνα περιπατῇς. 10. μὴ φοβεῖσθε, ἀλλ᾽ ἀγγείλατε ὅτι ἐδοκοῦμεν ἀκούειν² εἰς ἕκαστος τῇ ἰδίᾳ διαλέκτῳ λαλούντων αὐτῶν. 11. εἶπεν δ᾽ ὁ Ἰησοῦς· Ἐγείρεσθε, ἄγωμεν. καὶ ἔτι αὐτοῦ λαλοῦντος, ἰδοὺ Ἰούδας εἷς τῶν δώδεκα ἦλθεν καὶ μετ᾽ αὐτοῦ ὄχλος πολὺς μετὰ μαχαιρῶν ἀπὸ τῶν ἀρχιερέων καὶ πρεσβυτέρων τοῦ λαοῦ. καὶ εὐθέως προσελθὼν τῷ Ἰησοῦ εἶπεν, Χαῖρε,³ Ραββει.

Matt. 5.16; 6.13; 27.32; Mark 3.14-15; 6.8; Luke 8.22 (καὶ [third] — ἀνήχ.); 8.28 (δέομαι — βασ.); John 10.10; Heb. 13.13-15

Translate: 1. Let us take up our cross and follow Jesus to the end, trusting in his promises. 2. The guards told the shepherd that he was to keep⁴ his seven sheep beside the two rivers. 3. Do not remain here, lest the soldiers see us sitting by the fire. 4. Keep on hoping in the Lord; never say that he will leave his people. 5. Hail, king of the Jews! The soldiers called Jesus by this name, although they did not know that they were speaking the truth. 6. Depart in peace to your own land, for I will go with you in order that I may guard you.

¹ Common prepositional phrases are apt to omit the article.
² In CG ἀκούω took the gen. of a person instead of the acc. and this use is sometimes found in κ also.
³ Often a conventional greeting, *Hail*.
⁴ There is no analogy with the Latin sequence of tenses in Indirect Command and Purpose clauses. Present and aorist subjunctive are differentiated, as always, simply by the type of action.

81

There are few **Third declension adjectives** in the NT, but the student should be able to recognize case endings.

1. consonantal stems like ἡγεμών, no separate feminine:

foolish					
N.	ἄφρων	ἄφρον	N.	ἄφρονες	ἄφρονα
V.	ἄφρον	ἄφρον	V.	ἄφρονες	ἄφρονα
A.	ἄφρονα	ἄφρον	A.	ἄφρονας	ἄφρονα
G.	ἄφρονος	ἄφρονος	G.	ἀφρόνων	ἀφρόνων
D.	ἄφρονι	ἄφρονι	D.	ἄφροσι(ν)	ἄφροσι(ν)

2. original stem in -εσ, leading to contraction with dropping of σ, like ἔθνος, no separate feminine:

true					
N.	ἀληθής	ἀληθές	N.	ἀληθεῖς	ἀληθῆ
V.	ἀληθές	ἀληθές	V.	ἀληθεῖς	ἀληθῆ
A.	ἀληθῆ	ἀληθές	A.	ἀληθεῖς	ἀληθῆ
G.	ἀληθοῦς	ἀληθοῦς	G.	ἀληθῶν	ἀληθῶν
D.	ἀληθεῖ	ἀληθεῖ	D.	ἀληθέσι(ν)	ἀληθέσι(ν)

3. vowel stem (no noun counterpart) with separate feminine of 1st declension:

straight			
N.	εὐθύς	εὐθεῖα	εὐθύ
V.	εὐθύ	εὐθεῖα	εὐθύ
A.	εὐθύν	εὐθεῖαν	εὐθύ
G.	εὐθέος	εὐθείας	εὐθέος
D.	εὐθεῖ	εὐθείᾳ	εὐθεῖ
N.	εὐθεῖς	εὐθεῖαι	εὐθέα
V.	εὐθεῖς	εὐθεῖαι	εὐθέα
A.	εὐθεῖς	εὐθείας	εὐθέα
G.	εὐθέων	εὐθειῶν	εὐθέων
D.	εὐθέσι(ν)	εὐθείαις	εὐθέσι(ν)

4. a peculiar adjective, mentioned here because it occurs six times in the NT, *black*; feminine is 1st declension, the neuter is used as a noun meaning *ink*.

μέλας   μέλαινα   μέλαν   μέλανος   μελαίνης   μέλανος

Adverbs are formed from Third declension adjectives by changing ending ων of genitive pl. to ως:

ἀληθῶς, εὐθέως.

ἀληθής -ές	true	μάρτυς -υρος ὁ, ἡ	witness,
ἀσθενής -ές	sick, weak		martyr
ἄφρων -ον	foolish	μέλας -αινα -αν	black
βραχύς -εῖα -ύ	short, little	πλήρης -ες	full
γάμος -ου ὁ	marriage	σκεῦος -ους τό	vessel, im-
γονεύς -έως ὁ	parent		plement,
γρηγορέω	keep awake, watch		pl. goods
		ταχύς -εῖα -ύ	quick
εὐθύς -εῖα -ύ	straight	ταχύ	quickly[1]
καθεύδω	sleep	ὑγιής -ές	healthy, sound

Translate: 1. καὶ εὐθέως ἤκουσε φωνὴν ὁ πλούσιος λέγουσαν· Ἄφρον, ταύτῃ τῇ νυκτὶ δεῖ σε ἀποθανεῖν. 2. γρηγορεῖτε οὖν καὶ φυλάσσετε τὰ σκεύη τοῦ οἰκοδεσπότου μὴ κλεπτής τις ταχέως ἐλθὼν εὕρῃ ὑμᾶς καθεύδοντας. 3. ἀσθενὴς δέ τις προσπεσὼν τοῖς γόνασι τοῦ διδασκάλου προσεκύνησεν αὐτῷ καὶ ἐδεήθη ἵνα ἐλεήσῃ αὐτόν. 4. ἐπιστολὴν δὲ βραχεῖαν γράψω ὑμῖν, μὴ δοκῶ βούλεσθαι πολλὰ ὑμῖν προστάσσειν. 5. ἰδού, μέλαν ἐστὶ τὸ ἱμάτιον τούτου τοῦ παιδός, ἀποκτείναντος τοῦ ἡγεμόνος τὸν πατέρα αὐτοῦ. 6. τίνα εὑρήσομεν μάρτυρα πιστὸν καὶ ἀληθῆ; φοβοῦνται γὰρ πάντες τὴν δύναμιν τοῦ Καίσαρος. 7. καὶ ἤρξατο ὁ δαιμονιζόμενος κράζειν καὶ κλαίειν, οὐχ ὑγιὴς ὢν ἀλλ' ὑπ' ἐξουσίαν γενόμενος ἑπτὰ ἀκαθάρτων δαιμονίων. 8. εὐθέως οὖν μετανοείτωσαν οἱ ἄφρονες ἵνα λάβωσιν ἄφεσιν ἁμαρτιῶν πρὸ τῆς ὥρας τοῦ θανάτου. 9. προσκάλεσαι πάντας τοὺς

---

[1] The neuter sing. is used as an adverb along with the adverb proper ταχέως. There is also the common adverb εὐθύς along with εὐθέως.

πτωχοὺς καὶ τοὺς τυφλοὺς καὶ τοὺς χωλοὺς εἰς τὸν γάμον· οὔπω γὰρ πλήρης ἡ οἰκία μου.   10. δεῖ οὖν προσεύχεσθαι ἵνα μὴ ἔλθωμεν εἰς πειρασμόν· ἀσθενὴς γὰρ ἡ σάρξ.

Matt. 7.13; Mark 1.3b; 4.2-6; John 5.15-18; 8.26-27; Acts 6.8

Translate : 1. These scriptures are short, for the prophet was sick when he wrote and sent them forth to the churches. 2. In order to know my gospel you must truly keep my commandments in your hearts. 3. Those who keep awake will receive their full reward after the messenger comes from our master's vineyard. 4. Let no one continue to say foolish words, lest each persuade his brother to sin. 5. Do not ask the doctor to make you healthy, but confess your sins to the Lord in order that he may see your repentance and have mercy. 6. Behold, the day of the Lord will come quickly and then great will be the glory of the true martyrs, because they witnessed to their faith in order to find eternal life in heaven.

---

28 Contracted verbs with stem in α.   δύναμαι.   οὐ μή introducing a strong negation

Contracted verbs with stems in α. $a + \omega$, a drops out; $a + \epsilon = a$; $a + \epsilon\iota = \bar{a}$; $a + \eta = \bar{a}$; $a + o = \omega$; $a + ov = \omega$.

NB The only resultant combinations are a, $\bar{a}$, ω. It follows that the present indicative and subjunctive are the same in form.

honour *or* value

Present

	Indicative		Imperative
Active	Middle, Passive	Active	Middle, Passive
τιμῶ	τιμῶμαι	τίμα	τιμῶ
τιμᾷς	τιμᾷ	τιμάτω	τιμάσθω
τιμᾷ	τιμᾶται	τιμᾶτε	τιμᾶσθε
τιμῶμεν	τιμώμεθα	τιμάτωσαν	τιμάσθωσαν
τιμᾶτε	τιμᾶσθε		
τιμῶσι(ν)	τιμῶνται		

Infinitives τιμᾶν[1]   τιμᾶσθαι

Participles

   τιμῶν -ῶσα -ῶν   τιμῶντος   τιμῶσι   τιμώμενος -η -ον

Imperfect

Active	Middle, Passive
ἐτίμων	ἐτιμώμην
ἐτίμας	ἐτιμῶ
ἐτίμα	ἐτιμᾶτο
ἐτιμῶμεν	ἐτιμώμεθα
ἐτιμᾶτε	ἐτιμᾶσθε
ἐτίμων	ἐτιμῶντο

As with φιλέω, there is contraction only in present and imperfect; in all other tenses the stem lengthens, after a vowel or ρ to a long α (ἐάσω), after a consonant other than ρ to η (τιμάω τιμήσω), but there are exceptions (βοάω βοήσω, πεινάω πεινάσω).

NB ζάω *live* is irregular in its contraction, changing to η instead of α before ε, to ῃ instead of ᾳ before ει or ῃ. Hence such forms as: ζῇς, ζῇ, ζῆτε, infinitive ζῆν.

δύναμαι—this common verb, meaning *can*, is given here to avoid confusion with stems contracting in α, but belongs to a different group (cf. p. 113) in which the present and imperfect middle and passive are marked by the fact that the endings (differing slightly from λύω) are not linked to the stem by a connecting vowel. Contrast λύ-ομαι, τιμά-ομαι with δύνα-μαι. Similar are κάθημαι *sit*, κεῖμαι *lie*.

[1] NB The infinitive has no iota subscript.

Present indic.

δύνα-μαι	κάθη-μαι	κεῖ-μαι
δύνα-σαι, δύνῃ	κάθη-σαι	κεῖ-σαι
δύνα-ται	κάθη-ται	κεῖ-ται
δυνά-μεθα	καθή-μεθα	κεί-μεθα
δύνα-σθε	κάθη-σθε	κεῖ-σθε
δύνα-νται	κάθη-νται	κεῖ-νται

Imperfect indic.

ἠδυνά-μην	ἐκαθή -μην	ἐκεί -μην	
ἠδύνα-σο			
ἠδύνα-το	Infinitive	δύνασθαι κάθησθαι κεῖσθαι	
ἠδυνά-μεθα	Participle	δυνάμενος -η -ον	
ἠδύνα-σθε		καθήμενος -η -ον	
ἠδύνα-ντο		κείμενος -η -ον	

Other tenses follow regular conjugations. δύναμαι is a passive deponent, aorist ἠδυνήθην[1] with middle future δυνήσομαι; the imperfect sometimes has a regular augment, ἐδυνάμην. κάθημαι has a future καθήσομαι but otherwise this and κεῖμαι are only found in present and imperfect.

οὐ μή introducing a strong negation

οὐ μή is used with the aorist subj. or less often with future indic. to express a strong negative statement about the future.

αμην λέγω ὑμῖν, οὐ μὴ ἀπολέσῃ τὸν μισθὸν αὐτοῦ.

Verily I say unto you, he shall in no wise lose his reward (RV).

Matt. 10.42

NB In the NT this emphasis is often lost and translation must depend on the context.

ἀγαλλιάομαι[2] (M)	rejoice greatly, exult	βοάω	cry
		γεννάω	beget
		διψάω	thirst
ἀγαπάω[3]	love	δύναμαι	be able, can

[1] ἠδυνάσθη is found only in Mark 7.24.
[2] Almost always middle, but occasionally active.
[3] Used of the love between God and man.

ἐάω[1]	allow	οὐδέ, μηδέ	and not,
ἐρωτάω[2]	ask		nor, not
ζάω	live		even
ἰάομαι (M)	heal	πεινάω	be hungry
κάθημαι	sit	τιμάω	honour,
κεῖμαι[3]	lie		value
κοιμάομαι (P)	sleep		

Translate: 1. τὸν δὲ ἐρχόμενον πρός με οὐ μὴ ἐκβάλω ἔξω. 2. ὕστερον δὲ ἠρώτησαν αὐτόν τινες περὶ τῶν παραβολῶν. 3. καὶ νηστεύσας μετὰ τῶν θηρίων τεσσεράκοντα ἡμέρας ἐπείνασεν. 4. ἦν δὲ ὁ Πέτρος κοιμώμενος ἐν τῇ φυλακῇ. 5. τίμα τὸν πατέρα καὶ τὴν μητέρα σου ἵνα ζῇς μηδὲ κακῶς ἀπόλῃ. 6. καὶ ἐπηρώτησε τὸν ὄχλον ἀνάκεισθαι ἐπὶ τῆς γῆς· οἱ δὲ ὑπήκουσαν αὐτῷ. 7. καθημένων δὲ τῶν μαθητῶν περὶ αὐτόν, εἶπεν ὅτι ἀγαπᾷ ὁ Θεὸς πάντας τοὺς πεινῶντας καὶ διψῶντας καὶ ἐλεήσει αὐτούς. 8. εἰ θέλετε, δύνασθε ἰᾶσθαι πάντας τοὺς διὰ νόσον πάσχοντας καὶ ἀσθενεῖς ὄντας. 9. ἐγέννησεν ὁ Αβρααμ Ισαακ· γεννηθέντα δὲ ἤθελε καὶ ἀποκτεῖναι τὸν υἱόν, τοῦτο κελεύσαντος τοῦ Θεοῦ. 10. τίς ἐβόησεν ἐν τῇ ἐρήμῳ; τιμάσθω δὲ καὶ εὐλογείσθω οὗτος· καὶ γὰρ διὰ τὴν διδαχὴν αὐτοῦ ἀγαλλιῶνται πάντες οἱ κατοικοῦντες τὴν Ἰουδαίαν. 11. οὐκ εἴασεν ἡμᾶς ὁ βασιλεὺς πορευθῆναι παρὰ τὴν θάλασσαν· μὴ ἀγγείλωμεν τῷ ἡγεμόνι ὅτι πολλὰ πλοῖα ἔχει ὧδε. 12. οὐκ ἠδυνάμεθα ἀγοράσαι ἔλαιον ἐκεῖ εἰς τὸ ἰᾶσθαι τοὺς ἀσθενεῖς ὅτι οὐκ ἐπίστευσαν ἡμῖν οἱ ἀκούοντες τὸ εὐαγγέλιον.

Matt. 15.28; Mark 5.39-40; 12.34; Luke 5.29-31; 9.37-40; 16.13; 16.23-25; John 2.13-16; 4.39-40; 4.46-47; Rev. 2.11

Translate: 1. Those who love the Lord will in the last days see him coming upon the clouds in glory. 2. Who asked the guard to bring you bread and wine when you were hungry and thirsty? 3. We are not able even to eat bread because many are questioning us about Jesus' sayings. 4. Young man, cry that Jesus will heal the sick and make them healthy; for he will certainly not allow

---

[1] Irregular augment, imperfect εἴων, aorist εἴασα.
[2] Chiefly, like compound ἐπερωτάω, to ask questions, but also for request.
[3] Common compounds ἀνάκειμαι, κατάκειμαι recline, κατάκειμαι also lie abed.

them to suffer. 5. The faithful and holy ought to honour their rulers, whom God sent forth into the world in order that men might hear and obey their commandments. 6. Those who were reclining beside the king exulted when they heard that John was no longer alive.

---

29 Contracted verbs with stem in o. Questions direct and indirect. Deliberative subjunctive

Contracted verbs with stems in o. o drops out before ω and ου; o+ε=ου; o+ει=οι, o+η=οι, o+η=ω, o+o=ου. The only possible endings are ω, ου, οι.

πληρόω fill, fulfil

Present

| Active | | Middle, Passive | |
Indic.	Subj.	Indic.	Subj.
πληρῶ	πληρῶ	πληροῦμαι	πληρῶμαι
πληροῖς	πληροῖς	πληροῖ	πληροῖ
πληροῖ	πληροῖ	πληροῦται	πληρῶται
πληροῦμεν	πληρῶμεν	πληρούμεθα	πληρώμεθα
πληροῦτε	πληρῶτε	πληροῦσθε	πληρῶσθε
πληροῦσι(ν)	πληρῶσι(ν)	πληροῦνται	πληρῶνται

Imperfect

Active	Middle, Passive
ἐπλήρουν	ἐπληρούμην
ἐπλήρους	ἐπληροῦ
ἐπλήρου	ἐπληροῦτο
ἐπληροῦμεν	ἐπληρούμεθα
ἐπληροῦτε	ἐπληροῦσθε
ἐπλήρουν	ἐπληροῦντο

Imperatives

Active	Middle, Passive
πλήρου	πληροῦ
πληρούτω	πληρούσθω
πληροῦτε	πληροῦσθε
πληρούτωσαν	πληρούσθωσαν

Infin. $\pi\lambda\eta\rhoο\hat{υ}ν^1$ $\pi\lambda\eta\rhoο\hat{υ}σθαι$

Participles $\pi\lambda\eta\rho\hat{ω}ν$ -$ο\hat{υ}σα$ -$ο\hat{υ}ν$ $\pi\lambda\eta\rhoο\hat{υ}ντος$ $\pi\lambda\eta\rhoού\mu\varepsilonνος$ -η -$ον$

Questions not introduced by an interrogative

Direct questions

(a) Unprejudiced questions which do not expect any particular answer are occasionally introduced by the CG untranslatable $\hat{a}\rho a$, but usually there is no introductory particle, only a question mark. In speech there would have been an interrogatory inflexion of the voice:

$\hat{a}\rho a$ $\varepsilonὑρήσ\varepsilonι$ $πίστιν$ $ἐπὶ$ $τῆς$ $γῆς;$
Will he find faith upon the earth?   Luke 18.8

(b) $οὐχί$, a more emphatic form of $οὐ$, introduces a question which expects an affirmative answer:

$οὐχὶ$ $καὶ$ $οἱ$ $τελῶναι$ $τὸ$ $αὐτὸ$ $ποιοῦσιν;$
Do not the tax-collectors also do the same?   Matt. 5.46

(c) $μή$, $μήτι$ introduce a hesitant question (perhaps?) or a question expecting a negative answer, but translators are apt to omit it, leaving the negative to be inferred from the context:

$μήτι$ $οὗτός$ $ἐστιν$ $ὁ$ $υἱὸς$ $Δαυειδ;$
Surely this man is not the son of David?   Matt. 12.23
Is this the son of David? (RV).

Indirect questions are introduced by $εἰ$ if, whether, and as in Indirect Statement the tense of the original questions is vividly retained. There is no change of mood:

$ἐπηρώτησεν$ $εἰ$ $ὁ$ $ἄνθρωπος$ $Γαλιλαῖός$ $ἐστιν.$
He asked whether the man was a Galilean.   Luke 23.6

NB In κ $εἰ$ is sometimes found introducing even a Direct Question; if so, it cannot be translated:

$καὶ$ $ἐπηρώτησαν$ $αὐτὸν$ $λέγοντες,$ $Εἰ$ $ἔξεστιν$ $τοῖς$ $σάββασιν$
$θεραπεῦσαι;$
And they questioned him, saying, 'Is it lawful to heal on the sabbath?'   Matt. 12.10

---

[1] Note that the infinitive active is $\pi\lambda\eta\rhoο\hat{υ}ν$, not $\pi\lambda\eta\rhoο\hat{ι}ν$.

The Deliberative Subjunctive

This is used for rhetorical questions, but in κ this and the future indic. are often confused:

ἁμαρτήσωμεν, ὅτι οὐκ ἐσμὲν ὑπὸ νόμον ἀλλὰ ὑπὸ χάριν;

Are we to sin because we are not under law, but under grace?

Rom. 6.15

δικαιόω	justify	ὁράω[1]	see
ἐπιτιμάω	(w. dat.) rebuke, warn	πλανάω	lead astray, (passive) err, wander
ἤ	or	πληρόω	fulfil, fill (w. acc. and gen.)
κοινόω	make common, defile (ritually)	σιωπάω	be silent
μεριμνάω	be anxious, take thought	σταυρόω	crucify
		ὑπαντάω	(w. dat.) meet
ὁμοιόω	make like, compare	ὑψόω	exalt
		φανερόω	manifest, show

Translate: 1. μὴ μεριμνήσητε λέγοντες· Τί πίωμεν ἢ τί φάγωμεν; 2. καὶ περιβλεψάμενος ἠρώτησεν αὐτοὺς τί ἐλάλουν πορευόμενοι· οἱ δὲ ἐσιώπων. 3. μήτι δεῖ ἡμᾶς κοινοῦν τὰς χεῖρας καὶ τὸ στόμα ἐσθίοντας τὰ ἀκάθαρτα; 4. δικαιοῖ ὁ υἱὸς τοῦ ἀνθρώπου τοὺς ἁμαρτωλοὺς τοὺς ἀδίκως ὑψοῦντας ἑαυτούς; 5. προσελθὼν δὲ ἐκ τῶν μνημείων ὑπήντησεν αὐτῷ ἰσχυρός τις ᾧ οὐκ ἠδύνατο οὐδεὶς ἐπιβαλεῖν τὰς χεῖρας. 6. καὶ μετὰ τὸ σταυρωθῆναι ἐφανερώθη πολλοῖς ἵνα ὁρῶντες γινώσκωσι ὅτι ἠγέρθη ἐκ νεκρῶν. 7. οὐχὶ δώδεκα ὧρας ἔχει καὶ ἡ ἡμέρα καὶ ἡ νύξ; ὀφείλομεν οὖν γρηγορεῖν μηδὲ καθεύδειν κατακείμενοι. 8. ἐπερωτᾶτε εἰ ὑπάγει ὁ διδάσκαλος; λέγω δὲ ὑμῖν ὅτι μέλλει ἀναβαίνειν εἰς τὰ ὄρη καὶ ἐκεῖ πλανήσει πολλούς. 9. οὐχὶ ἀληθῶς ὁμοιοῖ οὗτος τὴν βασιλείαν τοῦ Θεοῦ ἀνθρώπῳ σπείραντι καλὸν σπέρμα ἐν τῷ ἀγρῷ αὐτοῦ; 10. μὴ φανερώσῃς σεαυτὸν τοῖς κατοικοῦσι τὴν κώμην μὴ ἐπιτιμᾷ μοι ὁ ἄρχων, ἐντελλόμενος μηκέτι ἰᾶσθαι ἐν ὀνόματι Ἰησοῦ. 11. πληροῖ τὴν πόλιν τῆς διδαχῆς αὐτοῦ.

[1] This has a double augment (ἐω-) in the otherwise regular imperfect and perfect. Future and aorist have no relation to the present stem, but are given with ὁράω in lexicons. The future, active in meaning, is middle in form, ὄψομαι (deponent), the aorist passive is ὤφθην. εἶδον is used as the aorist active.

Matt. 2.1-5a; 3.15 (οὔτ. — δικ.); Luke 4.22; 22.49; 22.52-53; John 2.11; 2.18-22; I Cor. 9.1a; II Cor. 11.22; James 5.13-15a

Translate: 1. Those who see angels are honoured, for God takes thought about them. 2. Does not Jesus justify mankind? Therefore do not be led astray by those who rebuke hungry and thirsty sinners. 3. Manifest thy power now and heal my daughter, I beg thee; but he was not able. 4. The master warned us not to meet him, asking if we wanted to announce to the governor that he was departing. 5. Surely you do not ask whether my words are true? 6. We are not anxious, for we know that Christ who likened us to his sheep will save us from our enemies in that day.

---

30 Demonstrative, relative and interrogative pronouns and adverbs. Subjunctive in indefinite clauses

Demonstratives	**Relatives**	**Interrogatives**
οὗτος, ὅδε[1]	⎰ ὅς, ἥ, ὅ who	τίς, τί[2]
this	⎱ ὅστις, ἥτις, ὅτι[3]	who?, what?, why?
ἐκεῖνος		(cf. p. 73)
that		
ὧδε, ἐνθάδε	οὗ, ὅπου	ποῦ[2]
here, hither	where, whither	where?, whither?
δεῦρο, δεῦτε		
hither		

[1] This is the definite article with suffix δε.

[2] The enclitic (cf. p. 154) forms of these four are found with indefinite meaning, *somebody, somewhere, at some time, somehow*.

[3] This is a combination of ὅς and τις, each declined separately, and in the NT is found only in nom. sing. and pl. and in the gen. sing. ὅτου (short form of οὗτινος) used with ἕως, μέχρις, ἄχρι meaning *until* (cf. p. 38).

ἐκεῖ, ἐκεῖσε		
there, thither		
ἐντεῦθεν, ἔνθεν	ὅθεν	πόθεν
hence	whence	whence ?
ἐκεῖθεν		
thence		
τότε	ὅτε	πότε[1]
then	when	when ?
οὕτως	ὡς, ὅπως	πῶς[1]
thus, so	how !, as	how ?
τοιοῦτος[2]	οἷος, ὁποῖος	{ ποῖος[3]
such	what sort !, as	{ ποταπός.
		what sort ?
τοσοῦτος[2]	ὅσος	{ πόσος
so big, so many	how big !, how	{ πηλίκος
	many !, as	how big ?, how many ?

The interrogatives are used to introduce both Direct and Indirect Questions. Occasionally the longer relative forms ὅπως and ὁποῖος are used as in CG for Indirect Questions, also the neuter ὅτι *why*, but this is more common in Direct Questions. Editors sometimes write as ὅ τι to avoid confusion with ὅτι *that* and ὅτι *because*:

καὶ ἐπηρώτησαν αὐτὸν λέγοντες, ῞Οτι λέγουσιν οἱ γραμ-
ματεῖς ὅτι ᾿Ηλείαν δεῖ ἐλθεῖν πρῶτον;
And they asked him, saying, Why do the scribes say that
Elijah must first come ?   Mark 9.11

In NT there is confusion between interrogative and exclamatory, but this will cause no difficulty, as English uses the same word for both. Compare:

πῶς δύσκολόν ἐστιν εἰς τὴν βασιλείαν τοῦ Θεοῦ εἰσελθεῖν.
How hard it is to enter the kingdom of God !   Mark 10.24
ὡς ὡραῖοι οἱ πόδες τῶν εὐαγγελιζομένων.
How beautiful are the feet of them that bring good tidings !
                                                 Rom. 10.15

---

[1] The enclitic (cf. p. 154) forms of these four are found with indefinite meaning, *somebody, somewhere, at some time somehow*.

[2] Prefixes τοι- and τοσ- followed by ουτος without initial τ:
   τοιοῦτος   τοιαύτη   τοιοῦτο (or τοιοῦτον).

[3] In K it may have a weaker meaning, *which?*, little different from τίς.

Where the relative, with demonstrative expressed or implicit, involves comparison, the English translation will be *as*:

παραλαμβάνουσιν αὐτὸν ὡς ἦν ἐν τῷ πλοίῳ.
They took him with them, as he was, in the boat.

Mark 4.36

(The longer forms κάθως and ὥσπερ are common in comparisons.)

οἷος ὁ ἐπουράνιος, τοιοῦτοι καὶ οἱ ἐπουράνιοι.
As is the heavenly man, so also are the heavenly.

I Cor. 15.48

ὅσοι ἥψαντο διεσώθησᾰν.
As many as touched him were made whole (saved).

Matt. 14.36

(Such clauses can often be translated as *all who*.)

Subjunctive in indefinite clauses (negative always μή)

ἄν or ἐάν, which cannot be pinpointed to any one translation, is used with subj. to make a clause indefinite, as 'ever' is often used in English.

1. Relative pronouns and adverbs

ὅτι ἂν λέγῃ ὑμῖν, ποιήσατε.
Do whatever he tells you.

John 2.5

ὅπου ἐὰν κηρυχθῇ τὸ εὐαγγέλιον
Wherever the gospel is preached

Mark 14.9

2. ἐάν as combination of εἰ and ἄν may be indefinite, *if ever*, or may refer to the future, *if*. With this conditional meaning ἐάν will always be the first word in its clause:

ἐὰν ὑμῖν εἴπω, οὐ μὴ πιστεύσητε.
If I tell you, you will not believe.

Luke 22.68

3. Temporal clauses, whether indefinite or referring (as often) to the future, which by its nature is regarded as indefinite:

ὅταν (i.e. ὅτε + ἄν) — the context must show whether this means *whenever* or *when* in reference to the future. Even if it is indefinite, *ever* is often omitted in translation.

93

οὐ γὰρ νίπτονται τὰς χεῖρας ὅταν ἄρτον ἐσθίωσιν.

For they do not wash their hands when they eat bread (RV).

Matt. 15.2

ἕως while, ἕως, μέχρι(ς), ἄχρι(ς) until (all three either alone or with genitive of relative neuter sing. οὗ, ὅτου) are very flexible, found either with or without ἄν:

οὐ μὴ παρέλθῃ ἡ γενεὰ αὕτη ἕως ἂν πάντα ταῦτα γένηται.

This generation shall not pass away until all these things come to pass.

Matt. 24.34

4. ἄν found sometimes with ὅπως in purpose clauses with subj. is a relic of CG and does not affect translation.

ἀδικέω	injure, do wrong	ἐπιθυμέω	(w. gen.) desire
ἀρνέομαι (M)	deny	θυσία -ας ἡ	sacrifice
ἐγγύς	(w. gen.) near	κατηγορέω	(w. gen.) accuse
εἰκών -όνος ἡ	image	ὑποτάσσω	(w. acc. and dat.) make subject
ἔμπροσθεν	(w. gen.) in front of		
		χώρα -ας ἡ	country

Translate: 1. ἀναβαίνω ἐκεῖσε ὅθεν ἦλθον. 2. πῶς δύνασθε ἀγαθὰ λαλεῖν πονηροὶ ὄντες; 3. ἰδέ, πόσα κατηγορεῖ σου. 4. τοιαύτην δὲ νῦν πάσχομεν θλῖψιν οἷα οὐδέποτε ὕστερον μέλλει γίνεσθαι. 5. ὅστις ἂν ἀρνῆται τὸν υἱὸν τοῦ ἀνθρώπου, τοῦτον οὐκ ὠφελήσουσι πολλαὶ θυσίαι. 6. ὅταν δὲ εὕρητε τὴν εἰκόνα ἐκείνην ἐν ταύτῃ τῇ χώρᾳ, γινώσκετε ὅτι ἐγγὺς ἤδη τὸ τέλος. 7. καὶ ὅπου ἂν μένωσιν οἱ φίλοι μου, ἐκεῖ μενῶ κἀγώ.[1] 8. ἐὰν δὲ θέλῃς ἰάσασθαι τοῦτον τὸν τυφλόν, εὐθὺς ἀναβλέψει. 9. τοσαύτην δ' οὐκ ἔχομεν πίστιν ὅσην οἱ πατέρες ἡμῶν. 10. καὶ ἕως ἂν ᾖ μεθ' ἡμῶν, δεῖ ὑποτάσσεσθαι αὐτῷ ὡς ἐξουσίαν ἔχοντι. 11. νῦν οὖν παραγγέλλω ὑμῖν ἵνα ὅστις ἂν ἀδικῇ ἄγηται ἔμπροσθεν τοῦ ἄρχοντος· οὗτος γὰρ ἐπιθυμεῖ κρῖναι ὥσπερ ἐνετείλατο

[1] Combination of καί and ἐγώ, recognizable by retention of the breathing, cf. also κἀκεῖ, κἀκεῖθεν.

αὐτῷ ὁ ἡγεμών. 12. ὅστις δ' ἂν λέγῃ κακὰ κατὰ τοῦ ῾Αγίου Πνεύματος, τοῦτον οὐκ ἐλεήσει ὁ Κύριος ἐν ἡμέρᾳ κρίσεως.

Matt. 15.29; Mark 2.16; 3.31-35; 6.38; 9.37; 11.33b; 12.41; 13.3-7; John 4.48; 16.21; Gal. 1.23-24; Heb. 7.4a

3I   Perfect active, middle and passive

Perfect

Active	Middle, Passive (identical)	
λέλυκα	λέλυμαι	
λέλυκας	λέλυσαι	
λέλυκε(ν)	λέλυται	
λελύκαμεν	λελύμεθα	
λελύκατε	λέλυσθε	
λελύκασι(ν) (-αν)	λέλυνται	
Infinitive λελυκέναι	λελύσθαι	Imperative
Participle λελυκώς -υῖα -ός	λελυμένος -η -ον	Passive
λελυκότος -υίας -ότος		2nd sing. λέλυσο
λελυκόσι(ν) -υίαις -όσι(ν)		2nd pl. λέλυσθε

(Note the accentuation of all these infinitives and participles.)

The Perfect may be recognized by (1) prefix (2) endings.

    (1) Prefix

1. Reduplication, i.e. initial consonant with ε is prefixed to the stem:

    (a) when verb begins with a single unaspirated consonant:

        γεγέννηκα   τετήρηκα   πεπίστευκα

(b) when verb begins with a single aspirated consonant (χ, φ, θ), the reduplication is with the unaspirated form (κ, π, τ):

κεχάρισμαι   πεφανέρωκα   τεθέαμαι

(c) when verb begins with guttural (κ, χ, γ), labial (π, φ, β), dental (τ, θ, δ) followed by liquid (λ, μ, ν, ρ) reduplication is with the first letter (or its unaspirated form, as in (b) above):

γέγραφα πέπραχα πεπλήρωκα τέθνηκα (from θνήσκω which is found only in the perfect and pluperfect, ἀπο-θνήσκω in all other tenses)

2. Augment instead of reduplication:

(a) when verb begins with double consonant ζ, ξ, ψ or σ+one or more consonants:

ἀπέσταλκα (ἀποστέλλω)   ἐξηραμμένος (ξηραίνω) ἐσπαρμένος (σπείρω)

(b) when verb begins with a vowel:

ᾔτηκα (αἰτέω)   ἦρκα (αἴρω)   ἴαμαι (ἰάομαι, i.e. ἰῶμαι)

(c) when verb begins with ῥ (rare), ρ is doubled and prefixed by the augment:

ἔρρωσθε (ῥώννυμι)   ἐρριζωμένος (ῥιζόω)

NB Since the augment is a substitute for reduplication it is an integral part of the perfect stem and is retained in infin. and participle.

(2) Endings

Perfect active — 1st (weak) and 2nd (strong) perfect endings differ only in that the weak perfect adds κ to the stem and follows rules, while the strong stem has no κ and must be learnt.

Weak

(a) verbs with a vowel stem (including contracted verbs, which lengthen vowel in all tenses except present and imperfect) add κ to stem:

μεμαρτύρηκα   πεπλήρωκα   γεγέννηκα

(*b*) verbs with stem ending in a consonant:

> Gutturals κ, χ, γ change to χ: πεφύλαχα (φυλάσσω)
> Dentals τ, θ, δ drop out: ἤλπικα (ἐλπίζω)
> Liquids λ, μ, ν, ρ often irregular, but κ added to stem, except that ν drops out: ἀπέσταλκα κέκρικα

Perfect middle and passive. The endings are those already learnt for δύναμαι (cf. p. 86). With consonantal stems 2nd pl. ends in - θε, infin. in - θαι. As there is no connecting vowel these stems may change before the following consonant, but the only unfamiliar combinations are with μ and τ, given below. The 3rd pl. is always periphrastic (cf. p. 70) and the periphrastic use of the verb *to be* with perfect participle is also found with other persons.

Guttural διώκω	Labial γράφω	Dental πείθω
δεδίωγμαι	γέγραμμαι	πέπεισμαι
δεδίωκται	γέγραπται	πέπεισται
δεδιωγμένοι -αι -α	γεγραμμένοι -αι -α	πεπεισμένοι -αι -α
εἰσί(ν)	εἰσί(ν)	εἰσί(ν)

Liquids

ἀποστέλλω	σπείρω	κρίνω	ξηραίνω
ἀπέσταλμαι	ἔσπαρμαι	κέκριμαι	ἐξήραμμαι
ἀπέσταλται	ἔσπαρται	κέκριται	ἐξήρανται
ἀπεσταλμένοι	ἐσπαρμένοι	κεκριμένοι	ἐξηραμμένοι
-αι -α	-αι -α	-αι -α	-αι -α
εἰσί(ν)	εἰσί(ν)	εἰσί(ν)	εἰσί(ν)

Some common irregular and strong perfects:

ἀκούω	ἀκήκοα	
ἀπόλλυμι	ἀπόλωλα	(strong is like middle in meaning, *have perished, am lost*)
γίνομαι	γέγονα[1]	γεγένημαι
γινώσκω	ἔγνωκα	ἔγνωσμαι
γράφω	γέγραφα	γέγραμμαι

[1] Both active and passive have the same meaning, *have become,* **have taken place**, but the active is far more common.

ἐγείρω[1]		ἐγήγερμαι	
	εἴρηκα		εἴρημαι (cf. λέγω p. 159)
ἔρχομαι	ἐλήλυθα		
εὑρίσκω	εὕρηκα		
-θνήσκω	τέθνηκα (simple form only, compound in other tenses)		
λαμβάνω	εἴληφα	εἴλημμαι	
πείθω	πέποιθα	πέπεισμαι (strong perfect intransitive, I trust, am confident)	
πάσχω	πέπονθα		

Meaning

In the NT the perfect is comparatively rare, so it is not given for many verbs which had the form in CG. The usual narrative tense is the aorist, which denotes simply that an event took place, while the perfect denotes that a past event still has present consequences. Compare ἀποθνήσκει he is dying, ἀπέθνησκε he was dying, ἀπέθανε he died, τέθνηκε he has died, i.e. he is dead.

1. In the indic. active the meaning can often be brought out by *have*:

   πεπληρώκατε τὴν Ιερουσαλημ τῆς διδαχῆς ὑμῶν.

   You have filled Jerusalem with your teaching (and it is still full).   Acts 5.28

2. In the indic. passive *has been* may be cumbersome and the present verb *to be* with a past participle more idiomatic. The common formula ὡς γέγραπται *as it has been written* (and still remains so) is translated *is written* RV, *stands written* NEB.

3. The passive participle has a peculiar nuance which often defies translation. *Crucified* would translate both σταυρωθείς and ἐσταυρωμένος, but the former refers to the crucifixion as a historical event only, the latter (I Cor. 1.23) implies the results of the crucifixion which are still operative. Sometimes, however, the distinction is blurred.

[1] CG ἐγρήγορα with intransitive meaning has been replaced in K by an easier regular present γρηγορέω *to keep watch, be awake*.

4. The imperative passive is only found twice in the NT. πεφίμωσο Mark 4.39, '*Be still*', is perhaps a more impressive adjuration than the aorist φιμώθητι Mark 1.25, as it implies *Be gagged and remain so*. ἔρρωσθε Acts 15.29 (ἔρρωσο added by some MSS in Acts 23.30) is a conventional formula, *farewell* (literally: *be in a state of having been strengthened*, from an obsolete verb ῥώννυμι).

γαμέω	marry	πάθημα -ατος τό	suffering
θεάομαι	behold	ῥιζόω	root
θεμελιόω	lay a foundation, ground	τελειόω	make perfect
νικάω	conquer	φιμόω	gag
ξηραίνω	dry up, wither	χαρίζομαι (M)	grant

Translate: 1. νενίκηκεν ὁ βασιλεὺς καὶ ἐλεύσεται πάλιν εἰς τὴν πατρίδα ἑαυτοῦ. 2. τετελείωκεν ὁ Θεὸς τὸν υἱὸν διὰ παθημάτων. 3. οὐχὶ κέκριται ὁ ἄρχων τοῦ κόσμου τούτου; 4. εὕρηκεν ὁ ποιμὴν τὰ πρόβατα τὰ ἀπολωλότα. 5. ἐρριζωμένοι καὶ τεθεμελιωμένοι ἐν ἀγάπῃ εἰσὶν οἱ ἅγιοι. 6. μέλας γέγονεν ὁ ἥλιος καὶ οὐκέτι δυνάμεθα ἰδεῖν τοὺς ἀστέρας. 7. ἐξήρανται ἡ χεὶρ τοῦ παραλυτικοῦ τούτου. 8. μακάριοι οἱ δεδιωγμένοι διὰ τὸν Χριστόν. 9. ὡς Ἰακωβ ὁ πατριάρχης, κἀγὼ γεγάμηκα δύο γυναῖκας καὶ διὰ τοῦτο πολλὰ πέπονθα. 10. ὅστις πέποιθεν ἐν τῷ Ἰησοῦ, οὗτος πέπεισται ὅτι δύναται σῶσαι τοὺς ἀπολωλότας. 11. ἐγήγερται ὁ Λάζαρος ἐκ τοῦ μνημείου καὶ ζῇ. 12. εἰλήφασιν τὰς ἐντολὰς ἀλλ' οὐ σεσωσμένοι εἰσίν. 13. κεχάρισταί σοι τοῦτο ὁ Κύριος.

Matt. 2.19-23; Mark 1.15; 7.29-30; John 1.43-48; 16.27-28a; Acts 18.1-3; Rom. 15.14; Gal. 6.14b; I John 1.1-4

Translate: 1. Christ risen from the dead has manifested himself to two women. 2. As it is written, Not a hair of your head shall perish. 3. Where shall we find those who have borne witness and are now dead? 4. What I myself have beheld and heard I shall proclaim among the Gentiles. 5. Behold, the withered hand has been healed. 6. Seeds which have been sown on bad ground do not bear fruit.

---

32 Pluperfect active, middle and passive. οἶδα. Accusative with infinitive or participle in indirect statement

Pluperfect

Active	Middle, Passive
ἐλελύκειν	ἐλελύμην
ἐλελύκεις	ἐλέλυσο
ἐλελύκει	ἐλέλυτο
ἐλελύκειμεν	ἐλελύμεθα
ἐλελύκειτε	ἐλέλυσθε
ἐλελύκεισαν	ἐλέλυντο

The pluperfect follows the perfect in stem formation. The augment is sometimes dropped, but the person-endings give a sure indication. It has a much more restricted use than the English pluperfect with *had* (which often corresponds to the Greek aorist denoting action prior to the main verb), for it is only used to show that the results of a past action continued in the past, as the perfect shows that they continue in the present: τέθνηκε *he is dead*, ἐτεθνήκει *he had died*, i.e. *he was dead*.

τεθεμελίωτο γὰρ ἐπὶ τὴν πέτραν.
For it had been founded upon the rock (and was still there).
Matt. 7.25

οἶδα, *know*, is a perfect from an obsolete present stem in ειδ, which is used with present meaning, the pluperfect with imperfect force.

Indicative			Subjunctive
Perfect		Pluperfect	Perfect
οἶδα		ᾔδειν	εἰδῶ[1]
οἶδας		ᾔδεις	εἰδῇς
οἶδε(ν)		ᾔδει	εἰδῇ
οἴδαμεν		ᾔδειμεν	εἰδῶμεν
οἴδατε (ἴστε Acts 27.4)		ᾔδειτε	εἰδῆτε
οἴδασι(ν) (ἴσασι Heb. 12.17)		ᾔδεισαν	εἰδῶσι(ν)

Imperative, only 2nd pl. ἴστε   Infinitive εἰδέναι

Participle εἰδώς -υῖα -ός   Future εἰδήσω

εἴωθα, *be accustomed*, is another perfect with present meaning from an obsolete present, but is conjugated regularly.

Indirect statement

1. By far the commonest construction is a clause introduced by ὅτι, already met (p. 43). Note also ὅτι 'recitative', when ὅτι is used like inverted commas to introduce the direct statement. This is easily recognizable in texts where capitals are used for direct quotation[2] and when it occurs is untranslatable:

   Καὶ λέγει αὐτοῖς ὁ Ἰησοῦς ὅτι Πάντες σκανδαλισθήσεσθε.
   And Jesus said to them, 'You will all fall away'.   Mark 14.27

2. Much rarer is a vestige of CG, an accusative and infinitive clause, in which the accusative represents the subject and the infinitive the verb of the direct speech.[3] The infinitive retains the tense of the direct speech, negative μή:

   Σαδδουκαῖοι . . . οἵτινες λέγουσιν ἀνάστασιν μὴ εἶναι.
   Sadducees . . . who say that there is no resurrection.
   Mark 12.18

---

[1] Not to be confused with εἶδον *I saw*, subj. ἴδω.

[2] This is an editorial convention, as there were no capitals in early MSS, and sometimes it is questionable whether ὅτι introduces a direct or indirect statement.

[3] In CG, when the subject of the infinitive verb is the same as that of the main verb, it is either omitted or is in the nominative case; when it is different from that of the main verb, it is in the accusative.

3. Occasionally the CG use of accusative with participle instead of with infinitive is found after verbs of knowing or perceiving:

ὡς εἶδον ἤδη αὐτὸν τεθνηκότα.

When they saw that he was already dead.   John 19.33

Principal Parts. Now that all tenses of the verb have been covered principal parts may be memorized; the conventional pattern is:

Present act.	Future act.	Aorist act.
λύω	λύσω	ἔλυσα
Perfect act.	Perfect pass.	Aorist pass.
λέλυκα	λέλυμαι	ἐλύθην

From these it is possible to form all other tenses:

(1) imperfect uses present stem and the only irregularity may lie in the augment; if so, this is given in the lists on pp. 155-61.

(2) middle future and aorist usually follow stem formation of active.

(3) pluperfect active and passive follow formation of perfect.

(4) future passive is formed from aorist passive (p. 45).

The student should look through the alphabetical list (p. 155) and gradually memorize all irregular verbs already met. From now on any new irregular verbs will be asterisked.

ἄρτι	now, just now	μόνος -η -ον	alone
βλασφημέω	rail, blaspheme	οἶδα *	know
εἴωθα	be accustomed	περιβάλλω	throw around,
ἐνδύω	put on		(middle) wear
κλίνη -ης ἡ	bed	σφραγίζω	seal
λευκός -ή -όν	white	φαίνω*	shine, (passive)
μόνον	(adverb) only		appear

Translate: 1. πότε ἦλθες; ἐγένετό ποτε προφήτης τις μέγας. ποῦ ἐστιν ἡ οἰκία σου; πόθεν ἔμαθες τοῦτο; ἔγραψά που τοῦτο. πόσους ἄρτους ἔχετε; ὅτι τοῦτο ἐποίησας; πῶς ἔχετε φόβον; ποταπὴ ἡ διδαχὴ αὕτη; 2. πρὸ τοῦ φανῆναι τὸν Ἰησοῦν συνελη-λύθει πολὺς ὄχλος. 3. ὁ δὲ εἰδὼς αὐτῶν τὴν ὑπόκρισιν εἶπεν αὐτοῖς, Τί με πειράζετε; 4. οὐκ ᾔδει οὐδεὶς ὅτι οὗτός ἐστιν ὁ Χριστός. 5. τεθεάμεθα σημεῖα διὰ τοῦ ὀνόματος Ἰησοῦ γεγενημένα καὶ νῦν πιστεύοντες ἐσόμεθα ἐν αὐτῷ. 6. ὁ δὲ Ἰωάννης ἦν ἐνδεδυμένος τρίχας καμήλου. 7. ἔλεγεν γὰρ ὁ Ἰωάννης τῷ Ἡρῴδῃ ὅτι Οὐκ ἔξεστίν σοι ἔχειν τὴν γυναῖκα τοῦ ἀδελφοῦ σου. 8. δεῖ οὖν τοὺς ἐσφραγισμένους βαπτίσματι πορεύεσθαι ἐν τῇ ὁδῷ τοῦ Κυρίου μὴ ἀρνουμένους τὰς ἐντολὰς αὐτοῦ. 9. αἱ δὲ γυναῖκες ἑωράκασι νεανίσκον καθήμενον ἐκ δεξιῶν περιβεβλημένον στολὴν λευκήν. 10. μήτι οἱ μάγοι εἰρήκασι τῷ Ἡρῴδῃ ὅτι εὑρήκασι τὸ παιδίον ὃ ἐζήτουν; 11. οὐχὶ βλασφημεῖτε, λέγοντες τοῦτον ἐκβαλεῖν δαιμόνια μόνον διὰ τοῦ διαβόλου; 12. καὶ ὡς εἰώθει, ἀναβὰς πρὸς τὸ ὄρος μόνος ἦν ἐκεῖ προσευχόμενος. 13. ἵνα πάντες εἰδῆτε τὴν ἀλήθειαν ἐρῶ[1] ὑμῖν τοῦτον μετὰ τὴν ἀνάστασιν αὐτοῦ ἀναβῆναι εἰς τὸν οὐρανόν.

Matt. 7.24-27; 25.11-13; 27.15; Mark 1.24b; 5.33; 6.14-20; 8.27-30; Luke 8.45-46; John 7.14-16; 9.16-22a; 21.12; Acts 9.19b-20; Rom. 4.1

Translate: 1. As it has been said by the prophet, No good thing can come out of this place. 2. Many soldiers have come just now in order to conquer the enemy quickly before they are able to flee. 3. Whoever knows that Christ taught thus, ought to send money to the tax-collectors. 4. The woman was lying[2] on the bed and the seven devils had gone out of her. 5. Surely you know in what authority he preached the gospel? 6. As it is written in this book, I will have mercy upon my people and no longer remember their sins.

[1] Contracted future, after liquid ρ, linked with λέγω (cf. p. 159).
[2] Pluperfect passive of βάλλω *had been cast*, i.e. *was lying*, or imperfect of κατάκειμαι.

-μι verbs. These are a small group of very common and peculiar verbs. Some share the peculiarity of having a present stem with a reduplicating prefix of initial consonant + ι. All, like δύναμαι, add endings direct to the stem without a linking vowel. The following three form a small section within the larger group:

δίδωμι	prefix δι,	stem proper δο,	meaning *give*	
τίθημι	prefix τι,	stem proper θε,	meaning *place, lay*	
-ἵημι	prefix ἱ,	stem proper ἑ,	meaning in itself *let go*, but only found in compounds.	

Present active

Indicative

δίδωμι	τίθημι	-ἵημι[1]
δίδως	τίθης	-ἵης
δίδωσι(ν)	τίθησι	-ἵησι(ν)
δίδομεν	τίθεμεν	-ἵεμεν
δίδοτε	τίθετε	-ἵετε
διδόασι(ν)	τιθέασι(ν)	-ἱᾶσι(ν)

Subjunctive

διδῶ	τιθῶ	-ἱῶ
διδῷς or διδοῖς[2]	τιθῇς	-ἱῇς
διδῷ or διδοῖ[2]	τιθῇ	-ἱῇ
διδῶμεν	τιθῶμεν	-ἱῶμεν
διδῶτε	τιθῆτε	-ἱῆτε
διδῶσι(ν)	τιθῶσι(ν)	-ἱῶσι(ν)

Imperfect active

ἐδίδουν	ἐτίθην
ἐδίδους	ἐτίθεις
ἐδίδου	ἐτίθει
ἐδίδομεν	ἐτίθεμεν
ἐδίδοτε	ἐτίθετε
⎰ ἐδίδοσαν	ἐτίθεσαν
⎱ ἐδίδουν[2]	ἐτίθουν[2]

Imperative active

δίδου	τίθει	-ἵει
διδότω	τιθέτω	-ἱέτω
δίδοτε	τίθετε	-ἵετε
διδότωσαν	τιθέτωσαν	-ἱέτωσαν

[1] A κ present tense form ἀφίω, regular, also exists, ἀφίομεν. The imperfect would be formed like τίθημι, but is not found in NT, though forms from ἀφίω as if an uncompounded verb, ἤφιον, ἤφιε are found.

[2] Examples of the constant tendency of κ to assimilate to familiar endings instead of using the obsolescent and more difficult forms.

Infinitive active

διδόναι   τιθέναι   -ἱέναι

Participle active

διδούς -οῦσα -όν   διδόντος -ούσης -όντος   διδοῦσι -δούσαις
τιθείς -εῖσα -έν   τιθέντος -είσης -έντος   τιθεῖσι -είσαις
-ἱείς -εῖσα -έν   -ἱέντος -είσης -έντος   -ἱεῖσι -είσαις

Future active is formed regularly by lengthening vowel stem:

δώσω   θήσω   -ἥσω

Aorist active. In κ the weak aorist, formed by lengthening the stem vowel in the normal way, then adding κ and the normal endings, is used both in singular and plural. In CG peculiar strong aorists were used in the plural. No examples of their use are found in the NT for τίθημι and -ἵημι, but all three verbs are given below, because it was from the strong aorist stem that aorist subj., infin., imperative, and participles were formed.

Indicative

ἔδωκα		ἔθηκα		-ἧκα		
ἔδωκας		ἔθηκας		-ἧκας		
ἔδωκε(ν)		ἔθηκε(ν)		-ἧκε(ν)		
ἐδώκαμεν	ἔδομεν	ἐθήκαμεν	ἔθεμεν	-ἥκαμεν	-εἷμεν	
ἐδώκατε	ἔδοτε	ἐθήκατε	ἔθετε	-ἥκατε	-εἷτε	
ἔδωκαν	ἔδοσαν	ἔθηκαν	ἔθεσαν	-ἧκαν	-εἷσαν	

Subjunctive   Imperative

δῶ	θῶ	ἀφῶ	δός	θές	ἄφες
δῷς, δοῖς	θῇς	ἀφῇς	δότω	θέτω	ἀφέτω
δῷ, δοῖ,	θῇ	ἀφῇ	δότε	θέτε	ἄφετε
δώῃ			δότωσαν	θέτωσαν	ἀφέτωσαν
δῶμεν	θῶμεν	ἀφῶμεν			
δῶτε	θῆτε	ἀφῆτε			
δῶσι(ν)	θῶσι(ν)	ἀφῶσι(ν)			

Infinitive

δοῦναι   θεῖναι   -εἶναι

Participle

δούς δοῦσα δόν	δόντος δούσης δόντος	δοῦσι(ν) -αις
θείς θεῖσα θέν	θέντος θείσης θέντος	θεῖσι(ν) -αις
-εἷς -εἷσα -έν	-έντος -είσης -έντος	-εἷσι(ν) -αις

Common compounds:

ἀνταποδίδωμι	give back in return
ἀποδίδωμι	give back, pay, (middle) sell
μεταδίδωμι	impart, share with
παραδίδωμι	hand over, betray, hand down
ἀφίημι	leave, let, forgive (i.e. remit acc. direct object to dat. indirect)
συνίημι	understand
ἐπιτίθημι	lay upon, impose
μετατίθημι	transfer, change
παρατίθημι	set before (w. acc. of direct object, dat. of indirect), middle, entrust
προστίθημι	add

The perfect active is formed by regular process of reduplication; the vowel of δο lengthens to ω, of θε and ἑ to ει before κ and the regular weak endings:

δέδωκα   τέθεικα   -εἷκα

μέρος -ους τό	part	πλοῦτος -ου ὁ	wealth
νομίζω	think	πωλέω	sell

Translate: 1. καὶ ἀφέντες τὰ δίκτυα ἐν τῷ πλοίῳ ἠκολούθησαν αὐτῷ. 2. ἰδοὺ ὁ παραδιδούς με ἤγγικεν. 3. τότε ἐπιθέντες τὰς χεῖρας αὐτοῖς προσηύξαντο οἱ ἀπόστολοι ἵνα δοῖ ὁ Κύριος καὶ τούτοις μέρος τι τοῦ Ἁγίου Πνεύματος. 4. διδόασιν οἱ ἅγιοι τὸν πλοῦτον αὐτῶν τοῖς χρείαν ἔχουσι. 5. καὶ ἐγένετο ἐν ἐκείνῃ τῇ ἡμέρᾳ προσέθηκεν ὁ Κύριος πολλοὺς τῷ πλήθει τῶν πιστευόν-των. 6. εὐθὺς οὖν ἐκέλευσεν αὐτοὺς παραθεῖναι τῷ ὄχλῳ τοὺς πέντε ἄρτους καὶ δύο ἰχθύας ὅτι ἅπαντες ἐπείνων καὶ συνεληλύθεισαν ἀπὸ τῆς πόλεως. 7. πόσον μισθὸν ἀπέδωκας ἐκείνοις τοῖς ἐσχάτοις ἐργάταις; 8. ἐνόμιζεν δὲ συνιέναι τοὺς ἀδελφοὺς ὅτι ὁ Θεὸς διὰ χειρὸς αὐτοῦ δίδωσι σωτηρίαν αὐτοῖς· οἱ δέ οὐ συνῆκαν. 9. οἴδατε ὅτι ὁ Θεὸς ἐν τῷ ἀποστεῖλαι τὸν Ἰησοῦν εἰς τὸν κόσμον μετέθηκε τὸν νόμον; 10. μήτι δεδώκατε πάσας τὰς γραφὰς τοῖς στρατιώταις εἰς τὸ φθαρῆναι αὐτάς; 11. ποῖον οἶνον δώσεις ἡμῖν ὅταν γαμήσῃ ὁ υἱός μου τὴν θυγατέρα σου; 12. παρεδίδουν οἱ προφῆται ῥήματα σοφὰ καὶ ὑγιῆ τοῖς βουλομένοις ἀκούειν. 13. καὶ ἐμβλέψας αὐτῷ ἠγάπησεν αὐτὸν καὶ εἶπεν αὐτῷ· Ὕπαγε, ὅσα ἔχεις πώλησον καὶ δὸς τοῖς πτωχοῖς. 14. οὔπω συνίημι.

Matt. 5.40; 6.27; 13.18-23; 22.18-22; 23.1-4; Mark 1.16-18; 6.24-30; 12.35-37; John 10.14-18; 12.44-50; 14.25-27; 19.30; Heb. 2.8

Translate: 1. After placing the corpse in the tomb he departed. 2. Let him who loves God keep on giving bread to the hungry. 3. Will you impart your power to me? 4. You ought to give pay to the attendants and not add the money to your own wealth. 5. Only God is able to forgive sins. 6. We handed down to our children the gospel which we received in order that they might hear the words of eternal life.

---

34 Middle and passive of δίδωμι, τίθημι, -ίημι. ὥστε

Present			Imperfect	
δίδομαι	τίθεμαι		ἐδιδόμην	ἐτιθέμην
δίδοσαι	τίθεσαι		ἐδίδοσο	ἐτίθεσο
δίδοται	τίθεται	ἀφίεται	ἐδίδοτο	ἐτίθετο
διδόμεθα	τιθέμεθα		ἐδιδόμεθα	ἐτιθέμεθα
δίδοσθε	τίθεσθε		ἐδίδοσθε	ἐτίθεσθε
δίδονται	τίθενται	ἀφίενται	ἐδίδοντο	ἐτίθεντο

Subjunctive present is not found, but would be: δίδωμι with ω replacing η, διδῶμαι, διδῷ, διδῶται, τίθημι, -ἵημι with regular endings, τιθῶμαι, τιθῇ, τιθῆται.

Imperative (-ἵημι, although not found, would be like τίθημι):[1]

δίδοσο	τίθεσο
διδόσθω	τιθέσθω
δίδοσθε	τίθεσθε
διδόσθωσαν	τιθέσθωσαν

Infinitive   δίδοσθαι   τίθεσθαι   -ἵεσθαι

Participle   διδόμενος -η -ον   τιθέμενος -η -ον   -ἱέμενος -η -ον

Future middle — formed regularly, like active:

    δώσομαι   θήσομαι   -ἥσομαι

Aorist middle — only strong forms are found:

Indicative		Imperative	
ἐδόμην	ἐθέμην	δοῦ	θοῦ
ἔδου	ἔθου	δόσθω	θέσθω
ἔδοτο ἔδετο	ἔθετο	δόσθε	θέσθε
ἐδόμεθα	ἐθέμεθα	δόσθωσαν	θέσθωσαν
ἔδοσθε	ἔθεσθε		
ἔδοντο	ἔθεντο		

Subjunctive   δῶμαι   θῶμαι

Infinitive   δόσθαι   θέσθαι

Participle   δόμενος   θέμενος

Aorist passive is formed regularly except that the stem vowel is not lengthened; but τίθημι changes initial θ of stem to τ:

    ἐδόθην   ἐτέθην   ἀφέθην

Future passive is derived regularly from the aorist:

    δοθήσομαι   τεθήσομαι   ἀφεθήσομαι

---

[1] -ἵημι usually follows the pattern of τίθημι, but when tenses and moods were hardly found even in CG they have been omitted here.

Perfect middle and passive — regular reduplication, but δίδωμι does not lengthen stem vowel and τίθημι, as in active, lengthens to ει:

δέδομαι   τέθειμαι[1]   -εῖμαι 3rd pl. ἀφέωνται

Principal parts

δίδωμι	δώσω	ἔδωκα	δέδωκα	δέδομαι	ἐδόθην
	(M) ἐδόμην				
τίθημι	θήσω	ἔθηκα	τέθεικα	τέθειμαι	ἐτέθην
	(M) ἐθέμην				

ὥστε, *so that, so . . . that, so as to*, is used with the acc. and infinitive to express a result, the acc. representing the subject of the infin.:

καὶ ἐθεράπευσεν αὐτούς· ὥστε τὸν ὄχλον θαυμάσαι . . .
He healed them so that the crowd marvelled.   Matt. 15.31

This is a flexible construction and sometimes the context will convey an idea of purpose:

συμβούλιον ἔλαβον . . . ὥστε θανατῶσαι αὐτόν.
They took counsel together . . . to put him to death.
                                                    Matt. 27.1

More rarely ὥστε is found with the indicative, which lends extra emphasis to the fact of the result:

οὕτως γὰρ ἠγάπησεν ὁ Θεὸς τὸν κόσμον, ὥστε τὸν Υἱὸν τὸν μονογενῆ ἔδωκεν.
God so loved the world that he gave his only begotten Son.
                                                    John 3.16

ἄλλος -η -ο[2]	other, another	ἀσθενέω	be weak, sick
ἀποτίθεμαι (M)	lay aside	διαθήκη -ης ἡ	testament,
ἁρπάζω*	snatch, carry away		covenant
		διαρπάζω*	plunder

[1] In CG κεῖμαι was used as the perfect passive of τίθημι and sometimes needs to be translated as such in NT, cf. Luke 2.34.
[2] Note the neuter in -ο, normal in demonstratives (cf. p. 26).

διατίθεμαι (M)	appoint, covenant	καινός -ή -όν	new
ἐκδίδομαι (M)	let out, lease	ὅπλον -ου τό	weapon
ἐκπλήσσομαι[1]	be amazed	τέρας -ατος τό	wonder, portent

Translate: 1. ἤγγελκας. κέκριται. ἀκηκόατε. εἴρηται. κέκρυπται. ἐγηγερμένος. ἐληλύθει. ἐσταύρωται. 2. οὕτως ἰσχυρὸς ἦν οὗτος ὥστε μηδένα δύνασθαι διαρπάσαι τὰ σκεύη αὐτοῦ. 3. πόσου[2] ἀπέδοσθε τὸν ἀγρόν; 4. ἀποθώμεθα οὖν τὰ ἔργα τοῦ σκότους, ἐνδυσώμεθα δὲ τὰ ὅπλα τοῦ φωτός. 5. ταύτην τὴν καινὴν διαθήκην διέθετο τῷ λαῷ ὁ Κύριος. 6. παρέθεντο οὖν τοὺς φίλους αὐτῶν τῷ Κυρίῳ προσευξάμενοι ἵνα πάντοτε φυλάσσῃ αὐτοὺς ὥστε μηδὲν φοβεῖσθαι. 7. καὶ ἀκούσαντες τὰ ῥήματα τοῦ Πέτρου πολλοὶ προσετέθησαν τῇ ἐκκλησίᾳ ὥστε ἐκπλήσσεσθαι τὸν ὄχλον καὶ εἰπεῖν ὅτι Οὐδέποτε τοιαῦτα ἑωράκαμεν. 8. καὶ ἔδωκεν ἐξουσίαν τοῖς μαθηταῖς ὥστε ποιεῖν πολλὰ σημεῖα καὶ τέρατα. 9. λέγω γὰρ ὑμῖν ὅτι δέδοται ἐξουσία μοι ὥστε ἀφεῖναι ἁμαρτίας τοῖς ἀνθρώποις. 10. ἄλλοις οὖν ἐκδώσεται ὁ κύριος τὸν ἀμπελῶνα. 11. καὶ νῦν εἰδώς σε[3] ὅτι δίκαιος εἶ παρακαλῶ ἵνα ἐλθὼν ἐπιθῇς τὰς χεῖρας τῷ δούλῳ μου τῷ ἀσθενοῦντι καὶ θεραπεύσῃς αὐτόν. 12. ἐὰν δὲ βλασφημήσῃ τις κατὰ τοῦ Ἁγίου Πνεύματος, οὐκ ἀφεθήσεται αὐτῷ ἡ ἁμαρτία μηδὲ μετανοοῦντι ἐξ ὅλης τῆς καρδίας.

Matt. 26.1-5; 27. 57-58; Mark 2.25-28; 3.20; 4.35-37; 15.47; Luke 7.44-50; II Cor. 8.1; Heb. 10.16-18

Translate: 1. This money, which was snatched by the robbers, will be added to the wealth of the rich, but nothing has been given to the poor. 2. My father used to give bread and water to those who were hungry and thirsty in prison. 3. He therefore sold his house and laid the money at the feet of the apostles so as to help the widows. 4. All your sins have been forgiven you (pl.), because you understand these sayings and receive them in your hearts. 5. After Jesus had been betrayed he was led by the guards before the high priest. 6. This girl has become so beautiful that all the men when they behold her wish to marry her.

[1] Usually imperfect, aorist ἐξεπλάγησαν only found in Luke 2.48.
[2] Genitive used to express price or value.
[3] It is common idiom to anticipate the subject of a ὅτι clause, but it will be omitted in translation.

110

ἵστημι is like the foregoing in many ways, but has individual peculiarities. Like them it has a reduplicating prefix to the present stem, but the initial σ of the stem proper στα has softened to an aspirate, giving ἱ. It is convenient here to add the few surviving forms of φημί *say* and -εἶμι *go*.[1]

Present indic. active			Imperfect active		
ἵστημι	φημί[2]		ἵστην		
ἵστης			ἵστης		
ἵστησι(ν)	φησί(ν)		ἵστη	ἔφη	-ῄει
ἵσταμεν			ἵσταμεν		
ἵστατε			ἵστατε		
ἱστᾶσι(ν)	φασί(ν)	-ιᾶσι(ν)	ἵστασαν		-ῄεσαν

Present subj. active		Imperative	
ἱστῶ	ἱστῶμεν	ἵστη	
ἱστῇς	ἱστῆτε	ἱστάτω	
ἱστῇ	ἱστῶσι(ν)	ἵστατε	
		ἱστάτωσαν	

The present and imperfect, meaning *cause to stand*, were falling into disuse because a regular and easier form ἱστάνω had come into use in κ.

Infinitive ἱστάναι -ἰέναι
Participle ἱστάς -ᾶσα -άν (like πᾶς πᾶσα πᾶν) -ἰών -ἰοῦσα
-ἰόν -ἰόντος

Future active is formed by lengthening vowel α to η regularly, στήσω.

[1] Distinguished from εἰμί *to be* by its accent; it was only in the 1st and 2nd sing. that the form coincided.
[2] φημί like εἰμί is enclitic.

Aorist active — 1st (weak) aorist is formed regularly by lengthening stem, adding σ and the normal aorist endings:

Indic. ἔστησα, etc.   Subj. στήσω, etc.   Imperative στῆσον, etc.
Infinitive στῆσαι   Participle στήσας -ασα -αν like λύσας.

ἔστην, 2nd (strong) aorist, is like ἔβην (p. 46), or the strong aorist passive, such as ἐγράφην. Further forms from the 2nd aorist of βαίνω and γινώσκω may now be learnt. The likeness of these aorist forms of γινώσκω to δίδωμι will be apparent.

Aorist subj.
active (strong)   Imperative

στῶ		γνῶ	στῆθι⟩	-βῆθι⟩	γνῶθι
στῇς		γνῶς	-στα ⟩	-βα ⟩	
στῇ	-βῇ	γνῷ, γνοῖ	στήτω	-βάτω	γνώτω
στῶμεν		γνῶμεν	στῆτε	-βατε	γνῶτε
στῆτε		γνῶτε	στήτωσαν	-βάτωσαν	γνώτωσαν
στῶσι(ν)		γνῶσι(ν)			

Infinitive   στῆναι   -βῆναι   γνῶναι

Participle   στάς -ᾶσα -άν, -βάς -βᾶσα -βάν like λύσας
             γνούς -οῦσα -όν   γνόντος γνούσης γνόντος like δούς.

The strong aorist is intransitive, meaning *stood*.

Perfect active — this is formed regularly by lengthening stem and endings, but note that reduplicating prefix is aspirated: ἕστηκα.

Infinitive   ἑστάναι (but note ἐξεστακέναι in Acts 8.11)

Participle   (1) weak   ἑστηκώς -υῖα -ός like λελυκώς
             (2) strong   ἑστώς -ῶσα -ώς (and -ός)
                          ἑστῶτος -ώσης -ῶτος

This peculiar strong participle, like the infinitive, is a relic of CG. Both participles are used indiscriminately with the same meaning. Pluperfect εἱστήκειν is conjugated regularly, but note augment. Perfect and pluperfect are both intransitive, perfect with present meaning, *stand*, pluperfect like imperfect, *was standing*.

112

Middle and Passive — present and imperfect both like δύναμαι.

Present[1]	Imperfect	Imperative
ἵσταμαι	ἱστάμην	ἵστασο
ἵστασαι	ἵστασο	ἱστάσθω
ἵσταται	ἵστατο	ἵστασθε
ἱστάμεθα	ἱστάμεθα	ἱστάσθωσαν
ἵστασθε	ἵστασθε	Infinitive ἵστασθαι
ἵστανται	ἵσταντο	Participle ἱστάμενος -η -ον

The deponent ἐπίσταμαι *know, understand* (in NT only in the present), is also like δύναμαι.

Middle future is regular, like active, στήσομαι.

Middle aorist is regular, like 1st active, ἐστησάμην (not found in NT).

Passive aorist, like δίδωμι, etc., does not lengthen stem vowel, but otherwise is regular, ἐστάθην.

Passive future is formed regularly from aorist, σταθήσομαι.

Middle and Passive perfect ἔσταμαι is not found in NT.

Passive forms sometimes need to be translated as passive, but more often *be made to stand* is equivalent to the intransitive *stand*.

Transitive, *cause to stand*:

Present active	ἵστημι
Imperfect active	ἵστην
Future active	στήσω
1st (weak) aorist active	ἔστησα

Intransitive, *stand* or *be made to stand* (passive):

Present middle and passive	ἵσταμαι
Imperfect middle and passive	ἱστάμην
Future middle	στήσομαι
Future passive	σταθήσομαι
Aorist passive	ἐστάθην
Perfect active (present meaning)[2]	ἕστηκα
Pluperfect active (imperfect meaning)	εἱστήκειν
2nd (strong) aorist active	ἔστην

[1] The present subjunctive middle and passive are not found in the NT, but would have regular endings, ἱστῶμαι, etc.

[2] Just as a regular form γρηγορέω supersedes the irregular perfect of ἐγείρω, ἐγρήγορα, a form στήκω is found alongside ἕστηκα.

113

Some compounds of ἵστημι:

ἀνθίστημι	intr. (w. dat.) stand against, oppose.
ἀνίστημι	tr. raise, intr. rise, stand up.
ἀποκαθίστημι	tr. restore, passive, be restored.
ἀφίστημι	tr. draw away, intr. depart, withdraw.
ἐξίστημι	tr. cause to stand outside (oneself), amaze, intr. stand outside oneself, be mad.
ἐφίστημι	intr. stand over, come upon.
καθίστημι	tr. set, constitute, intr. be constituted.
παρίστημι	tr. present, intr. be present, stand by.

ἀντί	(w. gen.) instead of, for	μικρός -ά -όν	small
ἐπιγινώσκω	come to know, recognize	ὑπάρχω	be, exist
ἐπίσταμαι	know, understand	τὰ ὑπάρχοντα	one's belongings

Parse:[1] δίδωσι, ἐπέθηκε, ἦφιε, προσετέθησαν συνῆκαν, παραθῶμεν, ἀπέδοσθε, ἀφεθήσεται.

Translate: 1. καὶ εὐθὺς εἷς τις τῶν παρεστηκότων ἐπηρώτησεν αὐτὸν λέγων, Οὐχὶ καὶ σὺ ἀκολουθεῖς τούτῳ; 2. καὶ ἀναστὰς ἀνέβη εἰς τὸ ἱερὸν ἵνα ἐκεῖ παραστήσῃ θυσίαν τῷ Θεῷ. 3. πότε μέλλεις ἀποκαθιστάνειν τὴν βασιλείαν τῷ Ἰσραηλ; 4. οὐ δυνάμεθα ἀντιστῆναι τῷ πονηρῷ, μὴ ὠφελοῦντος ἡμᾶς τοῦ Θεοῦ. 5. οἱ δὲ γραμματεῖς πάντες ἐξίσταντο ἐπὶ τῇ σοφίᾳ αὐτοῦ. 6. σήμερον ἕστηκα ἔμπροσθεν τοῦ κριτοῦ ὥστε χαίρειν τοὺς ἐχθρούς μου. 7. ὁ δὲ Παῦλος κατέστησε πρεσβυτέρους ἐν ἑκάστῃ πόλει καὶ θεὶς τὰ γόνατα[2] παρέθετο αὐτοὺς τῷ Κυρίῳ. 8. καὶ μετὰ τὸ παθεῖν παρέστησεν ἑαυτὸν ζῶντα τοῖς μαθηταῖς. 9. ὁ δὲ ἠρνήσατο λέγων, Οὔτε οἶδα οὔτε ἐπίσταμαι σὺ τί λέγεις. 10. καὶ ἔφη αὐτῷ, Ἀνάστηθι ἐπὶ τοὺς πόδας σου· ὁ δὲ ἐπιγνοὺς ὅτι

[1] To parse a verb give person, number, tense, mood, voice, meaning and, if irregular, principal parts, e.g. λύω 1st sing. present indic. active of λύω, loose. To parse noun or adjective, give case, number, nom. sing., gen. sing., gender and meaning. This is a dull, but testing and valuable exercise.

[2] This expression, *kneel*, is not normal Greek but reminiscent of the Latin *genua ponere*.

δύναται ἑστάναι καὶ περιπατεῖν ἐχάρη καὶ εὐλόγησε τὸν Θεὸν τὸν ἐλεήσαντα αὐτόν. 11. οὐ δεῖ τοὺς μὲν ἄφρονας καθίστασθαι ἄρχοντας, τοὺς δὲ δικαίους οἵτινες οἴδασι[1] δικαίως πράσσειν. 12. λῃσταὶ δέ τινες εὐθὺς ἐπιστάντες διήρπασαν τὰ ὑπάρχοντα καὶ ἔλιπον αὐτὸν ἐν τῇ ἐρήμῳ ἵνα φάγῃ τὰ θηρία αὐτόν. 13. καὶ γὰρ ἦλθεν ὁ υἱὸς τοῦ ἀνθρώπου δοῦναι τὴν ψυχὴν αὐτοῦ λύτρον ἀντὶ πολλῶν. 14. καὶ γὰρ τοῦτο καλῶς ἐπίσταμαι ὅτι ἀπεκατεστάθη ἡ χείρ μου ἡ ἐξηραμμένη.

Mark 3.23-26; 9.1; 11.1-7; Luke 8.55-56; 18.9-14; John 1.35-37; 19.25-27; Acts 8.34-38; 17.15; Rom. 13.1-3; I Cor. 15.1

Translate: 1. He stood up[2] and placed the sheep in front of the shepherd. 2. We shall not stand before him when he comes in the glory of his angels, for we have all betrayed him. 3. The guard made the prophet stand in the midst of the soldiers and ordered the others to stand away from him. 4. Many signs and wonders were done in that city so that the crowd was astonished at the power of the apostles. 5. The angel who stands before God tells him about men, but he will forgive them their sins. 6. The children were standing outside saying that they were hungry and thirsty.

36 δείκνυμι. πρίν, ὑπέρ

There is a small group of verbs which have the same endings in present and imperfect as the -μι verbs given above, but:

(1) otherwise, although often irregular in their parts, they conjugate like λύω.

(2) there is no reduplicating prefix, but -νυ- is inserted between the stem proper and the endings δείκ-νυ-μι (in ἀπόλ-λυ-μι

---

[1] οἶδα with the infin. means *know how to*.
[2] Cf. No. 2 in the Greek exercise. This use of this participle is common in the NT and often redundant.

softened to λυ), -ννυ- after a vowel, ζώ-ννυ-μι. All other tenses are formed from the stem proper: δείκ-, future δείξω, etc., ζώ-, future ζώσω, etc.

Present and imperfect indic. active; regular forms in -ύω have largely superseded the older -μι forms, but the following are found:

Present	1st sing.	δείκνυμι	3rd sing.	δείκνυσι(ν)
Imperative	2nd pl.	δείκνυτε
Infinitive		δεικνύναι
Participle		δεικνύς -ύσα -ύν, -ύντος

Present and imperfect indic. passive and middle; no forms in -ύω are found in the NT, but the following -μι forms:

δείκνυμαι
δείκνυται   ἐδείκνυτο
δεικνύμεθα
δείκνυνται   ἐδείκνυντο

Imperative 2nd pl. δείκνυσθε
Infinitive   δείκνυσθαι
Participle   δεικνύμενος -η -ον

The following are found in the NT:

δείκνυμι (-ύω)	show
ἀμφιέννυμι[1] (only ἀμφιέννυσι)	clothe
ἀπόλλυμι (-ύω)*	destroy (cf. p. 72)
ζώννυμι (-ύω)	gird
ὄμνυμι (-ύω)*	swear
σβέννυμι*	quench

πρίν or **πρὶν ἤ**[2] is used as a temporal conjunction meaning *before*; it has the following peculiarity: if the main verb is affirmative, πρίν is followed by an acc. and infin. clause.

κατάβηθι πρὶν ἀποθανεῖν τὸ παιδίον μου.
Come down before my child dies.   John 4.49

Otherwise, if main verb is negative, πρίν follows normal rules for temporal conjunctions (cf. pp. 38, 93).

[1] Perfect participle passive is ἠμφιεσμένος, as if uncompounded.
[2] ἤ was added because of the comparative force in the original adverb πρίν *earlier than*, i.e. *before*.

ἄξιος -α -ον	(w. gen.)	συλλαμβάνω	seize, arrest,
	worthy		conceive a
ἑορτή -ῆς ἡ	feast, festival		child
ἐργάζομαι (M)	work	ὑπέρ	(w. acc.) above,
εὐχαριστέω	give thanks		beyond,
μισέω	hate		(w. gen.) on
ὅμοιος -α -ον	(w. dat.) like		behalf of
ὀργή -ῆς ἡ	wrath		

Parse: ἀναστάς, σβέννυνται, ἑστάναι, ἀποκαθιστάνεις, δεῖξον, ἐπιγνοῦσα, ἀπολωλός, δείκνυσι.

Translate: 1. ἐζήτουν οἱ ἀρχιερεῖς καὶ οἱ γραμματεῖς πῶς συλλαβόντες τὸν Ἰησοῦν ἀπολέσωσιν αὐτόν, ἀλλὰ μὴ ἐν τῇ ἑορτῇ. 2. αἱ λαμπάδες σβέννυνται ὅτι οὐκ ἠγοράσαμεν ἔλαιον. 3. οἱ δὲ παρεστῶτες ἤρξαντο βλασφημεῖν καὶ ὀμνύναι λέγοντες ὅτι Οὗτος βούλεται ἀπολέσαι τὸν λαὸν ἡμῶν. 4. ὁ δὲ ἄγγελος ὃς καλεῖται Αβαδδων παρὰ τοῖς Ἰουδαίοις ἐν τῇ Ἑλληνικῇ γλώσσῃ ὄνομα ἔχει Ἀπολλύων. 5. καὶ ὤμοσα ἐν τῇ ὀργῇ μου ὅτι οὐ μὴ ἔλθωσιν εἰς ταύτην τὴν χώραν. 6. δεῖ οὖν ἕνα ἄνθρωπον μηδὲν πεπραχότα ἄξιον θανάτου ἀπολέσθαι ὑπὲρ πολλῶν, μὴ φοβούμενοι μισῶσιν ἡμᾶς οἱ Ῥωμαῖοι. 7. ὁ δὲ ἐργαζόμενος τὴν δικαιοσύνην οὗτος δείκνυσι τὰς ἐντολὰς τοῦ νόμου ἐπιγεγραμμένας ἐν τῇ καρδίᾳ αὐτοῦ. 8. καὶ εὐχαριστήσας ἐκέλευσε τοὺς ἄνδρας κατακεῖσθαι ἵνα ἄρτον παραθῶσιν αὐτοῖς οἱ μαθηταί. 9. ὁμοία δ᾽ ἐστιν ἡ βασιλεία τῶν οὐρανῶν γυναικὶ ἥτις ἀπώλεσεν ἀργύριόν τι καὶ εὑροῦσα τὸ ἀπολωλὸς ἐχάρη. 10. καὶ εἶπεν ὅτι Οὐκ ἐάσει ἡμᾶς ὁ Κύριος πειρασθῆναι ὑπὲρ ἃ δυνάμεθα· πρὶν γὰρ ἀπολέσαι τὸν διάβολον ἡμᾶς ἐλεύσεται εἰς τὸ σῶσαι. 11. οὕτως ἀμφιέννυσιν ὁ βασιλεὺς τοὺς παῖδας αὐτοῦ ὥστε ἐξίστασθαι τοὺς ὄχλους ἰδόντας ταῦτα τὰ καλὰ ἱμάτια. 12. καὶ νῦν παρακαλῶ σε, δεῖξόν μοι τὰς χεῖρας καὶ τοὺς πόδας σου ἵνα πιστεύω ἀναστῆναί σε ἐκ νεκρῶν μετὰ τὸ σταυρωθῆναι. 13. τοῦ δὲ Πέτρου ἐπιθέντος τὰς χεῖρας, καὶ τὰ μικρὰ τέκνα ἐπληρώθη Ἁγίου Πνεύματος. 14. μὴ ὀμόσῃς μηδέποτε.

Matt. 4.1-11; 25.7-8; Mark 4.38-41; John 10.9-10; 13.1-11; 14.29

117

Translate: 1. Before the soldiers arrested Jesus you (pl.) swore that you would certainly not deny him. 2. If you follow this man he will show you a big house, where you must prepare for (εἰς) the festival. 3. The apostle will work many signs and wonders, thus showing the true power of God. 4. The lost sheep are wandering on the mountain, for the wicked shepherd departed before finding them. 5. And you (sing.) swore in your anger saying, 'All those who hate good works shall perish'. 6. Rising he girded himself and went out to meet his master.

---

37 Comparison of adjectives and adverbs

In the NT **comparative adjectives** are not common and the super-lative even rarer, for the comparative may be used with the force of a superlative, as will emerge from the context. Complete rules for formation are given below, but sometimes there are no examples of these forms in the NT. The comparative regularly ends in -τερος -α -ον, the superlative in -τατος -η -ον.[1]

2nd declension — remove final ς of masc. sing., then

(1) if vowel in syllable preceding this o is long add -τερος -α -ον, -τατος -η -ον. ἰσχυρότερος (ἰσχυρότατος not in NT).

(2) if vowel in syllable preceding this o is short, lengthen to ω and add -τερος -α -ον, -τατος -η -ον. σοφώτερος, ἁγιώτατος.[2]

NB ὑψηλός ὑψηλότερος ὕψιστος

3rd declension

(1) adjectives like ἄφρων -ονος add -έστερος -α -ον, -έστατος -η -ον to stem (ἀφρονέστερος, ἀφρονέστατος not in NT).

[1] Whatever the accentuation of the positive adjective, in comparative and superlative the accent always retracts as far back as possible.
[2] The example has been changed in order to use a superlative which is found in the NT.

(2) adjectives like ἀληθής add -τερος -α -ον, -τατος -η -ον to stem -εσ, ἀκριβέστερος, ἀκριβέστατος.

(3) adjectives like εὐθύς add -τερος -α -ον, -τατος -η -ον to stem, βαρύτερος (βαρύτατος not in NT).

A few common adjectives form their comparative in the 3rd declension, their superlative in the 2nd, and need to be learnt; some of them have no positive of the same root.

μέγας	μείζων	μέγιστος
πολύς	πλείων, πλέων	πλεῖστος
	κρείσσων, κρείττων (better)[1]	κράτιστος (best)[2]
	ἐλάσσων, ἐλάττων ⎱ (less,	ἐλάχιστος (least)
	ἥσσων, ἥττων ⎰ worse)[3]	
	χείρων (worse)	

Comparatives of this kind are declined like ἄφρων, but admit of certain contractions:

Singular		Plural	
M.F.	Neut.	M.F.	Neut.
μείζων	μεῖζον	μείζονες, μείζους	μείζονα, μείζω
μείζονα, μείζω	μεῖζον	μείζονας, μείζους	μείζονα, μείζω
μείζονος	μείζονος	μειζόνων	μειζόνων
μείζονι	μείζονι	μείζοσι	μείζοσι

Two constructions are possible to express *than* after a comparative adjective:

1. ἤ *than* (cf. Latin *quam*) followed by a noun or pronoun in the same case as the preceding comparative:

    μείζων δὲ ὁ προφητεύων ἢ ὁ λαλῶν γλώσσαις.

    Greater is he who prophesies than he who speaks with tongues.   1 Cor. 14.5

2. comparative followed by a noun or pronoun in the genitive (cf. Latin *ablative of comparison*):

    ἔρχεται ὁ ἰσχυρότερός μου ὀπίσω μου.

    He who is mightier than I comes after me.   Mark 1.7

[1] The spelling variation between σσ and ττ is not a feature of κ, but of the Attic dialect and probably due to the Atticizing movement of the second century.

[2] In NT this is found only as a title, cf. Luke 1.3 κράτιστε Θεόφιλε.

[3] *Less* implies inferiority and so may mean *worse*.

119

Comparison of adverbs

Adverbs are regularly formed from adjectives and recognizable by the ending -ως, but some have no corresponding adjective and are the neuter sing. of the adjective used adverbially. From this latter come the comparative adverb, which is the neuter acc. sing. of the comparative adjective, and the superlative adverb, which is the neuter acc. pl. of the superlative adjective. Occasionally -ως is added to the comparative stem, περισσός, περισσοτέρως. There are few examples of regular forms, but the following irregular formations should be learnt:

ἐγγύς[1] (near)   ἐγγύτερον   ἔγγιστα
εὖ[1] (well)   βελτίον, κρεῖσσον, κρεῖττον
ἡδέως[2] (with pleasure, gladly)   ἥδιστα
καλῶς (well)   καλλίον (only found once in NT, with superlative force. Acts 25.10)
            μᾶλλον (more, rather)   μάλιστα (most, especially)
πολύ[3] (much)   πλεῖον, πλέον
ταχύ,[3] ταχέως (quickly)   ταχίον   τάχιστα
πόρρω[1] (far)   πορρώτερον

ἀκριβής -ές	careful, accurate	περισσός -ή -όν	excessive, abundant
βαρύς -εῖα -ύ	weighty, grievous	τέλειος -α -ον	perfect, mature
εὔκοπος -η -ον	easy	τίμιος -α -ον	precious, honourable
μέλος -ους τό	limb, member		
μωρός -ά -όν	foolish	ὑψηλός -ή -όν	high
ξύλον -ου τό	wood, tree		
ὀπίσω ⎱	(w. gen.) be-		
ὄπισθεν ⎰	hind, after		

---

[1] Not derived from adjectives.
[2] From an adjective ἡδύς -εῖα -ύ *sweet, pleasant*, which is not found in the NT.
[3] Neuter acc. sing. of the adjective used adverbially.

Translate: 1. φρονιμώτεραι ὑπάρχουσιν αὗται αἱ παρθένοι ἐκείνων τῶν μωρῶν· ἔλαιον γὰρ ἔχουσιν ἐν ταῖς λαμπάσιν ὥστε δύνασθαι ταχέως ὑπαντῆσαι τῷ νυμφίῳ. 2. ἁγιώτατος ἔστω ἐν πᾶσιν ὁ γάμος ἵνα μηδεὶς ἀποστῇ τῆς ἰδίας γυναικὸς αὐτοῦ. 3. ἀκριβέστερον γέγραφεν οὗτος ὁ γραμματεὺς ἢ πάντες οἵτινες ἐπείρασαν λόγον ποιήσασθαι περὶ τούτου τοῦ χρόνου. 4. ἐκεῖνοι οἱ ἄλλοι μάρτυρες ἠγάπησαν τὴν ἀλήθειαν μᾶλλον ἢ τὴν ζωήν. 5. ἐν δ' ἐκείνῳ τῷ ἱερῷ κεῖται σκεύη ἐκ ξύλου τιμιωτάτου. 6. καὶ ἐγένετο μετὰ τὸ ἐγγύτερον προσελθεῖν τοὺς παῖδας ἠθέλησεν ὁ Ἰησοῦς ἐπιθεῖναι τὰς χεῖρας ταῖς κεφαλαῖς αὐτῶν ἵνα εὐλογῇ αὐτούς. 7. ἀλλ' ὅστις ἂν θέλῃ τηρεῖν τὰς βαρυτέρας ἐντολὰς τοῦ νόμου, ὦ κράτιστε Θεόφιλε, οὗτος τηρήσει καὶ τὰς ἐλαχίστας. 8. ἔκραζον οὖν οἱ χείρονες πολῖται, καλλίον εἰδότες ὅτι οὐχ ἥμαρτες, λέγοντες ὅτι Δεῖ αὐτὸν τάχιστα σταυρωθῆναι. 9. ὁ δὲ Ὕψιστος ὁ ποιῶν καρπὸν τοῖς ἀνθρώποις δίδωσιν οὐχ ἧσσον τοῖς κακοῖς ἢ τοῖς ἀγαθοῖς. 10. περισσότερον οὖν γενήσεται οὐδὲν τῶν μελῶν ὑμῶν· ἐκ πάντων γὰρ καθέστηκε τὸ σῶμα. 11. ταχίον δὲ λαλήσω ὑμῖν ἐὰν δυνῶμαι· καὶ γὰρ πορρώτερον πορευόμενος ἢ ἤμελλον ἐλπίζω ἔγγιστα ἐλθεῖν. 12. καὶ ἠρώτησε, Τί ἐστιν εὐκοπώτερον, ἀκολουθεῖν μοι αἴροντας τὸν σταυρὸν ὑμῶν ἢ πίνειν καὶ ἐσθίειν μετὰ τῶν ἐθνῶν ἥδιστα μένοντας; 13. καὶ μείζω τούτων ὄψονται οἱ ἄνθρωποι ἐν ταῖς ἐσχάταις ἡμέραις ὅταν ἔλθῃ ὁ υἱὸς τοῦ ἀνθρώπου εὖ καὶ ἀκριβῶς κρῖναι τὸν κόσμον.

Matt. 5.17-20; 12.43-45; Mark 2.6-12; 4.1; Luke 7.28; John 1.50-51; 5.9b-14; 13.12-17; Acts 4.19-20; I Cor. 1.25; 13.13; 15.9-10

Translate:[1] 1. Those who are more mature ought to help the weaker brethren. 2. God is wiser than men, for he knows well why they are less honourable than the angels. 3. This covenant is newer than that, for God wishes to give another and better hope to mankind. 4. This sin is called worse, because all know that those who hate their brothers are not worthy of the forgiveness which God gives through his Son. 5. Christ has become higher than the angels, for he has greater glory and a better name. 6.

[1] In these sentences only forms that occur in the NT have been used.

What you have more abundantly you ought to impart to the poor who have less than you. 7. Those who save most money become rich, but the righteous will receive a greater reward in the kingdom of heaven.

---

38   Prepositions

In CG the meaning of prepositions was often determined by their cases, particularly where a preposition was used with two or three cases, but in κ this case differentiation is breaking down and the accusative is encroaching on the functions of other cases.

Proper Prepositions, used to form compounds:

1. found with one case only:

Accusative — basically 'motion towards.'

ἀνά in compounds often keeps the original meaning of *up*, but in NT is only found in phrase ἀνὰ μέσον, *in the midst* or *between*, and distributively:

τὸ ἀρνίον τὸ ἀνὰ μέσον τοῦ θρόνου ποιμανεῖ αὐτούς.
The lamb that is in the midst of the throne shall shepherd
     them.   Rev. 7.17

καὶ ἀπέστειλεν αὐτοὺς ἀνὰ δύο.
He sent them out two by two.   Luke 10.1

εἰς   *into*; but in the NT often replaces ἐν and has a locative meaning, *in*:

καὶ εἰσπορεύονται εἰς Καφαρναουμ.[1]   Mark 1.21

[1] For the sake of revision very simple examples have been chosen in which the vocabulary should be already known.

καὶ εἰς τὴν οἰκίαν πάλιν οἱ μαθηταὶ περὶ τούτου ἐπηρώτων
αὐτόν.   Mark 10.10

Genitive — basically 'motion away from'

ἀντί   instead of, for the sake of

NB common phrase ἀνθ' ὧν because.

ὁρᾶτε μή τις κακὸν ἀντὶ κακοῦ τινι ἀποδῷ.   I Thess. 5.15
καὶ ἰδοὺ ἔσῃ σιωπῶν καὶ μὴ δυνάμενος λαλῆσαι — ἀνθ' ὧν
οὐκ ἐπίστευσας τοῖς λόγοις μου.   Luke 1.20

ἀπό   from; usually simple motion, but may have causal sense.

ἦλθεν Ἰησοῦς ἀπὸ Ναζαρεθ τῆς Γαλιλαίας.   Mark 1.9
καὶ ἀπὸ τῆς χαρᾶς αὐτοῦ ὑπάγει καὶ πωλεῖ ὅσα ἔχει καὶ
ἀγοράζει τὸν ἀγρὸν ἐκεῖνον.   Matt. 13.44

ἐκ, ἐξ   out of

τὸ πνεῦμα τὸ ἀκάθαρτον φωνῆσαν φωνῇ μεγάλῃ ἐξῆλθεν ἐξ
αὐτοῦ.   Mark 1.26

NB ἐκ δευτέρου a second time, ἐκ δεξιῶν on the right

πρό   before; usually temporal, but may be local.

πρὸ γὰρ τούτων τῶν ἡμερῶν ἀνέστη Θευδᾶς.   Acts 5.36
φύλακες πρὸ τῆς θύρας ἐτήρουν τὴν φυλακήν.   Acts 12.6

Dative — basically for association, location, instrument.

ἐν   in, on, used of both place and time, sometimes instrumental by, which is generally explained as a Semitism, but
existed in CG.

ἦν δέ τις μαθητὴς ἐν Δαμασκῷ ὀνόματι Ἁνανίας.
                                                Acts 9.10
δύο ἐξ αὐτῶν ἐν αὐτῇ τῇ ἡμέρᾳ ἦσαν πορευόμενοι εἰς κώμην.
                                                Luke 24.13
ἐν τῷ ἄρχοντι τῶν δαιμονίων ἐκβάλλει τὰ δαιμόνια.
                                                Matt. 9.34

σύν   with
καὶ σὺν αὐτῷ σταυροῦσιν δύο λῃστάς.   Mark 15.27

2. found with two cases:

διά (w. acc.) *on account of*

καὶ ἔσεσθε μισούμενοι ὑπὸ πάντων τῶν ἐθνῶν διὰ τὸ ὄνομά
μου.   Matt. 24.9

(w. gen.) *through*, used of instrument, space, time.

ὁ δὲ Ἰωάννης — πέμψας διὰ τῶν μαθητῶν αὐτοῦ εἶπεν
αὐτῷ.   Matt. 11.2
ἔδει δὲ αὐτὸν διέρχεσθαι διὰ τῆς Σαμαρίας.   John 4.4
διὰ δεκατεσσάρων ἐτῶν πάλιν ἀνέβην εἰς Ἱεροσόλυμα.
                                                       Gal. 2.1
NB διὰ παντός *always, continually.*

κατά (w. acc.) *according to, in* or *at* (local and temporal),
distributive.

ἐγήγερται τῇ ἡμέρᾳ τῇ τρίτῃ κατὰ τὰς γραφάς.
                                                       I Cor. 15.4
καὶ ἀπῆλθεν καθ' ὅλην τὴν πόλιν κηρύσσων ὅσα ἐποίησεν
αὐτῷ ὁ Ἰησοῦς.   Luke 8.39
κατὰ τὸν καιρὸν τοῦτον ἐλεύσομαι.   Rom. 9.9
καὶ ἐπορεύοντο οἱ γονεῖς αὐτοῦ κατ' ἔτος εἰς Ιερουσαλημ.
                                                       Luke 2.41

NB κατ' ἰδίαν *privately,* κατὰ μονάς *alone,* κατ' ὄναρ *in a
dream,* καθ' ἡμέραν *daily,* καθ' ὅσον *inasmuch as,* κατὰ πεντήκοντα *by fifties* (indeclinable numeral).

(w. gen.) *against, throughout* (locative), *by* (object by which one
swears), *down from* (only once in NT, but common in compounds).

ἀφίετε εἴ τι ἔχετε κατά τινος.   Mark 11.25
γνωστὸν δὲ ἐγένετο καθ' ὅλης τῆς Ἰόππης.   Acts 9.42
ἄνθρωποι γὰρ κατὰ τοῦ μείζονος ὀμνύουσιν.   Heb. 6.16

καὶ ὥρμησεν ἡ ἀγέλη κατὰ τοῦ κρημνοῦ.
And the herd rushed down from the cliff.   Mark 5.13

μετά (w. acc.) *after* (both of time and place, more often the former)

μετὰ ταῦτα ἦν ἑορτὴ τῶν Ἰουδαίων.   John 5.1
ἔρχεται μετ᾽ ἐμὲ οὗ οὐκ εἰμὶ ἄξιος τὸ ὑπόδημα (*shoe*) τῶν
   ποδῶν λῦσαι.   Acts 13.25

(w. gen.) *with*

τέκνον, σὺ πάντοτε μετ᾽ ἐμοῦ εἶ.   Luke 15.31

περί (w. acc.) *around* (local), *about* (softening precise statement)

καὶ ἐκάθητο περὶ αὐτὸν ὄχλος.   Mark 3.32
καὶ· ἐξελθὼν περὶ τρίτην ὥραν εἶδεν ἄλλους ἑστῶτας —
                                            Matt. 20.3

(w. gen.) *concerning*

τοῖς ἀγγέλοις αὐτοῦ ἐντελεῖται περὶ σοῦ.   Matt. 4.6

ὑπέρ (w. acc.) *above, beyond*

οὐκ ἔστιν μαθητὴς ὑπὲρ τὸν διδάσκαλον οὐδὲ δοῦλος ὑπὲρ
   τὸν κύριον αὐτοῦ.   Matt. 10.24

(w. gen.) *on behalf of*

καὶ ὑπὲρ αὐτῶν ἁγιάζω ἐμαυτόν.   John 17.19

ὑπό (w. acc.) *under*

οὐ γάρ ἐστε ὑπὸ νόμον ἀλλὰ ὑπὸ χάριν.   Rom. 6.14

(w. gen.) *by* (of the agent)

ἐγὼ χρείαν ἔχω ὑπὸ σοῦ βαπτισθῆναι.   Matt. 3.14

3. **found with three cases:**

ἐπί (w. acc.) *upon* (with idea of motion towards), *upon* (purely
   local), *over* (set in authority), *against* (with idea of motion),
   over (a period of time), *in reference to*

ἀλλὰ ἐλθὼν ἐπίθες τὴν χεῖρά σου ἐπ᾽ αὐτήν, καὶ ζήσεται.
                                            Matt. 9.18
καθήσεσθε καὶ αὐτοὶ ἐπὶ δώδεκα θρόνους.   Matt. 19.28

125

συνκαλεσάμενος δὲ τοὺς δώδεκα ἔδωκεν αὐτοῖς δύναμιν καὶ
ἐξουσίαν ἐπὶ πάντα τὰ δαιμόνια.　　　　　　Luke 9.1
καὶ ἐπαναστήσονται τέκνα ἐπὶ γονεῖς.　　　Matt. 10.21
τοῦτο δὲ ἐποίει ἐπὶ πολλὰς ἡμέρας.　　　　Acts 16.18
καὶ πῶς γέγραπται ἐπὶ τὸν Υἱὸν τοῦ ἀνθρώπου —
　　　　　　　　　　　　　　　　　　　Mark 9.12

NB ἐφ' ὅσον inasmuch as; ἐπὶ τὸ αὐτό together (Acts).

(w. gen.) upon (local), over (set in authority), in the presence of, in
the time of

καὶ ὄψονται τὸν Υἱὸν τοῦ ἀνθρώπου ἐρχόμενον ἐπὶ τῶν
νεφελῶν τοῦ οὐρανοῦ μετὰ δυνάμεως καὶ δόξης πολλῆς.
　　　　　　　　　　　　　　　　　　　Matt. 24.30
τίς σε κατέστησεν ἄρχοντα ἐφ' ἡμῶν;　　　Acts 7.27
εἶπεν, Θέλεις εἰς Ἱεροσόλυμα ἀναβὰς ἐκεῖ περὶ τούτων
κριθῆναι ἐπ' ἐμοῦ;　　　　　　　　　　　Acts 25.9
καὶ πολλοὶ λεπροὶ ἦσαν ἐν τῷ Ισραηλ ἐπὶ Ἐλισαίου τοῦ
προφήτου.　　　　　　　　　　　　　　Luke 4.27

NB ἐπ' ἀληθείας in truth, truly

(w. dat.) on or at (local), over (set in authority), at (grounds of
emotion), on (on a basis of), against

ὅταν ἴδητε ταῦτα γινόμενα, γινώσκετε ὅτι ἐγγύς ἐστιν ἐπὶ
θύραις.　　　　　　　　　　　　　　　　Mark 13.29
ἀληθῶς λέγω ὑμῖν ὅτι ἐπὶ πᾶσιν τοῖς ὑπάρχουσιν αὐτοῦ
καταστήσει αὐτόν.　　　　　　　　　　　Luke 12.44
λέγω ὑμῖν ὅτι χαίρει ἐπ' αὐτῷ μᾶλλον ἢ ἐπὶ τοῖς ἐνενήκοντα
ἐννέα (99) τοῖς μὴ πεπλανημένοις.　　　　Matt. 18.13
γέγραπται, Οὐκ ἐπ' ἄρτῳ μόνῳ ζήσεται ὁ ἄνθρωπος.
　　　　　　　　　　　　　　　　　　　Matt. 4.4
πατὴρ ἐφ' υἱῷ καὶ υἱὸς ἐπὶ πατρί　　　　Luke 13.53

παρά (w. acc.) contrary to, beside (motion towards and local),
by comparison with or than (after comparative implicit or
expressed)

παρὰ τὴν διδαχὴν ἣν ὑμεῖς ἐμάθετε.　　　Rom. 16.17

126

περιπατῶν δὲ παρὰ τὴν θάλασσαν τῆς Γαλιλαίας εἶδεν δύο ἀδελφούς.   Matt. 4.18

εὗρον καθήμενον τὸν ἄνθρωπον — παρὰ τοὺς πόδας τοῦ Ἰησοῦ.   Luke 8.35

πλείονα θυσίαν Ἀβελ παρὰ Καιν προσήνεγκεν.   Heb. 11.4

(w. gen.) *from* (of persons)

ᾐτήσατο παρ' αὐτοῦ ἐπιστολὰς εἰς Δαμασκόν.   Acts 9.2

(w. dat.) *beside* (local or in fuller sense of at somebody's house), *in a person's eyes or judgment*

εἱστήκεισαν δὲ παρὰ τῷ σταυρῷ τοῦ Ἰησοῦ ἡ μήτηρ αὐτοῦ καὶ ἡ ἀδελφὴ τῆς μητρὸς αὐτοῦ.   John 19.25

καὶ εἰσελθόντες εἰς τὸν οἶκον Φιλίππου τοῦ εὐαγγελιστοῦ ὄντος ἐκ τῶν ἑπτὰ ἐμείναμεν παρ' αὐτῷ.   Acts 21.8

μὴ γίνεσθε φρόνιμοι παρ' ἑαυτοῖς.   Rom. 12.16

πρός (w. acc.) *to* (motion towards), *to* (after verbs of saying), *to* (in reference to), *with* or *at* (like παρά w. dat.)

ὕστερον δὲ ἀπέστειλεν πρὸς αὐτοὺς τὸν υἱὸν αὐτοῦ.   Matt. 21.37

καὶ ἀπεστάλην λαλῆσαι πρὸς σὲ καὶ εὐαγγελίσασθαί σοι ταῦτα.   Luke 1.19

Κύριε, πρὸς ἡμᾶς τὴν παραβολὴν ταύτην λέγεις ἢ καὶ πρὸς πάντας;   Luke 12.41

πρὸς σὲ ποιῶ τὸ πασχα μετὰ τῶν μαθητῶν μου.   Matt. 26.18

καὶ πᾶς ὁ ὄχλος πρὸς τὴν θάλασσαν ἐπὶ τῆς γῆς ἦσαν.   Mark 4.1

NB πρὸς καιρόν *for a time*

(w. gen.) only once in NT, *in the interest of*

τοῦτο γὰρ πρὸς τῆς ὑμετέρας σωτηρίας ὑπάρχει.
For this is for your safety.   Acts 27.34

(w. dat.) *at, by* (local) — rare

ὁ δὲ Πέτρος εἱστήκει πρὸς τῇ θύρᾳ ἔξω.   John 18.16

Translate: 1. μετὰ δὲ τὴν ἑορτὴν ἔστησαν περὶ τὴν πρώτην ὥραν ἐπὶ τοῦ ἡγεμόνος. 2. ἤμην δὲ καθεύδων πρὸς τὴν θάλασσαν καὶ κατ᾽ ὄναρ ἐδόκουν ἰδεῖν περιπατοῦντά τινα ἐπὶ τοῦ ὕδατος. 3. οὐδὲν εἰρήκασιν οὗτοι κατὰ τοῦ ναοῦ οὐδὲ παρὰ νόμον πείθουσιν ἡμᾶς μὴ δέχεσθαι τὰς ἐντολὰς τὰς παραδεδομένας παρὰ τῶν πατέρων. 4. καὶ εἶπεν ὅτι Διὰ τὴν δικαιοσύνην ὑμῶν σωθήσεσθε καὶ παρὰ τοῦ Θεοῦ λήμψεσθε δύναμιν ὥστε ἀποκρίνεσθαι πρὸς τοὺς κριτάς. 5. καὶ διὰ παντὸς ἑστὼς ἔσται ἐπὶ τοῦ οἴκου μου ἵνα ἀκριβέστερον διδῷ λόγον περὶ τῶν ὑπαρχόντων μου τοῖς τελώναις. 6. καὶ ἅπαντες οἱ παρεστῶτες ἐξίσταντο ἐπὶ ταύτῃ τῇ καινῇ διδαχῇ. 7. ἐπεὶ δὲ εἶδόν σε ὑπὸ τὸ δένδρον ἔγνων σε ὅτι ἀνὴρ εἶ κατὰ τὴν καρδίαν μου. 8. καὶ νῦν ἀντὶ τῶν παλαιῶν ἐπαγγελιῶν εἰλήφατε καινὴν χάριν. 9. αὕτη οὖν ἡ παρθένος ἣ εὗρε χάριν παρὰ τῷ Κυρίῳ ἔτεκεν υἱὸν κατὰ καιρόν. 10. ἐπὶ δὲ τούτου τοῦ προφήτου ἀπέθανον πολλοὶ ὑπὲρ τῆς πατρίδος ἀνθιστάμενοι τοῖς ἐχθροῖς. 11. πολλὰ πεπόνθατε, ἀλλ᾽ οὐ πειράσει ὑμᾶς ὁ Κύριος ὑπὲρ ὃ δύνασθε. 12. λέγω δὲ ὑμῖν ὅτι δώσω ἀνὰ πέντε δηνάρια ἐὰν ἔλθητε εἰς τὸν ἀμπελῶνα καὶ ἐργάζησθε σὺν τοῖς λοιποῖς τοῖς ἤδη ἀπεσταλμένοις.

Matt. 20.8-12; 27.19; Mark 10.44-45; Rom. 8.5-11; Heb. 2.10

---

39 Compound verbs

In κ the force of a preposition often survives and is easily recogniz-able, especially with verbs of motion (e.g. ἀνά, ἀπό, διά), but some compounds where the preposition was used with an intensifying force have either superseded the original verb (ἀποκτείνω, ἀπόλ-

λυμι) or can barely be distinguished from it in meaning (ἀναγ-
γέλλω, ἀπαγγέλλω).[1] Sometimes the prepositional prefix admits
two meanings, so causing ambiguity, or assumes a meaning remote
from that of the preposition itself. The following deserve attention:

ἀνά   (1) *up* — the usual meaning in compounds: ἀναβλέπω *look
           up*
       (2) *again*: also ἀναβλέπω *receive sight*
       (3) *back*: ἀνάκειμαι, ἀναπίπτω *recline*, ἀναχωρέω *depart*

μετά   may involve an idea of change: μεταμορφόω *transform*,
        μεταβαίνω *remove, depart*

παρά   from the meaning of *along* may get a bad sense of passing
        on one side: παραβαίνω *transgress*, παράπτωμα *transgres-
        sion*, παραιτέομαι *beg oneself off, excuse oneself, refuse*,
        παρακούω both *overhear* and *disregard* (hence ambiguity in
        Mark 5.36)

αἱρέω[2]	take; NB strong aorist εἷλον (often with weak endings), but irregular augment, so infin. ἑλεῖν, etc.		
ἀναιρέω	take up (only Acts 7.21), destroy, kill		
ἀφαιρέω	take away		
καθαιρέω	take down, pull down, destroy		
ἀναβλέπω	(1) look up; (2) see again, receive sight		
ἀναζάω	come to life again	ἐντρέπω	put to shame
		ἐντρέπομαι (P)	reverence
ἀναχωρέω	depart	ἐπιτρέπω	(w. dat.)
τρέπω*[2]	turn		permit

[1] Prepositions ending in a vowel (except περί) elide before a following vowel
and if this is aspirated they take the aspirated form — ἀπάγω, ἀφαιρέω. In C G
there was usually assimilation so that the ν of ἐν and σύν before a labial became
μ (ἐμβαίνω, συμβαίνω), before a guttural became γ (ἐγκαλέω); σύν before λ became συλ (συλλαμβάνω), though reverting to the original form before the augment (ἐνέβην, συνέλαβον, etc.) In K the preposition is more often unchanged, but
editors may vary in their spellings.
[2] When simple verbs were not obsolete but do not occur in the NT the simple
forms, not the compound, are given in the list of irregular verbs and their parts
on p. 155.

ἐγκαλέω	(w. dat.) accuse		self, beg off, refuse
ἐπικαλέω	surname	παρακούω	(w. gen.)
ἐπικαλέομαι (M)	invoke		overhear,
καταλύω	destroy, lodge	προσδέχομαι (M)	disregard look for,
μεταβαίνω	remove, de- part		expect, accept
μεταμορφόω	transfigure	συμβαίνω	happen
παραιτέομαι (M)	excuse one-	ὑπομένω	endure

Translate: περὶ τὸν θρόνον. κατὰ τοῦ ὄρους. μετὰ τοῦ ἀγγέλου. διὰ τῆς γῆς. ἔζη ἐπὶ τοῦ Ἡρῴδου. καταλύει παρὰ τῷ Πέτρῳ. σοφώτερός ἐστι παρὰ τοὺς ἀδελφοὺς αὐτοῦ. ἐπὶ ξύλου ἐσταυρώθη. ἐξεπλήσσοντο ἐπὶ τῇ διδαχῇ αὐτοῦ. 1. ὁ δὲ τυφλὸς ἀναβλέψας ἀπήγγειλε κατὰ τὴν πόλιν ὅσα πεποίηκεν αὐτῷ ὁ Ἰησοῦς. 2. ἀλλ᾽ ὅστις ἂν μὴ ἐντρέπηται τοὺς φίλους, οὗτος μέλλει παρακούειν καὶ σοῦ. 3. καὶ ἐπέτρεψε τοῖς δαιμονίοις εἰσελθεῖν εἰς τοὺς χοίρους. 4. οἱ δὲ ἀφέντες τὰ δίκτυα εἰς τὸ πλοῖον συνηκολούθησαν τῷ Ἰησοῦ. 5. δεῖ γὰρ τοὺς προσδεχομένους τὴν βασιλείαν τῶν οὐρανῶν ὑπομένειν τὰ συμβαίνοντα διὰ τὴν πίστιν. 6. οἱ δὲ ὑπηρέται παρέθηκαν τοῖς συνανακειμένοις τῷ ἡγεμόνι καλὸν οἶνον, τοῖς δὲ ἄλλοις οἶνον ἐλάσσω. 7. καὶ ἀνεχώρησαν εἰς τὴν ἰδίαν πατρίδα αὐτῶν μὴ ἀποκαλύψαντες τοῦτο τῷ βασιλεῖ. 8. καὶ καθελὼν τὸ σῶμα κατέθηκεν αὐτὸ ἐν καινῷ μνημείῳ. 9. οἱ δὲ κεκλημένοι εἰς τὸν γάμον πάντες ἤρξαντο παραιτεῖσθαι. 10. μεταβὰς δὲ ἀπὸ τῆς κώμης ἀνῃρέθη ὑπὸ τῶν ἤδη βουλομένων καταλῦσαι τὴν ἐξουσίαν αὐτοῦ. 11. καὶ ἐν τῷ ἀναγινώσκειν τὸν εὐνοῦχον τὸ βιβλίον ἰδοὺ εὐθὺς ἐπῆλθεν αὐτῷ ὁ Φίλιππος. 12. ἀλλ᾽ ἐπεὶ ἀνέζησεν ὁ νεκρὸς ἅπαντες οἱ παραπορευόμενοι, εἰδότες ὅτι ἀνέστησεν αὐτὸν ὁ Ἰησοῦς, συνεχάρησαν τῇ μητρὶ καὶ ἐπῆραν τὴν φωνὴν αὐτῶν εὐχαριστοῦντες τῷ Θεῷ.

Matt. 5.38-39b; 17.1-3; Luke 9.10-12; 15.1-7; Acts 1.23-26; 2.21; 23.27-29; James 4.11

40 Prepositional adverbs. Some case usages

Improper prepositions, which are not used to form compounds:

ἕνεκα (ἕνεκεν, εἵνεκεν) (w. gen.) *for the sake of*
  μακάριοι οἱ δεδιωγμένοι ἕνεκεν δικαιοσύνης.   Matt. 5.10
ἕως, μέχρι(ς), ἄχρι(ς) (w. gen.) *until, as far as*
  καὶ σύ, Καφαρναουμ, μὴ ἕως οὐρανοῦ ὑψωθήσῃ;
                                              Matt. 11.23

Prepositional Adverbs

A number of adverbs came to be used as prepositions also. The commonest, given below, were all used with the genitive:

ἀπέναντι, κατέναντι   *over against, opposite*
  ὑπάγετε εἰς τὴν κώμην τὴν κατέναντι ὑμῶν.   Mark 11.2

ἐγγύς   *near*
  ἐγγὺς τοῦ τόπου ὅπου ἔφαγον τὸν ἄρτον.   John 6.23

ἐκτός, ἔξω, ἔξωθεν[1]   *outside*
  καὶ ἐξέβαλον αὐτὸν ἔξω τοῦ ἀμπελῶνος.   Mark 12.8

ἔμπροσθεν   *before*, both of time and place
  καὶ συναχθήσονται ἔμπροσθεν αὐτοῦ πάντα τὰ ἔθνη.
                                              Matt. 25.32
ἐντός, ἔσω, ἔσωθεν   *within*
  ἡ βασιλεία τοῦ Θεοῦ ἐντὸς ὑμῶν ἐστιν.   Luke 17.21

ἐνώπιον   *before, in the presence of*
  ὁ δὲ ἀρνησάμενός με ἐνώπιον τῶν ἀνθρώπων ἀπαρνηθήσεται
  ἐνώπιον τῶν ἀγγέλων τοῦ Θεοῦ.   Luke 12.9

[1] The suffix -θεν properly denotes *from*. ἔσωθεν and ἔξωθεν sometimes keep this meaning, but are also simply locative, according to context.

ἐπάνω   *above, upon* (this is almost always a preposition, but ἄνω *above, again,* ἄνωθεν *from above, from the beginning,* are always adverbial).

   ἴσθι ἐξουσίαν ἔχων ἐπάνω δέκα πόλεων.   Luke 19.17

μεταξύ   *between*
   ἦν ὁ Πέτρος κοιμώμενος μεταξὺ δύο στρατιωτῶν.
                                                   Acts 12.6

ὄπισθεν, ὀπίσω   *after, behind*
   Ὁ ὀπίσω μου ἐρχόμενος ἔμπροσθέν μου γέγονεν.   John 1.15

πέραν   *across* — the adverb is often used with τό to mean *the other side.*
   ὁ ὄχλος ὁ ἑστηκὼς πέραν τῆς θαλάσσης.   John 6.22

πλήν   *except* (as an adverb, *but, however*)
   εἷς ἐστιν καὶ οὐκ ἔστιν ἄλλος πλὴν αὐτοῦ.   Mark 12.32

πλησίον   *near* — this is often used with the article to mean *the person near,* i.e. *one's neighbour.*
   τίς τούτων τῶν τριῶν πλησίον δοκεῖ σοι γεγονέναι τοῦ
   ἐμπεσόντος εἰς τοὺς λῃστάς;   Luke 10.36

ὑποκάτω   *below* (only a preposition, but κάτω *down,* only an adverb)
   Κάθου ἐκ δεξιῶν μου ἕως ἂν θῶ τοὺς ἐχθρούς σου ὑποκάτω
   τῶν ποδῶν σου.   Matt. 22.44

χάριν   *for the sake of,* acc. sing. of χάρις
   οὗ χάριν λέγω σοι, ἀφέωνται αἱ ἁμαρτίαι αὐτῆς αἱ πολλαί.
                                                   Luke 7.47

χωρίς   *apart, without*
   πῶς δὲ ἀκούσωσιν χωρὶς κηρύσσοντος;   Rom. 10.14

Some Case Usages

This list has been compiled to illustrate usages which might cause difficulties in translation when they do not correspond to the simple meaning of the case.

Nominative

This is sometimes found with the article instead of the vocative.

Ἡ παῖς, ἔγειρε. Luke 8.54

Accusative

1. respect — much less common than in CG.

ἀνέπεσαν οὖν οἱ ἄνδρες τὸν ἀριθμὸν ὡς πεντακισχίλιοι (5,000). John 6.10

NB Paul sometimes uses a superfluous τό with a prepositional phrase.

καὶ ἐξ ὧν ὁ Χριστὸς τὸ κατὰ σάρκα Rom. 9.5
in respect of that which is according to the flesh, which means no more than *according to the flesh*

The adverbial neuter acc. of some adjectives has already been met, πολύ, πολλά, ταχύ. Note also δωρεάν (acc. sing. of δωρεά *gift*) *freely, for nought* and μακράν *far off*, which have become adverbial.

2. extent both of time and of place

καὶ ἰδοὺ ἐγὼ μεθ᾽ ὑμῶν εἰμι πάσας τὰς ἡμέρας ἕως τῆς συντελείας τοῦ αἰῶνος. Matt. 28.20
τὸ δὲ πλοῖον ἤδη σταδίους (*furlongs*) πολλοὺς ἀπὸ τῆς γῆς ἀπεῖχεν. Matt. 14.24

3. point of time

Ἐχθὲς ὥραν ἑβδόμην ἀφῆκεν αὐτὸν ὁ πυρετός.
Yesterday at the seventh hour the fever left him. John 4.52

Genitive

1. possessive — often such words as *son, mother, wife* are to be supplied from the context.

προβὰς ὀλίγον εἶδεν Ἰάκωβον τὸν τοῦ Ζεβεδαίου.

Mark 1.19

2. separation, sometimes found with verbs, but more often ἀπό or ἐκ is added.

ἦ οὐκ ἀφίστατο τοῦ ἱεροῦ.   Luke 2.37

3. time 'within which'

καὶ διὰ παντὸς νυκτὸς καὶ ἡμέρας — ἦν κράζων

Mark 5.5

4. price

ἀπεκρίθη δὲ πρὸς αὐτὴν Πέτρος, Εἰπέ μοι, εἰ τοσούτου τὸ χωρίον ἀπέδοσθε;   Acts 5.8

5. comparison

κρείττων γενόμενος τῶν ἀγγέλων.   Heb. 1.4

6. descriptive, of age

ἦν γὰρ ἐτῶν δώδεκα.   Mark 5.42

7. subjective or objective, when a noun stands in the relation of a subject or object to a noun from a verbal root

τὰς ψυχὰς ὑμῶν ἡγνικότες ἐν τῇ ὑπακοῇ τῆς ἀληθείας
having purified your souls by obedience to the truth

I Peter 1.22

Dative

1. possessive, used with εἰμί and verbs of similar meaning

εἰσὶν ἡμῖν ἄνδρες τέσσαρες.   Acts 21.23

2. instrumental (used more often with ἐν)

χάριτί ἐστε σεσωσμένοι.   Eph. 2.5

3. causal

ἵνα τῷ σταυρῷ τοῦ Χριστοῦ μὴ διώκωνται.   Gal. 6.12

4. respect

Ιωσηφ δὲ ὁ ἐπικληθεὶς Βαρναβᾶς — Κύπριος τῷ γένει.

Acts 4.36

5. measure of difference with a comparative

αὐτὸς δὲ πολλῷ μᾶλλον ἔκραζεν.   Luke 18.39

134

6. 'time when' (often with ἐν)

σὺ σήμερον ταύτῃ τῇ νυκτὶ πρὶν ἢ δὶς ἀλέκτορα φωνῆσαι
τρίς με ἀπαρνήσῃ.   Mark 14.30

7. extent of time

ὡς ἔτεσιν τετρακοσίοις καὶ πεντήκοντα (450).   Acts 13.20

ἀπέχω	(w. acc.) have already, have in full,	διαλέγομαι (M, P)	converse, argue
		ὅριον -ου τό	boundary, pl. territory
	(w. gen.) be distant	παραγίνομαι	be at hand, arrive
ἀπέχομαι (M	(w. gen.) abstain from	τράπεζα -ης ἡ	table, bank
		τρέχω*	run

Give the gen. sing., dat. pl., gender, meaning of θάλασσα, δεσπότης, αἰών, φύλαξ, λαμπάς, γυνή, πατήρ, πούς, χείρ, σῶμα.

Translate: 1. τὸ θυγάτριόν[1] μου ἦν δέκα ἐτῶν καὶ τοσούτῳ σοφώτερα πασῶν τῶν φίλων ὥστε τούτου χάριν πολλοὺς θέλειν διαλέγεσθαι αὐτῇ. 2. καὶ ἔφη ὅτι νυκτὸς ἔκλεψαν τὸ ἀργύριόν σου καὶ καταθέντες εἰς πλοιάριον[1] ἀπήνεγκαν πέραν τῆς θαλάσσης ἔξω τῶν ὁρίων ἡμῶν. 3. καὶ πέντε ἡμέρας νηστεύσαντες ἑστῶτες ἦμεν ἔμπροσθεν τοῦ ἱερέως καὶ ἀπηγγείλαμεν αὐτῷ ὅτι χωρὶς ἁμαρτίας τετελέκαμεν πάντα ἃ προσέταξεν ἡμῖν. 4. ἀλλ' ὑποκάτω τῆς τραπέζης ἐσθίει ἄρτον πολλὰ κυνάρια[1] ἃ ὑπάρχει τῷ οἰκοδεσπότῃ. 5. καὶ ὅτε τρέχοντες ὄπισθεν τῶν στρατιωτῶν παρεγένοντο ἐγγὺς τῆς πόλεως ἡδέως ἀνέπεσαν ἐπὶ τῆς γῆς κατέναντι τοῦ ποταμοῦ. 6. ἀπέχει ἡ καρδία τῶν πονηρῶν μακρὰν τοῦ Κυρίου, πεφανερωμένον δὲ ἔσται τὸ ἔσω αὐτῶν τῇ ἡμέρᾳ τῆς κρίσεως. 7. ὦ γύναι, ἀφεθήσεται παραπτώματα τοιαῦτα· πολλῷ γὰρ χείρους οὗτοι οἱ πλησίον σου οἱ μὴ ὁμολογοῦντες ἁμαρτῆσαι ἐνώπιον τοῦ Θεοῦ. 8. ὁ μέν Ἰωάννης

[1] Mark has a fondness for such diminutives, sometimes with no change of meaning, as ὠτάριον from οὖς 14.47

ἐβάπτιζεν ὕδατι, οἱ δὲ μαθηταὶ πάντες πλὴν Ἰούδα τοῦ παραδόν-
τος τὸν Ἰησοῦν ἐβαπτίσθησαν ἐν πυρί. 9. πᾶσαν τὴν νύκτα
ἐπάνω κραββάτου ἤμην κατακείμενος μεταξὺ δύο ὑπηρετῶν.
10. τῷ μὲν σώματι ἀσθενής ἐστι, τῇ δὲ ψυχῇ ἰσχυρότερος διὰ
τὴν πίστιν Ἰησοῦ.

Matt. 2.14-15; 6.30; 10.29; 20.13-16; Mark 4.33-34; Luke
8.40-42a; 10.29-35; 16.26; 23.28; John 1.35-39; 3.1-3; 4.41-
42; Acts 10.5-6

Translate: 1. We abstain from wine on this day for the sake of
the weak. 2. For three years I used to dwell opposite this mountain in order to be near my mother. 3. Across the river you will
find some slaves standing outside the city. 4. I swear before God
that I bought these sheep for much money. 5. The rich man
already has his reward; however this poor man, Lazarus by name,
instead of tribulation will have much joy in heaven.

4I   Conditions

Conditions for purposes of translation may roughly be differentiated by the absence or addition of ἄν with the main verb.

I · Main verb (apodosis) without ἄν is a straightforward indicative
or imperative and the *if* clause (protasis) is either:

(a) εἰ with the indicative marking a simple matter of fact, negative οὐ.

εἰ ἐμὲ ἐδίωξαν, καὶ ὑμᾶς διώξουσιν.
If they persecuted me, they will also persecute you.

John 15.20

or (b) ἐάν with the subjunctive, negative μή.

(1) present subj. is either iterative (p. 93) or rather more tentative than the present indicative:

ἐὰν σκανδαλίζῃ σε ἡ χείρ σου, ἀπόκοψον αὐτήν.
If your hand causes you to stumble, cut it off (i.e. if ever). Mark 9.43

Compare Ἐὰν θέλῃς, δύνασαί με καθαρίσαι.
If you wish, you can make me clean (leper speaking hesitantly). Mark 1.40

εἰ θέλεις, ποιήσω ὧδε τρεῖς σκηνάς.
If you wish, I will make three booths here (Peter confidently). Matt. 17.4

(2) aorist subj. for a single event occurring in the future before the action of the main verb (cf. Latin future perfect):

Ἐὰν γὰρ ἀφῆτε τοῖς ἀνθρώποις τὰ παραπτώματα αὐτῶν, ἀφήσει καὶ ὑμῖν ὁ Πατὴρ ὑμῶν ὁ οὐράνιος.
For if you forgive men their trespasses, your heavenly Father will also forgive you. Matt. 6.14

Although there are these subtle distinctions between εἰ with the present or future indic. and ἐάν with the present or aorist subj., they become blurred in English, which usually translates them all by the present.

II · The addition of ἄν with the main verb marks the condition as unreal or unfulfilled, represented in English by *would* or more loosely *should*. The indic. is used in both clauses, the imperfect in reference to continuous action (both in present and past), the aorist for a single act in the past, negative in the *if* clause μή. Note also the frequent εἰ μή, meaning *except*.

137

εἰ γὰρ ἐπιστεύετε Μωϋσεῖ, ἐπιστεύετε ἂν ἐμοί.

For if you believed Moses, you would also believe me.

John 5.46

Κύριε, εἰ ἦς ὧδε, οὐκ ἂν ἀπέθανεν ὁ ἀδελφός μου.

Lord, if you had been here, my brother would not have died.

John 11.32

εἰ μὴ ὅταν ὁ Υἱὸς τοῦ ἀνθρώπου ἐκ νεκρῶν ἀναστῇ.

Except when the Son of Man should rise from the dead.

Mark 9.9

If protasis and apodosis refer to different times this is naturally marked by different tenses:

εἰ τὰ ἐπίγεια εἶπον ὑμῖν καὶ οὐ πιστεύετε, πῶς ἐὰν εἴπω ὑμῖν τὰ ἐπουράνια πιστεύσετε;

If I told you earthly things and you do not believe, how will you believe, if I tell you heavenly things? John 3.12

εἰ μὴ ἦν οὗτος κακὸν ποιῶν, οὐκ ἄν σοι παρεδώκαμεν αὐτόν.

If this man were not (doing wrong) a wrong-doer, we would not have handed him over to you. John 18.30

NB Sometimes ἄν is omitted, but the context will show that the condition was unfulfilled:

οὐκ εἶχες ἐξουσίαν κατ' ἐμοῦ οὐδεμίαν εἰ μὴ ἦν δεδομένον σοι ἄνωθεν.

You would have no authority against me if it had not been given you from above. John 19.11

τε is an enclitic connecting particle, a mark of a literary style. If immediately followed by καί it means *both — and*, but alone and following the word which it links to the preceding one it means *and*:

συνήγαγον πάντας οὓς εὗρον, πονηρούς τε καὶ ἀγαθούς.

They gathered together all whom they found, both bad and good. Matt. 22.10

ἐθαύμαζον ἐπεγίνωσκόν τε αὐτοὺς ὅτι σὺν τῷ Ἰησοῦ ἦσαν.

They marvelled and recognized that they had been with Jesus.

Acts. 4.13

ἀρέσκω*	(w. dat.) please	λυπέω	grieve
δεῖπνον -ου τό	supper	πορνεία -ας ἡ	fornication
κοπίαω	toil	προσέχω	(w. dat.) give
λοιπός -ή -όν	remaining, (as		heed to
	a noun, the	ψεύδομαι (M)	(w. acc.) de-
	rest)		ceive by
τὸ λοιπόν	(adverb) for		lying, (w.
	the rest,		dat.) tell lies
	henceforth		

Translate: 1. εἰ ἔτι ἀνθρώποις ἤρεσκον, Χριστοῦ δοῦλος οὐκ ἂν ἤμην. 2. ἐὰν ἁμαρτήσῃ ὁ ἀδελφός σου, ἐπιτίμησον αὐτῷ καὶ ἐὰν μετανοήσῃ ἄφες αὐτῷ. 3. εἰ προσέχετε τοῖς ψευδομένοις τε καὶ βλασφημοῦσι, ἴστε ὅτι οὐκέτι πιστεύσουσιν ὑμῖν οἱ λοιποί. 4. ἐὰν ἀπολύσῃ τις τὴν γυναῖκα, εἰ μὴ ἐπὶ πορνείᾳ, κατακριθήσεται ἐνώπιον τοῦ Θεοῦ. 5. εἰ ἠγαπᾶτε τοὺς λυποῦντας μισοῦντάς τε ὑμᾶς, οὐκ ἂν ἀποδιδόντες ἦτε αὐτοῖς κακὸν ἀντὶ κακοῦ. 6. εἴ τις δοκεῖ σοφὸς εἶναι ἐν ὑμῖν ἐν τῷ αἰῶνι τούτῳ, μωρὸς γενέσθω ἵνα γένηται σοφός. 7. οὔτε ἐμὲ οἴδατε οὔτε τὸν Πατέρα μου· εἰ γὰρ ἐμὲ ᾔδειτε, καὶ τὸν Πατέρα μου ἂν ᾔδειτε. 8. εἰ δέ τις Πνεῦμα Χριστοῦ οὐκ ἔχει, οὗτος οὐκ ἔστιν αὐτοῦ. 9. ἐὰν λυπῇ τις τὸν ἀδελφὸν αὐτοῦ, δεῖ αὐτὸν εὐθὺς μετανοεῖν, μὴ λυπῆται τὸ Ἅγιον Πνεῦμα. 10. εἰ γὰρ ἔγνωσαν, οὐκ ἂν τὸν Κύριον τῆς δόξης ἐσταύρωσαν. 11. εἰ μὴ παρεγενόμην ἐν ἐκείνῃ τῇ ἡμέρᾳ, οὐκ ἂν εἶδον τοὺς ὄχλους τρέχοντας πρὸς τὸν Ἰησοῦν. 12. εἰ μὴ ἐκοπιάσαμεν δι' ὅλης τῆς νυκτὸς οὔτ' ἂν ἐλάβομεν τοσούτους ἰχθύας οὔτ' ἂν νῦν εἴχομεν αὐτοὺς εἰς δεῖπνον.

Matt. 12.1-9; 23.29-31; 24.43; Luke 16.30-31; 17.3-6; John 14.1-7

Translate: 1. If ever men speak with tongues they ought not to say that they are wiser than the rest of the brothers. 2. Unless you see signs and wonders you will certainly not believe. 3. If the blind witness said this he lied to the rich judge. 4. If the governor allows us to keep this money we shall give it to the poor widow. 5. If you had read the scriptures you would have found these words. 6. If he were a sinner he would not be casting out demons.

139

Optative

As this is so rarely met in the N T only the forms of the regular
verb are given. The present active, middle and passive, are
recognizable by οι, 1st aorist active and middle by αι, 1st and 2nd
aorist passive by ει.

Present	Active		Middle, Passive
	λύοιμι		λυοίμην
	λύοις		λύοιο
	λύοι		λύοιτο
	λύοιμεν		λυοίμεθα
	λύοιτε		λύοισθε
	λύοιεν		λύοιντο

Aorist	Active	Middle	Passive
	λύσαιμι	λυσαίμην	λυθείην
	λύσαις	λύσαιο	λυθείης
	λύσαι[1]	λύσαιτο	λυθείη
	λύσαιμεν	λυσαίμεθα	λυθείημεν
	λύσαιτε	λύσαισθε	λυθείητε
	λύσειαν, λύσαιεν	λύσαιντο	λυθείησαν

The optative has no time distinction between present and aorist,
only the difference between continuous and momentary action which
is found in subjunctive, infinitive and imperative. Therefore like
them it drops the augment in the aorist. The 2nd (strong) aorist
active and middle, as in the infin., participle and imperative, takes
the present endings, φάγοι from ἐσθίω, γένοιτο from γίνομαι.

---

[1] Only in the optative does a final αι rank as long for accentuation. This
may serve to distinguish between the optative and the 1st aorist infinitive active,
e.g. λύσαι and λῦσαι.

NB δῴη — 3rd sing. 2nd aorist optative active of δίδωμι (δοῖ is a κ form of the 2nd aorist subj. active, cf. p. 105), δυναίμην, δύναιντο — 1st sing. and 3rd pl. present optative of δύναμαι, εἴη — 3rd sing. optative of εἰμί *to be*.

Uses of the Optative

1. Wishes, commonest survival in κ, negative μή. These are, with one exception, in the 3rd person.

χάρις ὑμῖν καὶ εἰρήνη πληθυνθείη.
Grace to you and peace be multiplied.   I Peter 1.2

δῴη ἔλεος ὁ Κύριος τῷ 'Ονησιφόρου οἴκῳ.
The Lord grant mercy to the house of Onesiphorus.

II Tim. 1.16

NB The common μὴ γένοιτο (literally: *may it not happen*) is translated in the RV as *God forbid*, in the NEB by a variety of expressions: *Certainly not! By no means. No, No! Of course not. I cannot believe it! Far from it! Never! No, never!*

2. Protasis of a condition viewed as a remote possibility, like CG:

κρεῖττον γὰρ ἀγαθοποιοῦντας, εἰ θέλοι τὸ θέλημα τοῦ Θεοῦ,
πάσχειν ἢ κακοποιοῦντας.
For it is better, if the will of God should so will, that ye
suffer for well-doing than for evil-doing.   I Peter 3.17

NB εἰ τύχοι is a formula found twice in Paul, literally *if it should happen by chance* (strong aorist optative from τυγχάνω *chance*), i.e. *maybe, perhaps*:

οὐ τὸ σῶμα τὸ γενησόμενον σπείρεις, ἀλλὰ γυμνὸν κόκκον
εἰ τύχοι σίτου ἤ τινος τῶν λοιπῶν.
You do not sow the body which shall be, but a bare grain
maybe of wheat or of any of the rest.   I Cor. 15.37

Lucan usage as a literary archaism, only in Luke and Acts.

1. Potential with ἄν in a direct statement or question, giving a note
of hesitancy, as opposed to blunt indicative (3 examples):

πῶς ἂν δυναίμην;
How would I be able? i.e. How could I?   Acts 8.31

141

2. Potential with ἄν in a reported question:

διηπόρει ὁ Πέτρος τί ἂν εἴη τὸ ὅραμα.
Peter was perplexed (literally: as to what the vision might be), i.e. about the meaning of the vision.   Acts 10.17

3. Optative replacing an original indic. or deliberative subj. after a historic main verb, in reported questions:

διελογίζετο ποταπὸς εἴη ὁ ἀσπασμὸς οὗτός.   Luke 1.29
She cast in her mind what manner of salutation this might be (RV).
She wondered what this greeting might mean (NEB).

Translations may vary and there is no rigid criterion.

In κ generally speaking οὐ is found with the indicative, μή with the infinitive, participle, imperative, subjunctive and optative.

ἄμεμπτος -ον	blameless	λογίζομαι (M)	reckon
ἀπώλεια -ας ἡ	destruction	πληθύνω	multiply
διαλογίζομαι (M)	consider	πυνθάνομαι (M)*	enquire
καταρτίζω	put in order, make perfect	τυγχάνω*	happen by chance

Translate: 1. εἶπεν δὲ Μαριαμ,[1] Ἰδοὺ ἡ δούλη Κυρίου· γένοιτό μοι κατὰ τὸ ῥῆμά σου. 2. Πέτρος δὲ εἶπεν πρὸς αὐτόν, Τὸ ἀργύριόν σου σὺν σοὶ εἴη εἰς ἀπώλειαν. 3. καὶ ἐπηρώτησαν τὸν πατέρα τί ἂν θέλοι καλεῖσθαι τὸ παιδίον. 4. αὐτὸς δὲ ὁ Θεὸς τῆς εἰρήνης ἁγιάσαι ὑμᾶς· καὶ ὑμῶν τὸ πνεῦμα καὶ ἡ ψυχὴ καὶ τὸ σῶμα ἀμέμπτως ἐν τῇ παρουσίᾳ τοῦ Κυρίου ἡμῶν Ἰησοῦ Χριστοῦ τηρηθείη. 5. ὥστε ἐπυθόμην εἰ βούλοιτο πορεύεσθαι εἰς Ἱεροσόλυμα. 6. ὁ δὲ τυφλὸς ἀκούσας ὄχλου διαπορευομένου ἐπυνθάνετο τί εἴη τοῦτο. 7. οὐδείς μοι παρεγένετο, ἀλλὰ πάντες με ἐγκατέλιπον· μὴ αὐτοῖς λογισθείη. 8. καὶ διελογίζοντο οἱ δώδεκα τίς ἂν εἴη μείζων αὐτῶν. 9. ἁμαρτήσωμεν, ὅτι οὐκ ἐσμὲν ὑπὸ νόμον ἀλλὰ ὑπὸ χάριν; μὴ γένοιτο. 10. Ὁ δὲ Θεὸς

[1] This is indeclinable transliteration of the Aramaic, but it is also found as Greek Μαρία -ας.

τῆς εἰρήνης, ὁ ἀναγαγὼν ἐκ νεκρῶν τὸν ποιμένα τῶν προβάτων τὸν μέγαν ἐν αἵματι διαθήκης αἰωνίου, τὸν Κύριον ἡμῶν Ἰησοῦν, καταρτίσαι ὑμᾶς ἐν παντὶ ἀγαθῷ εἰς τὸ ποιῆσαι τὸ θέλημα αὐτοῦ.

Mark 11.12-14; Luke 15.25-26; Acts 5.24; I Cor. 14.8-11; Gal. 3.21-25; II Thess. 2.16-17; 3.16

---

43   Some idioms

1. Attraction of the relative pronoun to case of antecedent.

   (*a*) antecedent retained:

   — περὶ πάντων, ὦ Θεόφιλε, ὧν ἤρξατο ὁ Ἰησοῦς ποιεῖν τε καὶ διδάσκειν.

   . . . about all the things, O Theophilus, which Jesus began both to do and teach (ὧν instead of ἃ by attraction)

   Acts 1.1

   (*b*) antecedent retained, but attracted into relative clause:

   κατέναντι οὗ ἐπίστευσεν Θεοῦ

   before God in whom he trusted (instead of Θεοῦ ᾧ)

   Rom. 4.17

   c) antecedent demonstrative omitted:

   μὴ πλείονα σημεῖα ποιήσει ὧν οὗτος ἐποίησεν;

   . . . will he do more signs than those which this man has done? (instead of τούτων (gen. of comparison) ἃ)

   John 7.31

2. τοῦ with the infinitive, i.e. genitive of articular infinitive, which may become a noun clause if the subject of the infin. is added in the acc. (cf. p. 52 for the use of πρό with such a clause).

(a) instead of a simple infin. after a noun or adjective which would normally govern the genitive:

Τῇ δὲ Ελεισαβετ ἐπλήσθη ὁ χρόνος τοῦ τεκεῖν αὐτήν.

Now Elisabeth's time was fulfilled that she should be delivered (RV) (literally: the time of her bearing a child).
Luke 1.57

ἐὰν δὲ ἄξιον ᾖ τοῦ κἀμὲ πορεύεσθαι, σὺν ἐμοὶ πορεύσονται.

And if it be meet for me to go also, they shall go with me (literally: worthy of my going also).   I Cor. 16.4

(b) CG use to express purpose instead of the simple infin.:

ἐξῆλθεν ὁ σπείρων τοῦ σπείρειν.

The sower went forth to sow.   Matt. 13.3

(c) purpose may shade into result:

ἰδὼν ὅτι ἔχει πίστιν τοῦ σωθῆναι.

Seeing that he had faith (so as) to be saved, i.e. made whole.   Acts 14.9

(d) CG construction of a negative infin. after verbs of hindering, preventing and the like, expressing a negative result:

καὶ ταῦτα λέγοντες μόλις κατέπαυσαν τοὺς ὄχλους τοῦ μὴ θύειν αὐτοῖς.

And with these sayings scarce restrained they the multitudes from doing sacrifice unto them. (RV)   Acts 14.18

NB The English idiom after such verbs is *from*, rather than *so as not to*.

(e) Luke-Acts and James, influenced by the LXX, are apt to use the genitive when the article is quite redundant and alien to Greek:

ἡμεῖς δὲ πρὸ τοῦ ἐγγίσαι αὐτὸν ἕτοιμοί ἐσμεν τοῦ ἀνελεῖν αὐτόν.

And we before he draws near are ready to slay him.
Acts 23.15

(τοῦ ἐγγίσαι is normal usage dependent on πρό, but ἕτοιμοι normally takes a simple explanatory infin.)

3. ἵνα clauses with subjunctive. Two main constructions should be familiar by now, ἵνα to introduce purpose, ἵνα to introduce a reported command or request. This latter was a development of κ existing alongside the cg infinitive construction, and in other ways too ἵνα clauses were used as equivalent to the infinitive.

(a) explanatory of a noun or adjective

Compare:

περὶ δὲ τῆς φιλαδελφίας οὐ χρείαν ἔχετε γράφειν ὑμῖν.
But concerning love of the brethren ye have no need that one write unto you.   I Thess. 4.9

οὐ χρείαν ἔχεις ἵνα τις σε ἐρωτᾷ.
You have no need that any one should ask you.

John 16.30

οὗ οὐκ εἰμὶ ἱκανὸς τὰ ὑποδήματα βαστάσαι.
whose shoes I am not fit to carry.   Matt. 3.11

Κύριε, οὐκ εἰμὶ ἱκανὸς ἵνα μου ὑπὸ τὴν στέγην εἰσέλθῃς.
Sir, I am not fit that you should enter under my roof.

Matt. 8.8

(b) equivalent to an infin. clause after a verb

Compare:

συμφέρει ἕνα ἄνθρωπον ἀποθανεῖν ὑπὲρ τοῦ λαοῦ.
It is expedient that one man should die for the people.

John 18.14

συμφέρει ὑμῖν ἵνα εἷς ἄνθρωπος ἀποθάνῃ ὑπὲρ τοῦ λαοῦ.
It is expedient for you that one man should die for the people.   John 11.50

οὐ θέλω δὲ ὑμᾶς κοινωνοὺς τῶν δαιμονίων γίνεσθαι.
I do not wish you to be in fellowship with demons. (Diglot)   I Cor. 10.20

θέλω ἵνα ἐξαυτῆς δῷς μοι ἐπὶ πίνακι τὴν κεφαλὴν Ἰωάννου τοῦ Βαπτιστοῦ.
I will that thou forthwith give me in a charger the head of John the Baptist. (RV)   Mark 6.25

(c) introducing a result:

Ραββει, τίς ἥμαρτεν, οὗτος ἢ οἱ γονεῖς αὐτοῦ, ἵνα τυφλὸς γεννηθῇ;

Rabbi, who did sin, this man or his parents, that he should be born blind? John 9.2

Finally there is the use of ἵνα to introduce a direct command. In most cases this is debateable and will be discussed in commentaries, but there is one clear instance:

ἕκαστος τὴν ἑαυτοῦ γυναῖκα οὕτως ἀγαπάτω ὡς ἑαυτόν, ἡ δὲ γυνὴ ἵνα φοβῆται τὸν ἄνδρα.

Each of you must love his wife as his very self; and the woman must see to it that she pays her husband all respect. (NEB) Eph. 5.33

ἀγνοέω	be ignorant	κωλύω	prevent
ἀθετέω	reject	μήν -ός ὁ	month
ἄνεμος -ου ὁ	wind	οἰκουμένη -ης ἡ	world
θύω	sacrifice	(i.e. γῆ)[2]	
ἐλεημοσύνη -ης ἡ	alms	συμφέρω	bring to-
ἱκανός -ή -όν	fit, suffi-cient[1]		gether, be expedient
κατέχω	keep back, restrain	τρόπος -ου ὁ	way, manner

Translate: 1. οὐκ εἰμὶ ἐγὼ ἱκανὸς ἵνα δοῖ ὁ Κύριός μοι ἔλεος. 2. οὕτως ἐλεύσεται ἐπὶ τῶν νεφελῶν ὃν τρόπον ἐθεάσασθε αὐτὸν πορευόμενον εἰς τὸν οὐρανόν. 3. ἐκάθητο καθ᾽ ἡμέραν πρὸς τὴν θύραν τοῦ ἱεροῦ τοῦ αἰτεῖν ἐλεημοσύνην παρὰ τῶν εἰσπορευομένων. 4. δὸς ἡμῖν ἵνα καθίσωμεν ἐγγὺς σοῦ ὅταν ἔλθῃ ἡ βασιλεία σου. 5. ὡς δὲ συνελθόντες ἐπὶ τὸ αὐτὸ ἠκούσαμεν ταῦτα, παρεκαλοῦμεν ἡμεῖς τε καὶ οἱ λοιποὶ τοῦ μὴ ἀπελθεῖν αὐτόν. 6. ἤμελλε γὰρ ὁ βασιλεὺς ζητεῖν τὸ παιδίον τοῦ ἀπολέσαι αὐτόν. 7. οἱ δὲ ὄχλοι ἐπείραζον κατέχειν αὐτὸν τοῦ μὴ ἀναχωρεῖν. 8. ἐὰν οὖν ἐπιθυμῆτε σωθῆναι, μηδὲν ἀθετεῖτε ὧν

[1] With words implying quantity it denotes a considerable amount, *ἱκανὸν χρόνον* for a long time.
[2] The inhabited earth, i.e. the civilized world.

παραδεδώκασιν ὑμῖν οἱ προφῆται. 9. συμφέρει ἵνα ἐν ἐκείνῳ τῷ μηνὶ θύηται τὸ πασχα. 10. ὁ δὲ Ἰησοῦς εἶπεν ὅτι οὐ θέλει ἵνα οἱ μαθηταὶ κωλύωσι τὰ παιδία τοῦ μὴ ἔρχεσθαι πρὸς αὐτόν. 11. ἄχρι ἧς ἡμέρας ἀνελήμφθη ὁ Κύριος ἠγνόουν οἱ ἀπόστολοι ὅτι δεῖ αὐτοὺς εὐαγγελίζεσθαι καθ᾽ ὅλην τὴν οἰκουμένην. 12. ἡμῖν τί ἀτενίζετε ὡς ἰδίᾳ δυνάμει πεποιηκόσιν τοῦ περιπατεῖν αὐτόν;

Matt. 24.45-47; Luke 1.19-20; 4.42; 5.7-11; 10.18-20; John 15.13; Rom. 6.17-18

---

44 Numerals

Cardinals

1-4 are declinable, 3rd declension adjectives (cf. p. 77).
5-100 are indeclinable.
200 and upwards are 2nd declension adjectives.
30-90 are recognizable by the ending -κοντα, 200-900 by the ending -κόσιοι.
Thousands are formed either by prefixing the numeral adverbs to the adjective χίλιοι, δισχίλιοι, twice 1,000, i.e. 2,000 or by using the cardinal with the collective noun χιλιάς -άδος ἡ (also adjectival, Rev. 7.4). The same principle holds for multiples of 10,000 (μύριοι, μυριάς -άδος ἡ).

Ordinals

These are always 2nd declension adjectives.

Numeral adverbs

After 1st to 3rd these are marked by the ending -κις.

The list below contains only numerals found in the NT. If the numerals 1 to 10, 20, 100, 1,000, 10,000 are memorized along with the rules given above, it should be possible to deduce the meaning of any numeral.

	Cardinals	Ordinals		Adverbials	
1	εἷς μία ἕν	πρῶτος -η -ον	1st	ἅπαξ	once
2	δύο	δεύτερος		δίς	twice
3	τρεῖς	τρίτος		τρίς	thrice
4	τέσσαρες	τέταρτος		τετράκις	4 times
5	πέντε	πέμπτος		πεντάκις	5 times
6	ἕξ	ἕκτος			
7	ἑπτά	ἕβδομος		ἑπτάκις	7 times
8	ὀκτώ	ὄγδοος			
9	ἐννέα	ἔνατος			
10	δέκα	δέκατος			
11	ἕνδεκα	ἑνδέκατος			
12	δώδεκα	δωδέκατος			
14	δεκατέσσαρες	τεσσαρεσκαιδέκατος			
15	δεκαπέντε	πεντεκαιδέκατος			
16	δέκα ἕξ				
18	δέκα ὀκτώ				
20	εἴκοσι(ν)				
30	τριάκοντα				
40	τεσσεράκοντα				
50	πεντήκοντα	πεντηκοστός			
60	ἑξήκοντα				
70	ἑβδομήκοντα			ἑβδομηκοντάκις	
80	ὀγδοήκοντα				
90	ἐνενήκοντα				
100	ἑκατόν				
200	διακόσιοι				
300	τριακόσιοι				
400	τετρακόσιοι				
500	πεντακόσιοι				
600	ἑξακόσιοι				
1,000	χίλιοι				
2,000	δισχίλιοι				
3,000	τρισχίλιοι				

Cardinals

4,000	τετρακισχίλιοι
5,000	πεντακισχίλιοι or χιλιάδες πέντε
7,000	ἑπτακισχίλιοι or χιλιάδες ἑπτά
10,000	μύριοι[1] or δέκα χιλιάδες
12,000	δώδεκα χιλιάδες
20,000	εἴκοσι χιλιάδες or δὶς μυριάδες
50,000	μυριάδες πέντε

δέσμιος -ου ὁ	prisoner	πολλάκις	often
δῶρον -ου τό	gift	χαλκός -οῦ ὁ	brass, money
ἐλεύθερος -α -ον	free		of small
κληρονομέω	inherit,		value
	obtain	χρυσίον -ου τό	gold
νέος -α -ον	young, new	χρυσός -οῦ ὁ	gold
πόλεμος -ου ὁ	war		

Translate: 1. κληρονομήσει οὖν ὁ νέος κληρονόμος τρεῖς ἀμπελῶνας ἔχοντας ἕνα ἕκαστον ἀνὰ ἑβδομήκοντα δένδρα. 2. ὁ δὲ ἕκτος ἐργάτης οὐκ ἤθελεν ἐργάζεσθαι ὥστε μόνον μισθὸν μικρὸν καθ᾽ ἡμέραν δέχεσθαι. 3. ἐν δὲ ἐκείνῳ τῷ πολέμῳ τῶν μὲν ἐλευθέρων ἀνῃρέθησαν τετρακισχίλιοι, τῶν δὲ δούλων χιλιάδες ἑπτὰ καὶ ἑξακόσιοι καὶ ἐνενήκοντα καὶ ἐννέα. 4. τῇ δὲ ἑβδόμῃ παρθένῳ ὑπάρχει οὔτ᾽ ἀργύριον οὔτε χρυσίον· πλήν, ἕνδεκα βούλονται γαμῆσαι αὐτὴν ὅτι καλή ἐστιν καὶ ἀγαθή. 5. ὁ δὲ νεώτερος τῶν δύο ποιμένων διελογίζετο ἐν ἑαυτῷ λέγων, Τί ποιήσω; πλανῶνται γὰρ ὀγδοήκοντα ἑπτὰ πρόβατα οὐδὲ πολλάκις ζητήσας δύναμαι εὑρεῖν τὰ ἀπολωλότα. 6. τῇ δὲ τρίτῃ ἡμέρᾳ ἀνέστη ἐκ νεκρῶν καὶ ἐφανερώθη ἐπάνω πεντακοσίοις ἀδελφοῖς. 7. ἀλλ᾽ ἐν τῇ πεντηκοστῇ (ἡμέρᾳ) συνηγμένοι ἦσαν εἰς Ιερουσαλημ ὡσεὶ ἑκατὸν εἴκοσι ἀδελφοί. 8. οὗτος θέλει ἵνα ἀγοράσωμεν ἐξ ἄρτους τριῶν δηναρίων εἰς τὸ παραθεῖναι ταύταις ταῖς ὀκτὼ χήραις. 9. καὶ ἔκραξαν φωνῇ μεγάλῃ οἱ μύριοι ἅγιοι εὐλογοῦντες τὸν Θεόν. 10. δεσμίους δὲ χιλίους ἤγαγον εἰς Δαμασκὸν ὧν τετρακοσίους ἔλιπον ἐκεῖ πεντακοσίους τε παρέδωκαν τῷ βασιλεῖ καὶ ἑκατὸν εὐθὺς ἀπέκτειναν. 11. τρὶς οὖν ἔφερον χρυσόν τε καὶ

[1] Used already in CG for countless multitudes.

χαλκόν, ὁ δὲ ἄρχων οὐκ ἤθελε λαβεῖν μήποτε εἴπῃ τις ὅτι δώροις πεισθεὶς μέλλει ἀδίκως κρίνειν. 12. ὁ δὲ δωδέκατος ὁ παραδοὺς τὸν Χριστὸν τέθνηκε· δεῖ οὖν ἡμᾶς τοὺς λοιποὺς ἔνδεκα ἐκλέξασθαι ἕνα μάρτυρα τῆς ἀναστάσεως.

Matt. 14.15-21; 18.21-22; 20.3-7; Luke 10.17; John 21.11; Acts 2.41; 27.37; I Cor. 15.5; 16.8; Rev. 13.18

45 Semitisms[1]

There are a number of secondary Semitisms in the NT when the Greek is possible but unidiomatic and probably influenced by a Semitic construction. Such are the redundant ἀναστάς and ἤρξατο and ἀποκριθεὶς εἶπεν (sometimes even used to begin speech, Matt. 28.5). RV meticulously translates these, but the NEB sometimes omits as inessential.

Major Semitisms (often found in OT quotations) are not only bad Greek but are apt to cause difficulty in translation, so the more common are given below:

1. A special form of the infinitive known as the infin. absolute was used in Hebrew to add emphasis to the verb. Attempts are made to reproduce this by:

   (a) dative of a noun cognate with the verb:

   > Ἐπιθυμίᾳ ἐπεθύμησα τοῦτο τὸ πασχα φαγεῖν μεθ' ὑμῶν πρὸ τοῦ με παθεῖν.
   >
   > With desire I have desired to eat this passover with you before I suffer. (Bad English, bad Greek — I have earnestly desired, Diglot.) Luke 22.15

[1] The term covers both Hebrew and Aramaic, which had many similarities. The only longer passages in the NT consistently showing distinctively Hebrew idiom are Luke 1-2 and parts of Revelation.

(b) participle along with the verb:

εὐλογῶν εὐλογήσω σε καὶ πληθύνων πληθυνῶ σε.

I will indeed bless you and multiply you. (Diglot)

Heb. 6.13 (Gen. 22.17)

(c) cognate accusative of noun along with verb:

καὶ ἐφοβήθησαν φόβον μέγαν.

And they feared exceedingly. Mark 4.41

2. impersonal use of ἐγένετο:

(a) parataxis, when the main verb stands without any connecting link (cf. p. 41):

Καὶ ἐγένετο ἐν ἐκείναις ταῖς ἡμέραις ἦλθεν Ἰησοῦς ἀπὸ Ναζαρεθ.

And it came to pass in those days that Jesus came from Nazareth. Mark 1.9

(b) with acc. (more rarely dat.) and infin. clause:

Ἐγένετο δὲ ἐν σαββάτῳ διαπορεύεσθαι αὐτὸν διὰ σπορίμων.

Now it came to pass on a sabbath that he was going through the cornfields. Luke 6.1

(c) linked with main verb by redundant, untranslatable καί:

Καὶ ἐγένετο ἐν μιᾷ τῶν ἡμερῶν καὶ αὐτὸς ἦν διδάσκων.

And it came to pass on one of those days that he was teaching. Luke 5.17

3. use of προστίθεμαι for repetition or proceeding to take action:

καὶ προσέθετο ἕτερον πέμψαι δοῦλον.

And again he sent another servant. Luke 20.11[1]

4. addition of a demonstrative pronoun after a relative. This was a necessary addition to the Semitic relative which was indeclinable, so that the demonstrative defined case, number and gender, but is untranslatable in English:

οὗ οὐκ εἰμὶ ἱκανὸς λῦσαι τὸν ἱμάντα τῶν ὑποδημάτων αὐτοῦ. Luke 3.16

the latchet of whose shoes I am not worthy to unloose

[1] Matthew and Mark in their parallel passages write πάλιν ἀπέστειλεν.

5. εἰς with acc. instead of predicative nom. or acc.:

καὶ ηὔξησεν καὶ ἐγένετο εἰς δένδρον.
And it grew and became a tree.   Luke 13.19

6. casus pendens, usually nominative, i.e. a noun left in the air,
   outside the construction of the sentence:

ὁ γὰρ Μωϋσῆς οὗτος, ὃς ἐξήγαγεν ἡμᾶς ἐκ γῆς Αἰγύπτου,
οὐκ οἴδαμεν τί ἐγένετο αὐτῷ.
For as for this Moses, who led us forth from the land of Egypt,
we do not know what has become of him.
                                     Acts 7.40 (Ex. 32.23)

7. descriptive genitive where Greek and English use adjective:

καὶ ἐπῄνεσεν ὁ κύριος τὸν οἰκονόμον τῆς ἀδικίας.
And his lord commended the unrighteous steward.
                                                      Luke 16.8

8. metaphorical use of υἱός or τέκνον with genitive; this may sometimes be retained, but note:

οἱ υἱοὶ τοῦ νυμφῶνος
literally: the sons of the bride-chamber, i.e. the bridegroom's
friends.   Mark 2.19

9. οὐ (μή) ... πᾶς where πᾶς is equivalent to indefinite, not ... any:

οὐδέποτε ἔφαγον πᾶν κοινὸν καὶ ἀκάθαρτον.
I have never eaten anything that is common and unclean.
                                                     Acts 10.14

10. prepositional phrases formed with πρόσωπον (face, person):

    (a) ἀπὸ προσώπου from, from the presence of

        Οἱ μὲν οὖν ἐπορεύοντο χαίροντες ἀπὸ προσώπου τοῦ
        συνεδρίου.
        So they went out from the Council rejoicing.   Acts 5.41

    (b) πρὸ προσώπου before, in front of

        καὶ ἀπέστειλεν ἀγγέλους πρὸ προσώπου αὐτοῦ.
        And he sent messengers ahead. (NEB)   Luke 9.52

11. distributive expressed by repetition either of cardinal number or of noun itself:

δύο δύο
two by two

Mark 6.7

καὶ ἀνέπεσαν πρασιαὶ πρασιαί.
And they sat down in ranks.

Mark 6.40

12. use of cardinal for ordinal numeral:

τῇ μιᾷ τῶν σαββάτων
On the first day of the week

Mark 16.2

Matt. 2.10; 10.14; Mark 1.1-2b; 6.39; 10.6-8; 13.20; Luke 3.17; 5.1-2; 15.17-20; 19.11; Acts 13.23-24; 20.7; James 5.16-18; Rev. 7.2; 17.6-7

ENCLITICS

These are words so weak that they throw back their accent onto the preceding word whenever possible, monosyllabic enclitics always losing their accent. They comprise:

(1) Present indicative of $εἰμί$[1] and $φημί$, except 2nd sing. $εἶ$ (pp. 25, 111).

(2) Unemphatic $με$, $μου$, $μοι$, $σε$, $σου$, $σοι$.

(3) Indefinite $τις$, $τι$ (p. 74), $ποτέ$, $που$, $πως$ (p. 92), $τε$ (p. 138), $γε$ (a literary emphasizing particle).

Rules for use:

1. Enclitic following such words as $ἄνθρωπος$ and $δοῦλος$ throws back an acute accent onto the ultimate: $ἄνθρωπός$ $τις$. $δοῦλός$ $τις$.

2. Enclitic following such words as $ἀδελφός$ throws back its accent so as to give a final acute instead of a grave: $ἀδελφός$ $τις$.

3. Enclitic following such a word as $λόγος$ cannot throw back its accent, as two acutes cannot stand on adjacent syllables; therefore monosyllabic enclitics lose their accent, but disyllabic keep it on the ultimate: $λόγος$ $τις$. $ὁ$ $λόγος$ $ἐστὶ$ $πονηρός$.

4. Enclitic following such a word as $γῆ$ loses its accent:

$γῆ$ $τις$. $ἡ$ $γῆ$ $ἐστι$ $καλή$.

NB Enclitics are to be distinguished from the small group of words which have no accent at all: $ὁ$ $ἡ$ $οἱ$ $αἱ$, $εἰς$, $ἐν$, $ἐκ$, $οὐ$, $ὡς$.

---

[1] If the verb *to be* is not used simply as a link verb between subject and predicative, but implies existence, it takes a regular accent, e.g.

$εἷς$ $ἐστιν$ $καὶ$ $οὐκ$ $ἔστιν$ $ἄλλος$ $πλὴν$ $αὐτοῦ$.
He is one and there is none other but he.   Mark 12.32

PRINCIPAL PARTS OF VERBS

PRESENT	FUTURE	AORIST	PERF. ACT.	PERF. PASS.	AORIST PASS.
ἀγγέλλω announce	ἀγγελῶ	ἤγγειλα		ἤγγελμαι	ἠγγέλην
ἄγω lead	ἄξω	ἤγαγον		ἦγμαι	ἤχθην
αἱρέω take	αἱρήσω	εἷλον		ᾕρημαι	ᾑρέθην
αἴρω take up	ἀρῶ	ἦρα	ἦρκα	ἦρμαι	ἤρθην
ἀκούω hear	ἀκούσω ἀκούσομαι	ἤκουσα	ἀκήκοα		ἠκούσθην
ἁμαρτάνω sin	ἁμαρτήσω	ἡμάρτησα ἥμαρτον	ἡμάρτηκα		
ἀνοίγω open	ἀνοίξω	ἀνέῳξα ἠνέῳξα ἤνοιξα	ἀνέῳγα	ἀνέῳγμαι	ἀνεῴχθην ἠνεῴχθην ἠνοίχθην
ἀποθνῄσκω die	ἀποθανοῦμαι	ἀπέθανον	τέθνηκα		
ἀποκτείνω kill	ἀποκτενῶ	ἀπέκτεινα			ἀπεκτάνθην

PRESENT	FUTURE	AORIST	PERF. ACT.	PERF. PASS.	AORIST PASS.
ἀπόλλυμι destroy	ἀπολῶ	ἀπώλεσα	ἀπόλωλα		
intr. perish	ἀπολοῦμαι	ἀπωλόμην			
ἀποστέλλω send forth	ἀποστελῶ	ἀπέστειλα	ἀπέσταλκα	ἀπέσταλμαι	ἀπεστάλην
ἀρέσκω please	ἀρέσω	ἤρεσα			
ἁρπάζω snatch	ἁρπάσω	ἥρπασα			ἡρπάσθην ἡρπάγην
-βαίνω come	-βήσομαι	-ἔβην	-βέβηκα		
βάλλω throw	βαλῶ	ἔβαλον	βέβληκα	βέβλημαι	ἐβλήθην
βούλομαι wish					ἐβουλήθην
γαμέω marry		ἐγάμησα ἔγημα	γεγάμηκα		
γίνομαι become	γενήσομαι	ἐγενόμην	γέγονα	γεγένημαι	ἐγενήθην
γινώσκω know	γνώσομαι	ἔγνων	ἔγνωκα	ἔγνωσμαι	ἐγνώσθην

Present	Future	Aorist	Perfect Act.	Perfect Mid./Pass.	Aorist Pass.
γράφω write	γράψω	ἔγραψα	γέγραφα	γέγραμμαι	ἐγράφην
δέομαι beg					ἐδεήθην
δίδωμι give	δώσω	ἔδωκα, ἐδόμην	δέδωκα	δέδομαι	ἐδόθην
δοκέω seem		ἔδοξα			
δύναμαι[1] be able	δυνήσομαι				ἠδυνήθην, ἠδυνάσθην
ἐάω[2] allow	ἐάω	εἴασα			
ἐγείρω rouse	ἐγερῶ	ἤγειρα		ἐγήγερμαι	ἠγέρθην
εἰμί be	ἔσομαι	ἤμην			
ἐντέλλομαι order	ἐντελοῦμαι	ἐνετειλάμην		ἐντέταλμαι	
ἔρχομαι come	ἐλεύσομαι	ἦλθον	ἐλήλυθα		

[1] Imperfect ἠδυνάμην, ἐδυνάμην.   [2] Imperfect εἴων.

PRESENT	FUTURE	AORIST	PERF. ACT.	PERF. PASS.	AORIST PASS.
ἐσθίω eat	φάγομαι	ἔφαγον			
εὑρίσκω find	εὑρήσω	εὗρον	εὕρηκα		εὑρέθην
ἔχω[1] have	ἕξω	ἔσχον	ἔσχηκα		
θέλω[2] wish	θελήσω	ἠθέλησα			
-ἵημι let go	-ἥσω	-ἧκα	-εἷκα	-εἷμαι	-έθην
ἵστημι stand	στήσω	ἔστησα ἔστην	ἕστηκα		ἐστάθην
καλέω call	καλέσω	ἐκάλεσα	κέκληκα	κέκλημαι	ἐκλήθην
κλαίω weep	κλαύσω	ἔκλαυσα			
κόπτω cut	κόψω	ἔκοψα			ἐκόπην
κράζω cry out	κράξω	ἔκραξα	κέκραγα		

[1] Imperfect εἶχον.   [2] Imperfect ἤθελον.

Present	Future	Aorist	Perfect Active	Perfect M/P	Aorist Passive
κρίνω judge	κρινῶ	ἔκρινα	κέκρικα	κέκριμαι	ἐκρίθην
κρύπτω hide		ἔκρυψα		κέκρυμμαι	ἐκρύβην
λαμβάνω take	λήμψομαι	ἔλαβον	εἴληφα	εἴλημμαι	ἐλήμφθην
λέγω say	ἐρῶ	εἶπον	εἴρηκα	εἴρημαι	ἐρρέθην ἐρρήθην
λείπω leave	λείψω	ἔλειψα ἔλιπον		λέλειμμαι	ἐλείφθην
μανθάνω learn		ἔμαθον	μεμάθηκα		
μέλλω[1] be about to	μελλήσω				
μένω remain	μενῶ	ἔμεινα	μεμένηκα		
μιμνήσκομαι remember	μνησθήσομαι			μέμνημαι	ἐμνήσθην
ξηραίνω wither		ἐξήρανα		ἐξήραμμαι	ἐξηράνθην
οἶδα know	εἰδήσω	ᾔδειν			

[1] Imperfect ἤμελλον.

PRESENT	FUTURE	AORIST	PERF. ACT.	PERF. PASS.	AORIST PASS.
ὄμνυμι swear		ὤμοσα			
ὁράω[1] see	ὄψομαι	εἶδον	ἑόρακα ἑώρακα		ὤφθην
πάσχω suffer		ἔπαθον	πέπονθα		
πείθω persuade	πείσω	ἔπεισα	πέποιθα	πέπεισμαι	ἐπείσθην
πίνω drink	πίομαι	ἔπιον	πέπωκα		ἐπόθην
πίπτω fall	πεσοῦμαι	ἔπεσον	πέπτωκα		
πυνθάνομαι enquire		ἐπυθόμην			
σβέννυμι quench	σβέσω	ἔσβεσα			
σπείρω sow		ἔσπειρα		ἔσπαρμαι	ἐσπάρην
σώζω save	σώσω	ἔσωσα	σέσωκα	σέσωσμαι	ἐσώθην

[1] Imperfect.

τελέω end	τελέσω	ἐτέλεσα	τετέλεκα	τετέλεσμαι	ἐτελέσθην
τίθημι place	θήσω	ἔθηκα ἐθέμην	τέθεικα	τέθειμαι	ἐτέθην
τίκτω bear	τέξομαι	ἔτεκον			ἐτέχθην
τρέπω turn		ἐτρεψάμην			ἐτράπην
τρέχω run		ἔδραμον			
τυγχάνω chance		ἔτυχον			
φαίνω appear	φανήσομαι φανοῦμαι	ἔφανα			ἐφάνην
φέρω bear	οἴσω	ἤνεγκον ἤνεγκα	ἐνήνοχα		ἠνέχθην
φεύγω flee	φεύξομαι	ἔφυγον	πέφευγα		
φθείρω destroy	φθερῶ	ἔφθειρα		ἔφθαρμαι	ἐφθάρην
χαίρω rejoice	χαιρήσομαι				ἐχάρην

CONSPECTUS FOR CONSULTATION AND REVISION

Verbs

Present: present stem + present endings.

	Active		Middle, Passive	
	Indic.	Subj.	Indic.	Subj.
	λύω	λύω	λύομαι	λύωμαι
	λύεις	λύῃς	λύει(-ῃ)	λύῃ
	λύει	λύῃ	λύεται	λύηται
	λύομεν	λύωμεν	λυόμεθα	λυώμεθα
	λύετε	λύητε	λύεσθε	λύησθε
	λύουσι(ν)	λύωσι(ν)	λύονται	λύωνται

NB The subjunctive is differentiated from the indicative by the lengthening of the vowels in the endings.

Imperative: present stem + endings for 2nd and 3rd persons; 1st persons are expressed by the subjunctive.

		Active	Middle, Passive
sing.	2	λῦε	λύου
	3	λυέτω	λυέσθω
pl.	2.	λύετε	λύεσθε
	3.	λυέτωσαν	λυέσθωσαν

Infinitive: present stem + ειν —λύειν.
                  present stem + εσθαι —λύεσθαι.

Participle: present stem + Third decl. endings
                  present stem + Second decl. endings

λύων λύουσα λῦον   λυόμενος -η -ον

Rules for the temporal augment:

1. ε   before initial consonant of stem
2. α   becomes   η
    αι   ᾳ
    ε   ῃ
    ο   ω
    οι   ῳ

Imperfect: prefix of temporal augment to present stem, +imperfect endings.

Indicative

Active	Middle, Passive
ἔλυον	ἐλυόμεν
ἔλυες	ἐλύου
ἔλυε(ν)	ἐλύετο
ἐλύομεν	ἐλυόμεθα
ἐλύετε	ἐλύεσθε
ἔλυον	ἐλύοντο

The imperfect has no subjunctive, imperative, infinitive or participle.

Future: stem +σ (Active, Middle) or +θησ (Passive) and present endings in all parts.

Indicative

Active	Middle	Passive
λύσω	λύσομαι	λυθήσομαι
λύσεις	λύσει(-ῃ)	λυθήσει(-ῃ)
λύσει	λύσεται	λυθήσεται
λύσομεν	λυσόμεθα	λυθησόμεθα
λύσετε	λύσεσθε	λυθήσεσθε
λύσουσι(ν)	λύσονται	λυθήσονται

Infinitive

λύσειν	λύσεσθαι	λυθήσεσθαι

Participle

λύσων λύσουσα λῦσον	λυσόμενος -η -ον	λυθησόμενος -η -ον

The future has no subjunctive or imperative.

See p. 166 for changes in consonantal stems before other consonants.

Verb to be

	Present		Future	Imperfect
Indic.	Subj.			
εἰμί	ὦ		ἔσομαι	ἤμην
εἶ	ᾖς		ἔσει(-η)	ἦσθα, ἦς
ἐστί(ν)	ᾖ		ἔσται	ἦν
ἐσμέν	ὦμεν		ἐσόμεθα	ἦμεν, ἤμεθα
ἐστέ	ἦτε		ἔσεσθε	ἦτε
εἰσί(ν)	ὦσι(ν)		ἔσονται	ἦσαν

Imperative

ἴσθι	Present infinitive	εἶναι
ἔστω, ἤτω	Future infinitive	ἔσεσθαι
ἔστε	Present participle	ὤν οὖσα ὄν
ἔστωσαν	Future participle	ἐσόμενος -η -ον

Aorist (1st, weak): temporal augment prefixed to stem $+\sigma$ (Active, Middle) or $+\theta$ (Passive), and aorist endings.

Indicative	Active	Middle	Passive
	ἔλυσα	ἐλυσάμην	ἐλύθην
	ἔλυσας	ἐλύσω	ἐλύθης
	ἔλυσε(ν)	ἐλύσατο	ἐλύθη
	ἐλύσαμεν	ἐλυσάμεθα	ἐλύθημεν
	ἐλύσατε	ἐλύσασθε	ἐλύθητε
	ἔλυσαν	ἐλύσαντο	ἐλύθησαν

Subjunctive: aorist stem+present endings (Active, Middle), +present Active endings, accentuation different (Passive).

	λύσω	λύσωμαι	λυθῶ
	λύσῃς	λύσῃ	λυθῇς
	λύσῃ	λύσηται	λυθῇ
	λύσωμεν	λυσώμεθα	λυθῶμεν
	λύσητε	λύσησθε	λυθῆτε
	λύσωσι(ν)	λύσωνται	λυθῶσι(ν)

Imperative	λῦσον	λῦσαι	λύθητι[1]
	λυσάτω	λυσάσθω	λυθήτω
	λύσατε	λύσασθε	λύθητε
	λυσάντων	λυσάσθωσαν	λυθήτωσαν

| Infinitive | λῦσαι | λύσασθαι | λυθῆναι |
| Participle | λύσας-ασα-αν | λυσάμενος-η-ον | λυθείς-εῖσα-έν |

Aorist (2nd strong): temporal augment+strong stem, imperfect endings (Active, Middle), weak aorist endings (Passive).

Indicative	Active	Middle	Passive
	ἔλαβον	ἐγενόμην	ἐγράφην
	ἔλαβες	ἐγένου	ἐγράφης
	ἔλαβε(ν)	ἐγένετο	ἐγράφη
	ἐλάβομεν	ἐγενόμεθα	ἐγράφημεν
	ἐλάβετε	ἐγένεσθε	ἐγράφητε
	ἔλαβον	ἐγένοντο	ἐγράφησαν

NB Subjunctive, imperative, infinitive, participle — strong stem + present endings (Active, Middle), +aorist endings (Passive).

Subjunctive	λάβω	γένωμαι	γράφω
Imperative	λαβέ	γενοῦ	γράφηθι[1]
	λαβέτω	γενέσθω	γραφήτω
	λάβετε	γένεσθε	γράφητε
	λαβέτωσαν	γενέσθωσαν	γραφήτωσαν
Infinitive	λαβεῖν	γενέσθαι	γραφῆναι
Participle	λαβών-οῦσα-όν	γενομένος-η-ον	γραφείς-εῖσα-έν

[1]NB Slight difference between weak and strong aorist endings.

Perfect: reduplication (see p. 95)+stem+perfect ending. In the strong perfect there is a strong stem (no κ), but the same endings.

Indicative	Active	Middle, Passive
	λέλυκα	λέλυμαι
	λέλυκας	λέλυσαι
	λέλυκε(ν)	λέλυται
	λελύκαμεν	λελύμεθα
	λελύκατε	λέλυσθε
	λελύκασι(ν)	λέλυνται

Subjunctive and imperative are rarely found.

Infinitive	λελυκέναι	λελύσθαι
Participle	λελυκώς-υῖα-ός	λελυμένος-η-ον

Pluperfect: temporal augment (sometimes dropped)+perfect stem as above+pluperfect endings.

Indicative	Active	Middle, Passive
	ἐλελύκειν	ἐλελύμην
	ἐλελύκεις	ἐλέλυσο
	ἐλελύκει	ἐλέλυτο
	ἐλελύκειμεν	ἐλελύμεθα
	ἐλελύκειτε	ἐλέλυσθε
	ἐλελύκεισαν	ἐλέλυντο

The pluperfect has no subjunctive, imperative, infinitive, or participle.

NB Consonantal stems in both perfect and pluperfect (Middle, Passive) form infinitive in -θαι, not -σθαι, 2nd person pl. in -θε not -σθε.

Consonantal stems: changes through combination with other consonants are clearly seen in the Principal Parts (see p. 102).

Gutturals κ, χ, γ (may be concealed by σσ in present stem):

δίωκω, διώξω, ἐδίωξα, δεδίωκα, δεδίωγμαι, ἐδιώχθην.

Labials π, φ, β (may be concealed by ππ in present stem):

γράφω, γράψω, ἔγραψα, γέγραφα, γέγραμμαι, ἐγράφην (ἐπέμφθην).

Dentals τ, θ, δ (may be concealed by ζ in present stem):

πείθω, πείσω, ἔπεισα, πέπεικα, πέπεισμαι, ἐπείσθην.

Examples of the perfect Middle and Passive are given below for reference, but will not be found often.

δεδίωγμαι	γέγραμμαι	πέπεισμαι
δεδίωξαι	γέγραψαι	πέπεισαι
δεδίωκται	γέγραπται	πέπεισται
δεδιώγμεθα	γεγράμμεθα	πεπείσμεθα
δεδίωχθε	γέγραφθε	πέπεισθε
δεδιωγμένοι εἰσί(ν)	γεγραμμένοι εἰσί(ν)	πεπεισμένοι εἰσί(ν)

Liquids λ, μ, ν, ρ have the same basic endings as other verbs, except in the future (contracted), but have such peculiarities and irregularities that no brief summary can be adequate (see pp. 71ff., 97).

Contracted verbs (contraction occurs only in present and imperfect; in all other tenses the stem vowel is lengthened, ε to η, α to η, o to ω).

Stem in ε: ε drops out before ω, ει, η, and ου; ε+ε=ει, ε+o=ου.

Present indicative		Imperfect indicative	
Active	Middle, Passive	Active	Middle, Passive
φιλῶ	φιλοῦμαι	ἐφίλουν	ἐφιλούμην
φιλεῖς	φιλεῖ(-ῇ)	ἐφίλεις	ἐφιλοῦ
φιλεῖ	φιλεῖται	ἐφίλει	ἐφιλεῖτο
φιλοῦμεν	φιλούμεθα	ἐφιλοῦμεν	ἐφιλούμεθα
φιλεῖτε	φιλεῖσθε	ἐφιλεῖτε	ἐφιλεῖσθε
φιλοῦσι(ν)	φιλοῦνται	ἐφίλουν	ἐφιλοῦντο

The subjunctive has the same endings as λύω.

Imperative		Infinitive	
Active	Middle, Passive	Active	Middle, Passive
φίλει	φιλοῦ	φιλεῖν	φιλεῖσθαι
φιλείτω	φιλείσθω	Participle	
φιλεῖτε	φιλεῖσθε	φιλῶν-οῦσα-ουν	φιλούμενος-η-ον
φιλείτωσαν	φιλείσθωσαν		

Stem in α: α drops out before ω; α+ε=α; α+ει or α+η=ᾳ; α+o or α+ου=ω.

Present indicative		Imperfect indicative	
Active	Middle, Passive	Active	Middle, Passive
τιμῶ	τιμῶμαι	ἐτίμων	ἐτιμώμην
τιμᾷς	τιμᾷ	ἐτίμας	ἐτιμῶ
τιμᾷ	τιμᾶται	ἐτίμα	ἐτιμᾶτο
τιμῶμεν	τιμώμεθα	ἐτιμῶμεν	ἐτιμώμεθα
τιμᾶτε	τιμᾶσθε	ἐτιμᾶτε	ἐτιμᾶσθε
τιμῶσι(ν)	τιμῶνται	ἐτίμων	ἐτιμῶντο

Indicative and subjunctive have the same endings.

Imperative		Infinitive	
Active	Middle, Passive	Active	Middle, Passive
τίμα	τιμῶ	τιμᾶν	τιμᾶσθαι
τιμάτω	τιμάσθω	Participle	
τιμᾶτε	τιμᾶσθε	τιμῶν -ῶσα -ῶν	τιμώμενος -η -ον
τιμάτωσαν	τιμάσθωσαν		

Stem in o: o drops out before ω or ου; o+ε or o+o=ου; o+ει or o+η=οι; o+η=ω.

Present indicative		Imperfect indicative	
Active	Middle, Passive	Active	Middle, Passive
πληρῶ	πληροῦμαι	ἐπλήρουν	ἐπληρούμην
πληροῖς	πληροῖ	ἐπλήρους	ἐπλήρου
πληροῖ	πληροῦται	ἐπλήρου	ἐπληροῦτο
πληροῦμεν	πληρούμεθα	ἐπληροῦμεν	ἐπληρούμεθα
πληροῦτε	πληροῦσθε	ἐπληροῦτε	ἐπληροῦσθε
πληροῦσι(ν)	πληροῦνται	ἐπλήρουν	ἐπληροῦντο

Subjunctive has the same endings as λύω, except for πληροῖς, πληροῖ, πληρῶτε.

168

| | Imperative | | Infinitive | |
| | Active | Middle, Passive | Active | Middle, Passive |

Imperative		Infinitive	
Active	Middle, Passive	Active	Middle, Passive
πλήρου	πληροῦ	πληροῦν	πληροῦσθαι
πληρούτω	πληρούτω	Participle	
πληροῦτε	πληροῦσθε	πληρῶν -οῦσα -ουν	
πληρούτωσαν	πληρούσθωσαν		πληρούμενος -η -ον

Nouns

Proper names

Semitic personal names and place names from the OT were usually transliterated and indeclinable, e.g. Αδαμ (printed without accents and without breathings in Kilpatrick's Bible Society edition). In the NT period Hellenization was more common. Some names fit into regular declension patterns: 1st: Ἰωάννης, Ζαχαρίας; 2nd: Ἰάκωβος; 3rd: Σίμων. In the 1st declension even some stems ending in a consonant are found with a nominative ending in -ας, not -ης, and a Dorian dialect form of the genitive in -α. Jesus too is peculiar; consistency cannot be expected. Μαριαμ co-exists with Μαρία, Ιερουσαλημ (indeclinable fem. sing.) with Ἱεροσόλυμα (2nd neuter plural), and a name may fluctuate between two declensions.

N.	Σατανᾶς	Ἰησοῦς	Μωϋσῆς[1]
V.	Σατανᾶ	Ἰησοῦ	Μωϋσῆ
A.	Σατανᾶν	Ἰησοῦν	Μωϋσεα -ῆν
G.	Σατανᾶ	Ἰησοῦ	Μωϋσέως
D.	Σατανᾷ	Ἰησοῦ	Μωϋσει -ῆ

[1] The two small dots over ϋ show that the two vowels were to be pronounced separately.

Except when there are Anglicized forms, e.g. Timothy, translators use the conventional Latinized forms of the Vulgate. 1st and 3rd declension forms accept transliteration, but in the 2nd declension -us replaces -os: $N\iota\kappa\acute{o}\delta\eta\mu os$, Nicodemus; in the plural -i replaces -οι: $\Phi\iota\lambda\iota\pi\pi o\iota$, Philippi. Consonantal changes are what one would expect: θ, χ, ϕ, ψ become th, ch, ph, ps, and a rough breathing is replaced by an initial h, $\dot{\epsilon}\rho\mu\hat{a}s$, Hermas. Consonantal $\dot{I}$ becomes J, $\dot{I}\eta\sigma ovs$, Jesus, κ (non-existent in Latin) becomes c, $K\iota\lambda\iota\kappa\acute{\iota}a$, Cilicia. There can be no differentiation between ϵ and η, both e, nor o and ω, both o. Short v becomes y, $K\acute{v}\pi\rho os$ Cyprus (Latin 2nd declension ending); ov represents Latin long u, $\ddot{A}v\gamma ovoros$, Augustus, οι becomes oe, $\Phi o\acute{\iota}\beta\eta$, Phoebe, αι becomes ae, $Ko\lambda o\sigma\sigma a\acute{\iota}$, Colossae.

The above are only rough guide-lines, but proper names are generally preceded by the article and this is a reliable means of identifying the case and gender of the noun.

GLOSSARY OF GRAMMATICAL TERMS

These, like all technical jargon, when once mastered offer a quick and easy means of reference. Terms already explained in the text are given reference only; terms of self-evident meaning are not included. Page references are normally to the first occurrence; where terms are mentioned only in passing, either in text or notes, the reference is given in brackets.

Active
: Form of verb when the subject does what the verb indicates: *I loose*; *she suffered*, p. 11. (Contrast with Middle, involving self-interest, p. 34; Passive, p. 37.)

Adjective
: Qualifies noun: *brave* soldiers, p. 20.

Adverb
: Modifies verb, adjective or another adverb: We fought *bravely*; *fairly* brave; *really* bravely, p. 53.

Antecedent
: The noun or pronoun to which the relative refers: *Herod*, who said this, is dead, p. 41.

Aorist
: See pp. 28, 49.

Apostrophe
: A symbol (') showing the omission of a letter: *Don't*, p. 23 n. 1.

Apposition
: Placing of a noun or pronoun alongside another noun or pronoun, both referring to the same thing: Herod, *the king*, said this, p. 31.

Article
: Adjective which limits a noun. **Definite** (the): *The* king, p. 12. **Indefinite** (a, an): *A* king, p. 74, usually not expressed in Greek.

Aspirate
: H sound, as in *H*erod, p. 10.

Augment
: See p. 22.

Breathing
: See p. 10.

Cardinal
: Numbers expressing quantity: *one*, *two*, *three*, p. 147.

Case
: Ending of a noun, pronoun, or adjective, to show its relationship to other words in the sentence. The cases are: **Nominative, vocative, accusative, genitive, dative**. For explanation of their functions, see p. 13.

Clause	Sentence or part-sentence containing a verb or verbal equivalent: When he spoke (subordinate clause), they all cheered (main clause); see p. 37. Subordinate clauses often found are:
	Temporal: *When he came,* I saw him.
	Conditional: *If he comes,* I shall see him.
	Causal: *Because he did this,* he was punished.
	Concessive: *Although he sinned,* he was forgiven.
	Purpose (final): *In order that he might escape,* he ran away.
	Relative: Herod, *who said this,* is dead.
Cognate	Sharing the same stem: *king* and *kingdom* (p. 42).
Comma	Smallest punctuation mark (,), dividing one word or phrase or clause from another.
Compound	Verbs, nouns, adjectives, adverbs with a prefix, often of a preposition, to the basic stem: *overturn, upstart, downhill*; sometimes α- (known as privative α and with a negative force) is prefixed, corresponding to the English *un-*: *unjust* (p. 21 n. 1).
Conjugation	System of endings used to express change of person, tense, etc. in a verb, p. 11. To **conjugate** a verb means to reproduce the different forms in the conventional order: 1st, 2nd, 3rd person singular, then plural.
Conjunction	Word linking words, phrases or clauses: *Until* he comes, I shall stay; boys *and* old men, p. 37.
Consonants	Letters other than the vowels (p. 11 n. 1).
Declension	A class of nouns (also pronouns, adjectives) which have similar case endings. There are three declensions, but these have sub-groups, p. 12. To **decline** a noun means to give its various case forms in the conventional order given in the Grammar.
Deliberative	Use of the subjunctive in questions deliberating in one's own mind as to a course of action: *What am I to do?*, p. 90.
Demonstrative	Adjective or pronoun which points out: *This, that, these, those*, p. 26.
Deponent	See p. 34.
Diphthong	Two vowels pronounced as one sound, p. 10.

Elision   Dropping of a final vowel before another word beginning with a vowel, p. 23.

Enclitic   See p. 25.

Gender   The grammatical class (' sex ') to which a noun belongs. In Greek most words for men and boys are masculine and most words for women and girls are feminine, but a few are neuter. Words for things may be grammatically masculine, feminine or neuter, p. 14.

Genitive absolute   See p. 69.

Hiatus   When one vowel follows another and the two are pronounced separately, with a stop of breath between: *Anna is* here, p. 11, n. 1.

Historic   Describes tenses used in narration of past events, p. 28. The **historic present** is the present tense used instead of the past in vivid narration, common in the gospels, p. 27.

Hortatory   Subjunctive used to exhort and encourage: *Let us pray*, p. 79.

Idiom   Inexplicable turn of speech peculiar to any one language (p. 67).

Imperative   Mood of verb used to express a command: *Give* me the money; *let all lay down* their arms, p. 75.

Imperfect   See p. 22.

Indicative   Mood of verb used to express a matter of fact: *He loves* me; *are* they here? p. 11.

Indirect statement, command, question   These depend on a main verb of saying or thinking. Compare **indirect** statement: We said *that Christ was Lord*, with **direct** statement: We said: ' *Christ* is *Lord* ', p. 43.

Infinitive   Mood of verb used to express the action itself, without reference to a particular person or number, which in English employs the preposition ' to ': She liked *to dance* (i.e. dancing). When the article is prefixed (**articular infinitive**) the infinitive is used as an indeclinable neuter noun, taking its case from the case of the article: *By dancing* she won fame, pp. 48–52.

Interjection	Exclamation inserted in a sentence, p. 77 n. 1. (There is no exclamation mark in Greek.)
Intransitive verb	A verb which by its very meaning cannot take an object: She *rejoiced*, p. 46.
Middle	See p. 34.
Mood	Form of verb showing manner in which a verb is being used (p. 114). The moods are: **Indicative, infinitive, imperative, subjunctive, optative**.
Neuter	Grammatically a noun or pronoun which is neither masculine nor feminine in gender. Note that possibly it may not denote a thing, but may refer to a person, because the grammatical gender does not necessarily coincide with the real gender: τέκνον means ' child ', p. 14.
Noun	Name of person, place or thing, p. 12.
Number	Term used to state whether a word is singular or plural: *king, kings* (p. 114 n. 1).
Object	Person or thing affected directly or indirectly by the action of the verb: He gave *the beggar* (indirect) *the money* (direct); in English this would be more often expressed by ' to the beggar ', p. 13.
Oblique	Any case other than the nominative, from which cases were thought to slant (p. 31).
Optative	Mood named from its use to express a wish (cf. option), p. 140.
Ordinal	Numeral adjective expressing position in a series *first, second, third*, p. 147.
Parse	See p. 114 n. 1.
Participle	Part of verb declined like an adjective: *Broken* pieces; the *ruling* man, i.e. the ruler, p. 56 n. 2. They may be used either adjectivally in relation to a noun, p. 64, or adverbially when they are linked closely with a verb, p. 66.
Particle	Small Greek word used to link or emphasize: *and, but, for, therefore*, p. 16.
Passive	See p. 37.
Perfect	See p. 98.
Periphrastic	See p. 70.

Person	Used grammatically in reference to verbs, p. 11, pronouns, p. 30:
	1st person, *I* (sing.), *we* (plural).
	2nd person, *thou* (sing.), *you* (plural).
	3rd person, *he, she, it* (sing.), *they* (plural).
Phrase	Group of words, not a complete clause or sentence, which expresses a single idea: *In the beginning* (prepositional phrase) (p. 18).
Pluperfect	See p. 100.
Predicate (complement)	1. Noun or adjective used after intransitive verb and referring back to the subject: He became *king*, p. 25.
	2. Noun or adjective stating effect of transitive verb on direct object: Caesar made him *governor*.
Preposition	Indeclinable word used before a noun or pronoun to express a relation in time, space, etc.: *After* the flood, *in* the city, *with* God, *against* the king, pp. 122–7.
Prolate	Describes an infinitive used with a verb which requires an infinitive to explain and extend its meaning: He began *to teach*, p. 50.
Pronoun	Word used instead of a noun to refer to a person, place or thing: *Who* (interrogative, p. 73) does not know that *those* (demonstrative, p. 26) *who* (relative, p. 41) persecute *me* (personal, p. 30) condemn *themselves* (reflexive, p. 32)?
Reduplication	See p. 95.
Reflexive	Pronoun referring back to the subject of the verb: He killed *himself*, p. 32.
Relative	Word introducing a clause which describes the person or thing just mentioned: Jesus, *who* was crucified, p. 41.
Semi-colon	Punctuation mark (·), English ;, more weighty than the comma: blessed are the meek; for they shall inherit the earth, p. 18.
Stem	Basic form of verb or noun distinct from personal or case endings: λύ-ω, λόγ-ος, p. 15.
Subject	Person or thing governing the action of the verb: *The king* rules, p. 13.

Subjunctive	Mood used in various constructions, but so named because it is often found in a subordinate clause linked with the main verb by a conjunction, p. 79.
Syllable	Word or part of a word pronounced as a whole in itself: *God* (monosyllable), *ungodly* (three syllables), p. 11.
Tense	Form of verb to indicate time or completeness of action in present, past or future, p. 22; but see p. 49 for aorist peculiarities.
Transitive verb	Verb taking an object: God *loved the world*, p. 113.
Verb	Word to state that something happens: I *seek*, p. 11.
Voice	Form of verb differentiating between Active, Middle and Passive (p. 114 n. 1).
Vowels	Letters to represent sounds a e i o u (p. 10).

HINTS ON TRANSLATION

Do not rush in headlong, seizing on any word you happen to know and translating it immediately, regardless of case or context. Read through the whole sentence slowly and carefully. If the structure is complicated, take each clause in the order given in the Greek. Within a clause look for the *verb* and any qualifying adverb that goes with it. A subordinate clause will have a conjunction before the verb, but in a simple sentence the verb is usually at the beginning and, if there is none, you must supply the verb ' to be '. If the verb is in the first or second person, this is expressed by the ending and a pronoun is only added for emphasis. If the verb is in the third person, look for a *subject* in the *nominative*; if there is none, supply ' he, she, it, they ' according to the context. With the verb ' to be ' and the like, both subject and predicate will be in the nominative, but the latter can usually be distinguished by the omission of the article. There may also be a *vocative*, easily distinguishable even when the ending is that of the nominative, because of context and frequent prefix of ὦ. If the verb is passive, look out for an agent (ὑπό +*genitive*) and/or instrument (*dative*). Now see whether there is a *direct object* in the *accusative* and/or *indirect object* in the *dative*. All these may be qualified by adjectives or possessive genitives. When you have this skeleton, prepositional phrases, etc., should fall easily into place. Remember that Greek word-order within a clause is extremely flexible and cannot be a guide to the same extent as in English. In questions the only means of differentiating from a statement may be the question mark at the end of a sentence.

As a matter of style, it is better to translate the Historic Present by a past tense, ' Jesus said ' rather than ' Jesus says ', and also to use ' you ' for both ' thee ' and ' thou ', to conform with current usage. Modern translations tend to omit some introductory particles, on the grounds that they were becoming otiose, add little to the meaning and are contrary to English style, though AV and RV translate them meticulously. Examinees will be wise to translate them all in order to show that they do know the meaning.

Finally, familiarity with the English of the NT may be dangerous rather than helpful. Do not rely on your memory. The synoptists often use slightly different wording and you may dredge up from your memory a Lucan translation which will not fit the Marcan or Matthean Greek. Even when the text is unique and known by heart, as e.g. the Nunc Dimittis, stop and see how the Greek and the translation are matched. It is in order to be able to do this that you are learning Greek.

GREEK INDEX

This contains only words treated in the text or given in the vocabularies. Reference is to pages. An asterisk shows that the parts of this verb or its uncompounded form are given in the list, pp. 156-61.

178

αὐτός	31	γραμματεύς	61	δικαίως		53
ἀφαιρέω*	129	γραφή	38	δίκτυον		23
ἄφεσις*	65	γράφω*	11	διψάω		86
ἀφίημι*	106	γρηγορέω	83	διώκω		29
ἀφίστημι*	114	γυνή	58	δοκέω*		80
ἄφρων	82			δόξα		17
ἄχρι	37, 94			δοξάζω		65

Δ

Β

		δαιμόνιον	14	δούλος		14
				δύναμαι*		86
-βαίνω*	46	δέ	17	δύναμις		61
βάλλω*	23	δεῖ	53	δύο		77
βαπτίζω	38	δείκνυμι (-ύω)	116	δῶρον		149
βαπτιστής	19	δεῖπνον	139			
βαρύς	120	δέκα	29			
βασανίζω	44	δένδρον	29		**Ε**	
βασιλεία	17	δεξιός	77			
βασιλεύς	60	δέομαι*	50	ἐάν	93, 137	
βαστάζω	29	δέσμιος	149	ἐάω*		87
βιβλίον	23	δεσμός	33	ἐγγίζω		70
βλασφημέω	102	δεσπότης	19	ἐγγύς		94
βλέπω	11	δεῦρο, δεῦτε	91	ἐγείρω*		73
βοάω	86	δέχομαι	36	ἐγκαλέω*		130
βούλομαι*	50	διά	124	ἐγώ		30
βραχύς	83	διάβολος	36	ἔθνος		60
		διαθήκη	109	εἰ	77, 89, 137	
		διάκονος	44	εἶδον*		42
Γ		διαλέγομαι	135	εἰκών		94
		διαλογίζομαι	142	εἰμί*		25
γαμέω*	99	διαρπάζω*	109	εἶπον*		42
γάμος	83	διατάσσω	50	εἰρήνη		17
γάρ	17	διατίθεμαι*	110	εἷς		77
γεννάω	86	διδάσκω	26	εἰς		122
γῆ	29	δίδωμι*	104	εἰσέρχομαι*		44
γίνομαι*	40	διέρχομαι*	44	εἴωθα		102
γινώσκω*	23	δίκαιος	21	ἐκ		123
γλῶσσα	19	δικαιοσύνη	17	ἕκαστος		80
γονεύς	83	δικαιόω	90	ἐκβάλλω*		23
γόνυ	57			ἐκεῖ		41

179

ἐκεῖθεν	92	ἐπερωτάω	87	**Z**	
ἐκεῖνος	26	ἐπί	125		
ἐκεῖσε	92	ἐπιγινώσκω*	114	ζάω	87
ἐκκλησία	17	ἐπιθυμέω	94	ζητέω	15
ἐκκόπτω*	29	ἐπικαλέω*	130	ζωή	23
ἐκλέγομαι	36	ἐπίσταμαι	114	ζώννυμι	116
ἐκπλήσσομαι	110	ἐπιτάσσω	50		
ἐκτός	131	ἐπιτίθημι*	106	**H**	
ἔλαιον	59	ἐπιτιμάω	90	ἤ	90, 119
ἐλάσσων	119	ἐπιτρέπω*	129	ἡγεμών	56
ἐλάχιστος	119	ἑπτά	80	ἡδέως (ἥδιστα)	120
ἐλεέω	38	ἐργάζομαι	117	ἤδη	70
ἐλεημοσύνη	146	ἐργάτης	38	ἥλιος	54
ἐλεύθερος	149	ἔργον	12	ἡμεῖς	31
ἐλπίζω	80	ἔρημος	19	ἡμέρα	17
ἐλπίς	55	ἔρρωσθε	99	ἡμέτερος	21
ἐμός	21	ἔρχομαι*	42	ἥσσων	119
ἔμπροσθεν	94	ἐρωτάω	87		
ἐν	123	ἐσθίω*	42	**Θ**	
ἐνδύω	102	ἔσχατος	21		
ἕνεκα	131	ἔσω, ἔσωθεν	131	θάλασσα	17
ἐνθάδε	91	ἕτερος	44	θάνατος	15
ἔνθεν	92	ἔτι	70	θαυμάζω	59
ἐντέλλομαι*	80	ἑτοιμάζω	29	θεάομαι	99
ἐντεῦθεν	92	ἔτος	61	θέλημα	70
ἐντολή	17	εὖ	54	θέλω*	50
ἐντός	131	εὐαγγελίζομαι	54	θεμελιόω	99
ἐντρέπω*	129	εὐαγγέλιον	14	θεός	14
ἐνώπιον	131	εὐθέως	83	θεραπεύω	11
ἐξέρχομαι*	44	εὐθύς	44, 82	θεωρέω	65
ἔξεστι	53	εὔκοπος	120	θηρίον	80
ἐξίστημι*	114	εὐλογέω	65	θλῖψις	61
ἐξουσία	17	εὑρίσκω*	11	θρίξ	58
ἔξω, ἔξωθεν	131	εὐχαριστέω	117	θυγάτηρ	58
ἑορτή	117	ἐφίστημι*	114	θυγάτριον	135
ἐπαγγελία	65	ἐχθρός	33	θύρα	59
ἐπάνω	132	ἔχω*	17	θυσία	94
ἐπεί	59	ἕως	37, 94	θύω	146

181

παρακούω*	130	πλοῦτος	106	πτωχός	26
παράπτωμα	129	πνεῦμα	56	πυνθάνομαι*	142
παρατίθημι*	106	ποδαπός	92	πῦρ	65
παρθένος	19	πόθεν	92	πωλέω	106
παρίστημι*	114	ποιέω	15	πῶς	17
πᾶς	73	ποιμήν	56		
πάσχω*	40	ποῖος	92	Ρ	
πατήρ	58	πόλεμος	149		
πατρίς	56	πόλις	60	ῥῆμα	56
πείθω*	21	πολλάκις	149	ῥιζόω	99
πεινάω	87	πολύς	23		
πειράζω	47	πονηρός	21	Σ	
πέμπω	11	πορεύομαι	38		
πέντε	41	πορνεία	139	σάββατον	17
πέραν	132	πόρρω	120	σάρξ	56
περί	125	πόσος	92	σβέννυμι*	116
περιβάλλω*	102	ποταμός	38	σημεῖον	17
περιβλέπομαι	38	πότε	33	σήμερον	74
περιπατέω	21	ποτήριον	65	σιωπάω	90
περισσός	120	ποῦ	56	σκανδαλίζω	77
πηλίκος	92	πούς	58	σκεῦος	83
πίνω*	33	πράσσω	29	σκότος	70
πίπτω*	40	πρεσβύτερος	70	σός	21
πιστεύω	11	πρίν	116	σοφός	47
πίστις	61	πρό	123	σοφῶς	53
πιστός	21	πρόβατον	33	σπείρω*	47
πλανάω	90	πρός	127	σπέρμα	65
πλεῖστος	119	προσδέχομαι	130	σταυρός	2
πλέων	119	προσέρχομαι*	44	σταυρόω	90
πλῆθος	61	προσεύχομαι	36	στήκω	113
πληθύνω	142	προσέχω*	139	στόμα	56
πλήν	132	προσκαλέομαι*	36	στρατιώτης	44
πλήρης	83	προσκυνέω	80	σύ	31
πληρόω	90	προστάσσω	50	συλλαμβάνω*	117
πλησίον	132	προστίθημι*	106	συμβαίνω*	130
πλοιάριον	135	προφήτης	19	συμφέρω*	146
πλοῖον	14	πρωΐ	74	σύν	124
πλούσιος	26	πρῶτος	21	συνάγω*	33

183

συνέρχομαι*	44	τρέχω*	135	φιμόω		99
συνίημι*	106	τρίτος	77	φοβέομαι		44
σφραγίζω	102	τρόπος	146	φρόνιμος		59
σώζω*	11	τυγχάνω*	142	φυλακή		44
σῶμα	56	τυφλός	26	φύλαξ		55
σωτήρ	55			φυλάσσω		29
σωτηρία	41			φωνή		44

Υ

		ὑγιής	83	φῶς		70

Τ

		ὕδωρ	58	**Χ**		
ταχέως	83	υἱός	19			
ταχίον	120	ὑμεῖς	31	χαίρω*		47
τάχιστα	120	ὑμέτερος	21	χαλκός		149
ταχύς	83	ὑπάγω*	68	χαρά		54
τε	138	ὑπακούω*	68	χαρίζομαι		99
τέκνον	14	ὑπαντάω	90	χάρις		58
τέλειος	120	ὑπάρχω	114	χείρ		58
τελειόω	99	ὑπέρ	125	χείρων		119
τελέω*	15	ὑπηρέτης	44	χήρα		44
τέλος	61	ὑπό	125	χρεία		54
τελώνης	33	ὑποκάτω	132	Χριστός		44
τέρας	110	ὑπομένω*	130	χρόνος		41
τέσσαρες	56	ὑποτάσσω	94	χρυσός (-ίον)		149
τεσσεράκοντα	47	ὕστερον	47	χωλός		36
τηρέω	15	ὑψηλός	120	χώρα		94
τίθημι*	104	ὕψιστος	118	χωρίς		132
τίκτω*	40	ὑψόω	90			
τιμάω	85			**Ψ**		
τίμιος	120					
τίς	73	**Φ**		ψεύδομαι		139
τοιοῦτος	92					
τόπος	44	φαίνω*	102	**Ω**		
τοσοῦτος	92	φανερόω	90			
τότε	26	φέρω*	42	ὧδε		41
τράπεζα	135	φεύγω*	40	ὡς		37, 47
τρεῖς	77	φημί	111	ὠτάριον		135
τρέπω*	129	φθείρω*	73	ὠφελέω		54
		φιλέω	15			

ENGLISH–GREEK VOCABULARY

Only words from the exercises for translation into Greek are included. Prepositional usage should be carefully checked. An asterisk shows that the parts of this verb or its uncompounded form are given in the list pp. 156-61.

A

able (be)	δύναμαι*
about	περί
abstain	ἀπέχομαι*
abundantly (more)	περισσοτέρως
across	πέραν
add	προστίθημι*
afraid (be)	φοβέομαι
after	μετά
again	πάλιν
against	ἐπί, κατά
age	αἰών
all	πᾶς
allow	ἐάω*
already	ἤδη
also	καί
although	καίπερ
always	πάντοτε
angel	ἄγγελος
anger	ὀργή
announce	ἀγγέλλω*
another	ἕτερος
answer	ἀποκρίνομαι*
anxious (be)	μεριμνάω
apostle	ἀπόστολος
approach	ἐγγίζω
arrest	συλλαμβάνω*
as	ὡς
ask (for)	αἰτέω
astonish	ἐξίστημι*

at	ἐπί, παρά
attendant	ὑπηρέτης
authority	ἐξουσία

B

bad	κακός
baptist	βαπτιστής
baptize	βαπτίζω
be	εἰμί*
bear (child)	τίκτω*
bear witness	μαρτυρέω
beautiful	καλός
because	ὅτι
because of	διά
become	γίνομαι*
bed	κλίνη
before	πρό
beg	δέομαι*
begin	ἄρχομαι
behold	θεωρέω
behold !	ἰδού
believe	πιστεύω
beside	παρά
betray	παραδίδωμι*
better	κρείσσων
big	μέγας
bless	εὐλογέω
blessed	μακάριος
blind	τυφλός
blood	αἷμα
boat	πλοῖον

body	σῶμα	contrary to	παρά
book	βιβλίον	corpse	νεκρός
both — and	καί — καί, τε — καί	covenant	διαθήκη
		cross	σταυρός
boy	παῖς	crowd	ὄχλος
bread	ἄρτος	cry	βοάω
bring	φέρω*	cry out	κράζω*
brother	ἀδελφός		
build	οἰκοδομέω		

D

but	ἀλλά, δέ		
buy	ἀγοράζω	daughter	θυγάτηρ
by (agent)	ὑπό	day	ἡμέρα
by (local)	παρά	death	θάνατος
		deed	ἔργον
		demon	δαιμόνιον

C

		deny	ἀρνέομαι
call	καλέω*	depart	ἀπέρχομαι*
carry	βαστάζω	desert	ἔρημος
cast out	ἐκβάλλω*	destroy	φθείρω*
certainly not	οὐ μή	devil (sing.)	διάβολος
child	τέκνον	(pl.)	δαιμόνια
child (little)	παιδίον	die	ἀποθνήσκω*
choose	ἐκλέγομαι	disciple	μαθητής
Christ	Χριστός	disease	νόσος
church	ἐκκλησία	do	ποιέω
city	πόλις	doctor	ἰατρός
clothes	ἱμάτια	dog	κύων
cloud	νεφέλη	door	θύρα
cock	ἀλέκτωρ	drink	πίνω*
come	ἔρχομαι*	drive	ἄγω*
come down	καταβαίνω*	dwell	κατοικέω
come up	ἀναβαίνω*		
command	κελεύω		
command- ment	ἐντολή		

E

		each	ἕκαστος
condemn	κατακρίνω*	ear	οὖς
confess	ὁμολογέω	earth	γῆ
conquer	νικάω	eat	ἐσθίω*

end	τέλος	full	πλήρης
enemy	ἐχθρός		
enter	εἰσέρχομαι*		
eternal	αἰώνιος	**G**	
evangelize	εὐαγγελίζομαι	gather to-gether	συνάγω*
even	καί		
everything	πάντα	gentiles	ἔθνη
evil	πονηρός	gird	ζώννυμι
exult	ἀγαλλιάομαι	girl	παρθένος
eye	ὀφθαλμός	glorify	δοξάζω
		glory	δόξα
		go	ἔρχομαι*
F		go out	ἐξέρχομαι*
faith	πίστις	good	ἀγαθός
faithful	πιστός	gospel	εὐαγγέλιον
fall	πίπτω*	governor	ἡγεμών
fast	νηστεύω	grace	χάρις
fear	φοβέομαι	great	μέγας
festival	ἑορτή	greater	μείζων
field	ἀγρός	guard	φύλαξ
find	εὑρίσκω*	guard (verb)	φυλάσσω
finish	τελέω*		
fire	πῦρ		
first	πρῶτος	**H**	
fish	ἰχθύς	hail !	χαῖρε
five	πέντε	hair	θρίξ
flee	φεύγω*	hand	χείρ
flesh	σάρξ	hand down	παραδίδωμι*
follow	ἀκολουθέω	happy	μακάριος
foolish	ἄφρων	hate	μισέω
foot	πούς	have	ἔχω*
for (particle)	γάρ	head	κεφαλή
forgive	ἀφίημι*	heal	θεραπεύω
forgiveness	ἄφεσις	healthy	ὑγιής
forty	τεσσεράκοντα	hear	ἀκούω*
four	τέσσαρες	heart	καρδία
from	ἀπό, παρά	heaven	οὐρανός
fruit	καρπός	help	ὠφελέω

her (acc.)	αὐτήν	just now	ἄρτι
here	ὧδε	justify	δικαιόω
hide	κρύπτω*	justly	δικαίως
high	ὑψηλός		
him (acc.)	αὐτόν		
holy	ἅγιος	**K**	
honour	τιμάω	keep	τηρέω
hope	ἐλπίς	keep awake	γρηγορέω
hope (verb)	ἐλπίζω	kill	ἀποκτείνω*
house	οἶκος	king	βασιλεύς
householder	οἰκοδεσπότης	kingdom	βασιλεία
how?	πῶς	know	γινώσκω*
however	πλήν		
hunger	πεινάω		
husband	ἀνήρ	**L**	
		lake	θάλασσα
		lame	χωλός
I		lamp	λαμπάς
		land	γῆ
I	ἐγώ	last	ἔσχατος
if	εἰ, ἐάν	later	ὕστερον
if ever	ἐάν	law	νόμος
immediately	εὐθύς	lay	τίθημι*
impart	μεταδίδωμι*	lead	ἄγω*
in	ἐν	lead astray	πλανάω
in order that	ἵνα, ὅπως	lead away	ἀπάγω*
instead of	ἀντί	learn	μανθάνω*
into	εἰς	leave	λείπω*
		less (adj.)	ἐλάσσων
		less (adverb)	ἧσσον
J		lest	ἵνα μή, μή
		life	ζωή
Jesus	Ἰησοῦς	liken	ὁμοιόω
Jew	Ἰουδαῖος	listen	ἀκούω*
John	Ἰωάννης	live	ζάω
Jordan	Ἰορδάνης	loaves	ἄρτοι
journey	πορεύομαι	look round	περιβλέπομαι
joy	χαρά	loose	λύω
judge	κριτής		
just	δίκαιος		

lord	κύριος	name (verb)	ὀνομάζω
lose	ἀπόλλυμι*	nation	ἔθνος
love	ἀγάπη	native land	πατρίς
love (verb)	ἀγαπάω,	near	ἐγγύς
	φιλέω	necessary (is)	δεῖ
		need	χρεία
		net	δίκτυον
M		never	οὐδέποτε,
			μηδέποτε
make	ποιέω	new	καινός
man	ἄνθρωπος,	night	νύξ
	ἀνήρ	no	οὐ
manifest	φανερόω	no longer	οὐκέτι, μηκέτι
mankind	οἱ ἄνθρωποι	nor	οὐδέ, μηδέ
many	πολλοί	now	νῦν
martyr	μάρτυς		
marvel	θαυμάζω		
master	δεσπότης		
mattress	κράββατος	**O**	
mature	τέλειος		
meet	ὑπαντάω	obey	ὑπακούω*
mercy (have)	ἐλεέω	observe (keep)	τηρέω
messenger	ἄγγελος	oil	ἔλαιον
midst (in the)	ἐν μέσῳ	old	παλαιός
mighty work	δύναμις	on	ἐν, ἐπί
miracle	σημεῖον	on account of	διά
money	ἀργύριον	one	εἷς
most	πλεῖστος	only (adverb)	μόνον
mother	μήτηρ	open	ἀνοίγω*
mountain	ὄρος	opposite	κατέναντι
mouth	στόμα	order	προστάσσω
much	πολύς	other	ἕτερος
must	δεῖ	others	οἱ δέ,
my	ἐμός		ἄλλοι
		ought	ὀφείλω
		our	ἡμέτερος
		out of	ἐκ
N		outside	ἔξω
		own	ἴδιος
name	ὄνομα		

	P	remain	μένω*
		repentance	μετάνοια
pass by	παράγω*	report	ἀγγέλλω*
pay	μισθός	rest	λοιποί
pay (verb)	ἀποδίδωμι*	reveal	ἀποκαλύπτω
peace	εἰρήνη	reward	μισθός
people	λαός	rich	πλούσιος
perish	ἀπόλλυμαι*	righteous	δίκαιος
persecute	διώκω	righteously	δικαίως
persuade	πείθω*	righteousness	δικαιοσύνη
pity	ἐλεέω	river	ποταμός
place	τόπος	road	ὁδός
place (verb)	τίθημι*	robber	λῃστής
power	δύναμις		
pray	προσεύχομαι		
preach	κηρύσσω		**S**
prepare	ἑτοιμάζω		
priest	ἱερεύς	sabbath	σάββατον
prison	φυλακή	saint	ἅγιος
proclaim	κηρύσσω	salvation	σωτηρία
promise	ἐπαγγελία	same	ὁ αὐτός
prophet	προφήτης	save	σώζω*
pursue	διώκω	saviour	σωτήρ
		say	λέγω*
		saying	ῥῆμα
	Q	scriptures	γραφαί
		see	βλέπω,
question	ἐρωτάω		ὁράω*
quickly	ταχέως	seed	σπέρμα
		seek	ζητέω
	R	self	αὐτός
		sell	ἀποδίδομαι*
raise (from dead)	ἐγείρω*	send	πέμπω
		send forth	ἀποστέλλω*
read	ἀναγινώσκω*	seven	ἑπτά
rebuke	ἐπιτιμάω	sheep	πρόβατον
receive	δέχομαι	shepherd	ποιμήν
recline	ἀνάκειμαι	short	βραχύς
rejoice	χαίρω*	show	δείκνυμι
release	λύω		

sick	ἀσθενής		temple	ἱερόν
sign	σημεῖον		tempt	πειράζω
silver	ἀργύριον		ten	δέκα
sin	ἁμαρτία		than	ἤ
sin (verb)	ἁμαρτάνω*		that	ἐκεῖνος
sinner	ἁμαρτωλός		that (con-	ὅτι
sit	καθίζω		junction)	
slave	δοῦλος		them (acc.)	αὐτούς
snatch	ἁρπάζω*		then	τότε
so	οὕτως		there	ἐκεῖ
so as (that)	ὥστε		therefore	οὖν
soldier	στρατιώτης		thirst	διψάω
some	οἱ μέν,		this	οὗτος
	τινές		three	τρεῖς
son	υἱός		through	διά
sow	σπείρω*		throw	βάλλω*
speak	λαλέω		to	πρός
spirit	πνεῦμα		tomb	μνημεῖον
stand	ἵστημι*		tongue	γλῶσσα
stand away	ἀφίστημι*		tooth	ὀδούς
stand up	ἀνίστημι*		tree	δένδρον
star	ἀστήρ		tribulation	θλῖψις
still	ἔτι		true	ἀληθής
stone	λίθος		truly	ἀληθῶς
suffer	πάσχω*		trust	πιστεύω
surely?	οὐχί		truth	ἀλήθεια
surely . . . not?	μήτι		try	πειράζω
swear	ὄμνυμι*		two	δύο
sword	μάχαιρα			

T

U

take	λαμβάνω*		under	ὑπό
take thought	μεριμνάω		understand	συνίημι*
take up	αἴρω*		unjust	ἄδικος
talk	λαλέω		unrighteous	ἄδικος
tax-collector	τελώνης		until	ἕως
teach	διδάσκω		upon	ἐπί

V

village	κώμη
vineyard	ἀμπελών
voice	φωνή

W

walk	περιπατέω
warn	ἐπιτιμάω
water	ὕδωρ
way	ὁδός
weak	ἀσθενής
wealth	πλοῦτος
well (adverb)	εὖ
what?	τί
when	ὅτε
when?	πότε
where	οὗ
whether	εἰ
while	ἕως
who	ὅς
who?	τίς
whole	ὅλος
why?	τί
wicked	πονηρός
widow	χήρα

wife	γυνή
wise	σοφός
wisely	σοφῶς
wish	θέλω*
with	σύν, μετά
wither	ξηραίνω*
witness	μάρτυς
witness (verb)	μαρτυρέω
woman	γυνή
wonder	τέρας
word	λόγος
work	ἔργον
work (verb)	ἐργάζομαι
workman	ἐργάτης
world	κόσμος
worse	χείρων
worthy	ἄξιος
write	γράφω*
writing	γραφή

Y

year	ἔτος
you (sing.)	σύ
young man	νεανίας
your (sing.)	σός
(pl.)	ὑμέτερος